INCOMPARABLE
BUDGERIGARS

ALL ABOUT THEM
Including Instructions for Keeping, Breeding and
Teaching them to Talk

By

PERCY GLADSTONE FRUDD

Chairman and Show Manager of the " YORKSHIRE OBSERVER "
ANNUAL BUDGERIGAR AND FOREIGN BIRD SHOW

British Library Cataloguing-in-Publication Data
A catalogue record for this book is available from the
British Library

Aviculture

'Aviculture' is the practice of keeping and breeding birds, as well as the culture that forms around it, and there are various reasons why people get involved in Aviculture. Some people breed birds to preserve a specific species, usually due to habitat destruction, and some people breed birds (especially parrots) as companions, and yet others do this to make a profit. Aviculture encourages conservation, provides education about avian species, provides companion birds for the public, and includes research on avian behaviour. It is thus a highly important and enjoyable past time. There are avicultural societies throughout the world, but generally in Europe, Australia and the United States, where people tend to be more prosperous, having more leisure time to invest. The first avicultural society in Australia was The Avicultural Society of South Australia, founded in 1928. It is now promoted with the name Bird Keeping in Australia. The two major national avicultural societies in the United States are the American Federation of Aviculture and the Avicultural Society of America, founded in 1927. In the UK, the Avicultural Society was formed in 1894 and the Foreign Bird League in 1932. The Budgerigar Society was formed in 1925.

Some of the most popular domestically kept birds are finches and canaries. 'Finches' are actually a broader category, encompassing canaries, and make fantastic domestic birds, capable of living long and healthy lives if given the requisite care. Most species are very easy to breed, and usefully do not grow too large (unlike their larger compatriot the budgerigar), and so do not need a massive living space. 'Canary' (associated with the *Serinus canaria*), is a song bird is native to the Canary Islands, Madeira, and the Azores – and has long been kept as a cage bird in Europe, beginning in the 1470s. It now enjoys an international following, and the terms *canariculture* and *canaricultura* have been used in French, Spanish and Italian respectively, to describe the keeping and breeding of canaries. It is only gradually however (a testament to its growing popularity) that English breeders are beginning to use such terms. Canaries are now the most popular form of finch kept in Britain and are often found still fulfilling their historic role of protecting underground miners. Canaries like budgies, are seed eaters, which need to dehusk the seed before feeding on the kernel. However, unlike budgerigars, canaries are perchers. The average life span of a canary is five years, although they have been known to live twice as long.

Parakeets or 'Budgies' (a type of parrot) are another incredibly popular breed of domestic bird, and are originally from Australia, first brought to Europe in the 1840s. Whilst they are naturally green with yellow heads and black bars on the wings in the wild, domesticated budgies come in a massive variety of colours. They have the toes and beak typical of parrot like birds, as in nature they are climbers; budgies are hardy seed eaters and their strong beak is utilised for dehusking seeds as well as a climbing aid. When kept indoors however, it is important to supplement their diet of seeds with fresh fruit and vegetables, which would be found in the wild. Budgies are social birds, so it is most important to make sure they have company, preferably of their own kind. They do enjoy human companionship though, and may be persuaded, if gently stroked on the chest feathers to perch on one's finger. If not kept in an aviary, they need a daily period of free flight, but great care must be taken not to let them escape.

Last, but most definitely not least, perhaps the most popular breed of domestic bird, is the 'companion parrot' – a general term used for *any* parrot kept as a pet that interacts with its human counterpart. Generally, most species of parrot can make good companions. Common domestic parrots include large birds such as Amazons, African Greys, Cockatoos, Eclectus, Hawk-headed Parrots and Macaws; mid-sized birds such as Caiques, Conures, Quakers, Pionus, Poicephalus, Rose-Ringed parakeets and Rosellas, and many of the smaller types including Budgies, Cockatiels, Parakeets, lovebirds, Parrotlets and Lineolated Parakeets. The *Convention on International Trade in Endangered Species of Wild Fauna and Flora* (also known as CITES) has made the trapping and trade of all wild parrots illegal, because taking parrots from the wild has endangered or reduced some of the rarer or more valuable species. However, many parrot species are still common; and some abundant parrot species may still be legally killed as crop pests in their native countries. Endangered parrot species are better suited to conservation breeding programs than as companions.

Parrots can be very rewarding pets to the right owners, due to their intelligence and desire to interact with people. Many parrots are very affectionate, even cuddly with trusted people, and require a lot of attention from their owners. Some species have a tendency to bond to one or two people, and dislike strangers, unless they are regularly and consistently handled by different people. Properly socialized parrots can be friendly, outgoing and confident companions. Most pet parrots take readily to trick training as well, which can help deflect their energy and correct many behavioural problems. Some owners successfully use well behaved parrots as therapy animals. In fact, many have even trained their parrots to wear parrot harnesses (most easily accomplished with young birds) so that they can be taken to enjoy themselves outdoors in a relatively safe manner without the risk of flying away. Parrots are prey animals and even the tamest pet may fly off if spooked. Given the right care and attention, keeping birds is usually problem free. It is hoped that the reader enjoys this book.

THE IDEAL BUDGERIGAR

Reproduced by kind permission of the Budgerigar Society

CONTENTS

7

LIST OF ILLUSTRATIONS

List of Illustrations

All other Photographs by A. D. FIRTH, 110, Duchy Avenue, Bradford, *in conjunction with the Author.*

Line Drawings by the Author.

INTRODUCTORY

"A FASCINATING LITTLE FELLOW"

SOME, who pick up this book, will probably wonder who "A Fascinating Little Fellow" really is. If you will read these stories I feel sure that you will agree that he *is* a fascinating little chap. Of course I refer to THE BUDGERIGAR (*Melopsittacus undulatus*, Shaw).

"Penelope and her Pierrot" and other stories included in this book are based on incidents taken from the lives of these handsome pets. They are founded upon true incidents and are not pure, unadulterated fiction as the cynic might suppose.

I dare say I shall be accused of 'window dressing' my stories. Well, if adding dialogue to make the stories interesting is 'window dressing', then I plead guilty; but let me assure my readers who may not be aware of the fact—Budgerigars *can* be taught to talk. There are many thousands of them in the British Isles who are speaking freely, and since these stories first appeared in *The Yorkshire Observer* their number has increased many times over.

But it is not the faculty of being able to reproduce human speech alone which makes them so fascinating, but because they are on their own initiative born mimics, mischievous and probably the most intelligent of all birds.

Hardy, quite inexpensive to keep; and, requiring the very minimum of attention to keep in a perfectly healthy condition, they are no burden on the exchequer of even the humblest person who would wish to avail himself of their pleasant companionship.

11

Introductory

This volume is not intended to be a scientific treatise on the upkeep and management of these pets—there are many books already available for the expert—but is written primarily to interest the reader in these gorgeous creatures, and then to tell him in plain, simple language how to train and keep them as they should be kept.

These stories have brought many hundreds of new ' fanciers ' to our ranks in the North ; but, of far more importance, they have been the means of many more people acquiring a new ' friend '. This fact is of sufficient importance to make it imperative that I should explain how these stories first came into being (they are unique in the fact that never before have such stories about birds been published), and at the same time pay a tribute to certain gentlemen who made the *general public* in the north of England ' budgie-conscious ', for the first time.

In June, 1936, while engaged in promoting The Yorkshire Budgerigar Society, I went along with Mr. J. W. Whitworth, the first secretary of the society, to Mr. O. B. Stokes, editor of *The Bradford Telegraph and Argus*, to see if we could not persuade this gentleman to give us some publicity for our pets.

Mr. Stokes was so interested that he secured for us an interview with Mr. F. H. Timperley, the General Manager of The Bradford and District Newspaper Co. Ltd., who quickly turned a sympathetic ear towards us. It is to this gentleman of vision that all budgerigar fanciers, all people who have since acquired them as pets, owe a deep debt of gratitude for his foresight and the help that he gave us.

Before the discussion had proceeded very far, Mr. Timperley suggested that he should promote a show, on lines which had hitherto been unthought of, to help to make the people of the North budgie-conscious, if I would find the necessary organization from the fanciers of the West Riding to work the show.

Introductory

The title of the show was agreed to be, The First Annual Yorkshire Observer Budgerigar and Foreign Bird Show ; and it was then that Mr. S. Oddy, editor of that paper, came into the picture. I shall ever remember this gentleman as one of the kindest, most sympathetic of all men.

During my discussion with Mr. Oddy on the publicity which should be given to the show in his paper, the question was mooted of placing before the public matter pertaining to the budgerigar in a novel form, such as these stories. He encouraged and advised me, with the result that " Penelope and her Pierrot " and other stories were written by me and published by him in his newspaper.

If ever success should crown my efforts as an author I shall owe it all to Mr. Oddy, who helped me so much.

Next I would like to mention Mr. W. I. Noddle, the Sales Manager of this company. To him fell the secretarial duties connected with the project. It was with Mr. Noddle that I spent most of the time I was engaged upon this show. A more tireless, efficient colleague I have yet to find. In the short space of ten weeks we had everything ready ; and whatever praise has come to me for my part, as chairman and show-manager of that colossal undertaking, must be shared by Mr. Noddle, for without his help I could never have done it. Tribute must also be paid to my assistant show-manager, Mr. Harold Parkinson and my committee of forty enthusiastic people whose one aim seemed to be ' to succeed '. Working as one man they were a wonderful team of which I was proud to be the head.

Then came the show itself. It was only then that the true genius of Mr. F. H. Timperley was seen. He is a born showman ; he can visualize the finished product—and in this case it was *par excellence*. Here I must mention the name of Mr. John Dennison. It was

Mr. Dennison and his assistants who did the hard work. We created a world's record—1,507 entries staged magnificently. The South, up to this time the recognized leaders, suddenly became aware that the North had taken the initiative.

The beginners class of 117 was astounding. This was proof positive that people had read these stories in the paper and had fallen for ' This Fascinating Little Fellow '.

This year, 1937, we established a new world's record of 1,747 entries, thus giving the world something to think about, as well as a difficult task to accomplish, if they would beat this figure. Upwards of 15,000 people visited the show each year in the two days it was held.

After many requests to put these stories in book form I decided to do so. Now read about this fascinating little fellow for yourself and see if *you* can resist his spell.

PART ONE

TRUE STORIES OF INCIDENTS IN THE LIVES
OF BUDGERIGARS IN THE AUTHOR'S AVIARIES,
AND THOSE OF HIS FRIENDS

PENELOPE AND HER PIERROT

CHAPTER I

PENELOPE AND HER PIERROT

A Budgie Idyll that almost ended in tragedy

" Penelope loved a Pierrot on the Portobello Pier,
And when he sang his lay
Penelope was not far away, she would stay all day."

A SIMPLE ditty. The sort of thing one used to hear before " Pierrots " became " Concert Parties " or " Follies ".

I heard this song ages and ages ago—about 1908, I believe. Basking in the sun on a glorious summer's afternoon, I lay listening to a pierrot troupe at Whitley Bay; when a gun from the " Spanish Battery " situated in the entrance to the Tyne boomed forth. Sudden y remembering that there was to be gun practice and an old ship sunk, I went off to Tynemouth to see the fun, and straightways forgot all about " Penelope and her Pierrot ".

.   .   .   .   .

Now, in the year 1934, Greywing Olive Budgerigars were very scarce. It was a 'New Shade', and not many people had them. There was great excitement in our aviaries that year—we had bred our first baby greywing olive budgerigar.

She was a little gem. How we fussed over her! Dr. Dafoe and the ' Quins ' were easily out-shone. All visitors to our aviaries were invited to ' Come up and see our baby greywing olive '. Eventually this reached the ears of one, ' Mae West ', who said, " Who is this Olive person ? " and remarked petulantly, " You should come up and see ME sometime," thereby gaining everlasting fame.

When this precious mite was about eight weeks old she was liberated with the rest of her family into a large flight, here to exercise and develop into an adult budgerigar.

She was a vivacious little creature, and spent much time watching her reflection in the water-pot, as she tucked the feathers behind her ears. Oh yes, budgies have ears. Besides, it was the fashion in 1934.

Later she developed into a beautiful young lady, and had learnt all the rudiments of budgie love. Having her eyes conveniently placed one on either side of her head by nature, she was able, whilst watching her reflection with one eye, to keep in view with the other a certain young gentleman not far away, and notice the effect that her preening and sprucing produced upon him.

Now in the next flight was a greywing cobalt budgie. He was a year older than G.W.O. He had been ' run over '—a term that we use when we allow a budgie to develop rather than take a wife, to get size and become a better show bird. This he had done, and he was now a big handsome fellow, having many wins to his credit.

But G.W.C. was by no means slow, he was rather quick on the uptake. He had spotted G.W.O. the very first day she had been turned into the flight next to him. Unfortunately for him the partition between them consisted of a double row of netting with a space of two inches in the centre.

I watched him as he clung to his side of the wire, making love to G.W.O. It was love at first sight. He knew every move of the game.

He would fly swiftly to the netting and give his call, which invariably brought G.W.O. to a position opposite him. He would then 'rub noses' on the wire and tap it with his beak, in a succession of sharp taps. His mask and feathers stood out like a ruffle round his neck, while he crooned his lay. The notes of his song were sweet, and they fell on the ears of G.W.O. like drops of sheer liquid delight. He would dart away like an arrow in flight; a swift loop, a dive and he was back again in the same spot, repeating the performance again and again.

One day, as I watched this play, I found myself humming quietly a little tune that I had dismissed with indifference from my mind about twenty-six years previously—'Penelope loved a Pierrot on the Portobello Pier', and then, 'Penelope loved a Pierrot in an aviary quite near'.

G.W.C. reminded me of a pierrot with his white, close-fitting skull-cap, his mask all stuck out like a ruffle, his spots like pom-poms, his grey satin coat, his blue pants and sash. So, subconsciously, a tune that had meant nothing at all had suddenly seemed to 'fit' after a lapse of many years. Thus G.W.C. became 'Pierrot' and G.W.O. became 'Penelope'.

> " Her mother had said, ' Come away, my dear,'
> But Penelope said, ' No fear, Ma dear,
> From my Pierrot, my hero, my Pierrot
> On the Portobello Pier.' "

Penelope's mother was a cross-tempered old grey-wing mauve. We thought that she must have been crossed in love; but eventually found out that her hubby, 'Yellow Olive', had, in the excitement of seeing her first eggs inadvertently put his foot on one and crushed it, so that she had sat upon a sticky yolk and rather 'mucked up' her latest in pantees.

A trifle maybe, yet she never seemed to get over it. Anyway, she scolded Penelope rather badly, saying the usual, "No good will come of this, etc., etc.," and being 1934, not 1908, Penelope just replied, " Sez you! "

The course of true love never did run smooth, and a terrible accident occurred that nearly resulted in a tragedy for poor little Penelope. Of late, she had been copying Pierrot's dives and loops, but she varied hers with a quick dash to a swing, where, suspended head downwards, she would slide down the wire until her feet touched the wood. Then a somersault in mid-air, a quick recovery, a dash, a swerve and she was back upon the wire opposite Pierrot.

One day she slipped. Over-confidence had let her down. The loop at the top of the swing had become loose and instead of sliding down the wire as usual, she found herself suspended in mid-air, head downwards, unable to get free. The numbered ring upon her leg had slipped over the projecting point of the wire, and there she hung, screaming and struggling to get free.

Her screams upset Pierrot, who added his to the din, and her mother of course added a vibrant, "I told you so."

My wife rushed into the aviary, and to her horror found poor Penelope in a terrible state. Her frantic struggles had broken her thigh, the flesh had given way, the bone protruded. Blood was streaming down her body; she was a pitiful sight. My wife swiftly disengaged the leg and took Penelope into the house and endeavoured to stop the bleeding.

I came home shortly afterwards. I looked at Penelope and shook my head.

" She is too far gone," I exclaimed, and prepared to put her quickly and painlessly out of her misery, when the old song again came to my mind. " What a climax to such a beautiful romance," I said.

But wait. There was just one chance in a million.

" Get wool, Iglodine and silk thread," I cried, and, taking out my nail scissors, sterilized them by the simple method of holding over a burning match.

Penelope and Her Pierrot

One quick ' snip ' and the flesh parted. So did
Penelope—with a leg. The bone was trimmed, the
wound bathed in Iglodine, the stump was tied round
with some silk thread and covered with a tiny pad of
boracic wool.

Poor Penelope was far gone, so we put her into a
cage without perches. It was touch and go, but we
fed her often with a fountain pen filler, and she hung
on to life. In twenty-four hours she began to eat some
soaked seed. Eventually, in about two weeks, Penelope pulled off her bandage with her strong beak, and
behold—a clean healed stump was revealed.

Now she was removed to a cage with perches, and
she soon learnt how to balance herself on one foot.
It was a very tiring job, and she often came down and
laid her body on the floor of the cage, to rest her weary
leg.

Her strength regained, a very demure Penelope was
returned to the flight. It was a heart-rending sight;
we had thought that her dream of love had ended.
However, she clung to the wire with her beak and
one remaining leg, but she could not respond to Pierrot's
song of love. She was unable to use her beak and
hang on at the same time, and so she was bereft of
speech, and could only listen.

Old Pierrot was nearly bowled over at her plight;
but his love was strong and true, so he never let her
see that. He still sang his lay, if anything, stronger
than ever.

Our hearts bled for them, and so impressed were
we with Pierrot's fidelity we determined on a daring
experiment. They were both put into a breeding pen.
They were united at last; their joy was unbounded.
The nest was hung, and we fixed a double perch close
to the entrance to enable Penelope to get in or out
more easily.

We thought that she would never make that tiny

21

hole that served as the entrance to her miniature ' Villa '.
But love soon found a way, and in about two weeks'
time Penelope was sitting on four beautiful white eggs.
Joy came to the heart of Pierrot. The eggs were fertile,
and in due course four tiny pink chicks were hatched
—and each had two tiny legs.

Penelope and Pierrot were almost hysterical with
joy. The chicks lived and prospered. They, in turn,
went to the shows and brought home many prizes.

Both Penelope and Pierrot are now ' pensioned
off '. I see them as I write. Her head is tucked up
into his neck, his head encircles hers as he tickles her
off-side ear, so tenderly with his beak. Her eyes are
half closed, and in the deepening shadows she listens
to a radio in the distance broadcasting the ' golden
voice ' of Grace Moore singing ' One Night of Love '.

We sigh happily as we fix the padlocks for the
night. We have just seen a perfect ending to a perfect budgie idyll that might well have been a tragedy.

TOLD TO A PEPPER POT

CHAPTER II

TOLD TO A PEPPER POT

A Feathered Prodigy Confounds the Critics

" Hello, everybody ! This is Beauty Metcalfe calling—
I'll be seeing you ! "

Tap ! Tap ! Tap ! went his tiny beak upon the rim
of the pepper-pot.

" Where's Georgie-Porgie-Porgie ? I beg your par-
don ! Ha ! Ha ! Jolly good ! "

My mouth opened as though to laugh, my eyes had
already assumed the proportions of dinner plates. It
was unbelievable ; it was uncanny. I could not speak.
A feeling of awe had taken possession of me. I felt
that I was hoist with my own petard. For the past
two years I had boosted the ' talking budgie ', and in
that time had heard hundreds of these fascinating little
fellows displaying their linguistic abilities ; and yet,
until I had made the acquaintance of Beauty Metcalfe
in person, I had seen and heard nothing. Now I felt
very foolish.

" Humpty Dumpty, sat on a wall,
    Humpty Dumpty had a great fall,
  And all the King's horses (pronounced *h*orsis) and
    all the King's men
  Couldn't put Humpty together again."

Before I had time to register my surprise, he was at
it again—with a true Oxford accent, too.

" Every time I look, the monkey's on the table.
  Get a stick—get a stick! and knock him off,
  And Pop! goes the weasel. . . . Jolly good!"
" You say it, Beauty. . . . Ha! ha!"
He laughed at his own joke.

He danced up and down, he bowed and rubbed his nose on now dented top of that famous pepper-pot. What action! His neck was arched, his spotless white bib stood out in front of him like a ruffle —he was proud! He turned quickly, ran to the edge of the table, cocked his head sideways and looked at me.

" Hey diddle diddle. . . . Go on, you say it!"

I gasped! His eye held me spellbound. It was bold and extraordinarily bright—there was a look of profound intelligence in it. I must have looked for all the world like a credulous youngster standing open-mouthed before a Punch and Judy show, for Beauty simply chuckled and scampered back to his pepper-pot. Never had I heard such a melodious expression of exultation, never had any budgie in my recollection shown such vivacity.

" Little Bo-Peep has lost her sheep . . . " word perfect and with flawless delivery, was followed instantaneously by—

" Little Miss Muffet sat on a tuffet . . . "

" Doesn't he ever get mixed up?" I asked.

" Oh yes, sometimes. He gets terribly excited like a precocious young child," said his Mistress, " He goes too fast, and then . . . . . he only chuckles and says, 'Say it again, Beauty,' so we cannot scold him."

" Sing a song of sixpence . . . . "

He went through that with lightning speed. I tried to say the words, silently, in time with him, but got badly tongue-tied. He must have known, for he gave me such a look from the corner of his eye.

Told to a Pepper-pot

" You say it, Beauty ! "

I felt snubbed.

" Good-night ! "

I deserved that. For nearly twenty minutes he had given me excerpts from his repertoire, without pause. Who was I but a mere scribbler ? while he—he was a " Star "

On the night of December 2nd, 1937, for almost thirty minutes, Beauty Metcalfe, a lovely, deep blue budgerigar, held the world astonished as they listened in to the recording of his thrilling chatter. There was not the slightest shadow of doubt ; he scooped the pool.

Many critics said that the record had been joined up ; that no living bird could have spoken for so long a period without pause or prompting. But I assure all those people who listened in to North Regional that night that this was a perfectly true recording of the most famous talking bird in the whole world. ' Beauty ' had made history. Henceforth that fascinating little fellow—" The Incomparable Budgerigar " —will be known as the perfect copyist of human speech.

It was with a feeling of regret that I took my leave —but tiny children such as he have to be asleep long before we ' burners of the midnight oil ' ; it was long past ten o'clock. Yet I felt deep a reverence for that pioneer who first gave us the means of recording for all time one of the marvels of nature.

On February 26th, 1938, " Beauty " again took the world by storm when he featured in " In Town To-night " broadcast. Was he not 'Incomparable' ?

A mere morsel of gorgeously coloured feathers, Beauty Metcalfe is worth many times his weight in gold. May he have a long and happy life.

CHAPTER III

BATTLES OF A FATHER OF " QUADS "

Richard the Lion-hearted " Budgie "

RICHARD, the strong silent budgie was very hand-some and very sedate. Whereas Beauty ' talked ' quite a lot, he only ' thought '. Sitting on his doorstep or perch, he always brought to my mind ' The Thinker ' by Rodin.

It takes many kinds of budgies to make ' budgie-dom '; but there, Richard occupies no mean place.

Richard was a family man ; his duty was to produce and rear winners if possible for his master, Mr. G. He took his job seriously, and was very house-proud.

When we first made his acquaintance, Richard was the father of four tiny baby chicks ; he was fond of his wife, and very proud of the ' detached ' villa which hung on the aviary wall, housing his family.

My word ! he had a busy time. Being the father of ' Quads ', and with a wife to feed into the bargain, was no sinecure for Richard. How he worshipped those babies ! All day long he journeyed to and fro to the seed-pot and then to the nest. Only the choicest seeds did he pick out, the remainder he carefully dropped over the edge of the pot to save further re-sorting. Time and time again he filled his crop and then dis-gorged the seed into that of his wife, who partially digested it before passing it on to her babies.

He never left the house empty-handed, either ; he always brought out the dried excreta on his return

BATTLES OF A FATHER OF QUADS

journeys. So did Richard keep his home sweet and clean.

At eventide, when his family were all fed and settled down for the night, only then did he rest. Filling his crop for the last time that day, he settled down on the tiny perch outside the entrance to his home to meditate upon the responsibilities of a father of ' Quads '.

Eventually the great day arrived when the first chick left the nest. He was just like velvet; his first suit spotless, he looked just like a tiny ball of green, yellow and black fluff. Old Richard had a field-day; he rushed his family duties and then put his young son through his paces.

Lessons in flying, fighting and feeding were all part of the curriculum. The latter was nearly Richard's undoing, for young Dick soon learnt to crack seed for himself, and, the foolish boy mistaking something for 'Niger' seed, in ignorance he ate it, became ill and quickly died.

Richard, almost heart-broken himself, had to bear silently the wrath of Mr. G., who blamed him for not having fed and taken due care of his offspring.

In due course chick No. 2 came out of the nest, only to meet the same fate as his elder brother. Things began to get warm at Sherburn House. Richard could not talk ! Not a word left his tongue ; in silence he bore the tempest.

Quad No. 3 followed, and soon he was relegated to the dust-bin. The temperature, by this time, was at fever heat.

Quoth Mr. G., " One more chick—one more chance ! If this one goes, then you go too."

Poor old Richard ! Why had someone not taught him to speak in his childhood days ? Had he had Beauty's education he might have told a thing or two, but his lips were sealed.

One day he overheard his young mistress reciting 'Gelert's Grave', all about 'Llewellyn and his dog'. A cold shiver ran down his spine—visions of the 'vengeful sword' flashed to his mind, and he determined to do or die in the attempt. Something had to be done or his life would be forfeit.

Now, while Richard had been soliloquizing on his doorstep at eventide, he had seen and heard, in the twilight, something which had upset even his calm serenity.

Scampering feet; pairs of bright, black eyes flashing up at him; long, sharp teeth crunching up seed—the very same teeth that he had seen making short work of the wood around the flight—these sent him all goosey.

Chick No. 4 must have been born on Friday the 13th, for in spite of his father's watchful eye, he, too, went the way of all flesh. This last mishap fairly staggered Richard; he thought, 'Someone will have to die'—well, it should not be him. But what protection were feathers against teeth which ate through wood?

He braced himself up; with his 'old school cry' gurgling in his throat, for that was the best he could do in the way of speech, he swooped down and grabbed one of the intruders by the scruff of the neck. It was a battle royal, but Richard won! Judging by the feathers, fur and blood lying about it must have been a sanguinary conflict. The rest of the field fled, and Richard resumed his family duties, for by this time his wife was laying her second round of eggs.

Daylight came, and with it Mr. G. He found the dead chick; he almost exploded with wrath, but wait —what is this? A dead mouse! Great Scot! He looked around—the little bits of 'Niger seed' were mouse droppings . . . the poor little Quads had eaten them, knowing no better. That dreaded disease 'enteritis' had done the rest.

28

It was not the end of Richard, however. Saved by the strength of his beak, but it had been a narrow escape. He was now 'Public Hero No. 1', but still he was silent, so Mr. G. told the tale for him.

Three other mice followed. 'An eye for an eye,' thought Richard—four chicks—four mice! But what it had cost him to fight those battles one will never know.

Still, he did get his reward. Later, he was sent to a show, a red ticket adorned his cage, people fussed over him, and Richard was prouder than ever.

Chapter IV

THE ADVENTURES OF THE PRODIGAL SON

How Samson was Cured of Wanderlust

SAMSON was a skyblue budgie, the only one in a nest of light greens; it was probably this difference of colour which made his parents dote on him in his childhood, for he was pampered and spoilt. He soon outgrew all his brothers and sisters and developed into an adult budgie of wonderful physique, hence his name Samson.

As a young man, he was both churlish and swelled-headed. He seemed to be very dissatisfied with his lot, and often vented his temper upon the rest of his relations. We thought it was perhaps a case of ' familiarity breeding contempt ', and that a change of surroundings would do him good, so we moved him to another flight among fresh companions.

The experiment failed, however, for he soon made their lives most miserable with his arrogance and over-bearing manners. My wife and I were at a loss to make him more contented and happy; we had tried to tame him, and often coaxed him, but he did not respond to kindness and become more amiable. At last we put his father, a four-year-old budgie, into the flight with him. Pa was a level-headed, sedate budgie, and we thought that perhaps he might bring Samson to heel somewhat.

THE ADVENTURES OF THE PRODIGAL SON

This later move was also doomed to failure, for Samson bullied the old man terribly. Not one good feature did he seem to have inherited from his parents, and we were about to give him up as a bad job when one day, quite by accident, we found the cause of the trouble.

In the garden, near to the flight where Samson exercised, was a bird-bath. Here many wild birds came to drink and to pick up the crumbs which we put out for them in the hard times, when natural food was scarce.

We had previously noted that when the dull-looking sparrows came to feed and bathe, Samson habitually turned up his nose (beak in his case) in an expression of contempt and muttered something which sounded very much like 'Swine!' Surely it was not these harmless creatures who came and went as they pleased which made Samson discontented? No! he considered them far below his dignity; it was another visitor to our garden who was the root of the mischief.

She was beautiful; her body was sleek and very shapely; the jet-black feathers with their even markings and over all a wonderful glossy sheen, suited her well. Her black feet; brilliant yellow beak and bold black eyes completed her ravishing 'ensemble'.

Miss Delilah Starling was as bad as she was beautiful, and her flashing eyes were filled with cunning. She was feared by most of the others who came to feed. Many a poor little sparrow received a vicious peck for having the temerity to come too near.

We noticed that Miss Delilah hung round the flight where Samson lived and openly flirted with him. One day we saw them in serious conclave, so decided to see what was 'in the wind'. We did not get all of the conversation, but we did hear something like this—

Samson: "If only I could get out of here! I feel positively stifled!"

Delilah : " My dear, a big strong handsome man like you should be king of the open spaces."

Samson : " Oh, Miss Delilah, you make me feel my position. If I were out of this prison, I would make you my Queen."

Delilah : " You wonderful cave-man ! You *shall* be out of here. Listen, and I will tell you of a plan I've thought out. . . . Sh-h, bend a little closer, we might be overheard. . . ."

We missed the rest of the conversation, but I thought it wise to remove Samson before more damage should be done by this dark temptress, so I took the net, and prepared to take him from that flight. As I bent my head to enter the low doorway of the flight I felt a rush of wind past my ear, just over my shoulder, and I had the horrible experience of seeing Samson flying swiftly through the air towards Cottingley.

This cunning witch of a Delilah had whispered and told Samson not to dart high and hit the safety portion over the door, but to dive low past my head. He had done so, and was free !

Our hearts were heavy ; we knew what lay ahead of Samson. The Autumn had set in ; the nights were cold and heavy with dew, maybe mist and frost. The grasses had long since shed their seeds ; food was hard to obtain even for the wild birds, who were more experienced than Samson. Only a slow and painful death from starvation awaited him unless he had the sense to return, but we had little hope of that, knowing him.

On first obtaining his freedom Samson forgot all about Delilah, so exciting was his new-found liberty ; he spent the first few hours racing, darting, looping and gliding in sheer ecstasy. It was painful yet wonderful to behold ; budgies are like swifts in flight, a fact you will soon realize if ever your pet escapes.

It had been early morning when Samson had made his getaway and his crop had been almost empty ; so quickly had the dash been planned that he had had no chance to replenish it with seed. His exertions made him hungry, so he fed on grass which was mostly withered and not very palatable, and which he soon found was not very sustaining.

His hunger temporarily abated, he bethought himself of Delilah and his ' kingdom ', so away to the chimney-stacks he hied in search of her.

Samson did not get the reception he had anticipated. Delilah saw him approaching. " Here comes the little swanker," she said to her companions. " Let's give him beans ! "

Delilah had betrayed him to the Philistines ; they set about him with a will. It was fortunate for Samson that he was quick in flight, for he managed to outwit the attackers, but not before he had received many wounds and lost a few feathers.

He espied a huge tree and paused in his flight to rest ; but to his horror a big black bird, a giant to him and possessing a terrible beak, snapped at him as he would have alighted on the bough. Luck again saved him ; a side swerve and a nose-dive beneath the branch and he was away, but he left his tail in the beak of a big black crow.

Samson was in a terrible state by eventide. He had been chased hither and thither, and now the rooks coming in to roost frightened the very life out of him ; so, seeing an opening at the top of a barn, he flew in and settled on a rafter in the gathering darkness in an endeavour to sleep and so regain his strength.

He did not remain undisturbed very long. As the night closed in, and he was dozing with his head tucked beneath his wing, something ghostly brushed past him and he awoke with a start. A bat had dropped from its inverted position above him and flapped its ungainly wings in flight to the opening through which Samson had entered the barn.

Samson shivered with fright; he thought of the cosy, peaceful aviary which he had left that morning, and felt anything but a king just then. Suddenly the moon broke through the clouds and a dull shaft of light shone through the opening straight on to him— and also on to a pair of flashing eyes belonging to a great barn owl, who had a horrible curved beak much stronger than his, and long sharp talons. The owl was about to seize him, to make supper from his well-nourished body, when that tiny flash of light into his eyes made him blink, and before he had recovered Samson had shot like a bullet from a rifle through that hole—into the night.

He had ' wind up ' properly now ; he flew as though all the devils in Hades were on his tail—or where it used to be. The moon went back behind the clouds, the night was pitch black, the wind bitterly cold, but on went Samson in sheer terror, until at last he could fly no further, and he dropped like a stone . . . he knew not where.

Fortunately, without encountering any obstacle, he fell into some long wet grass, which partially broke his fall, and he lay shivering, too frightened and too weak to move, scarcely daring to breathe.

Sounds of things moving in the darkness filled him with fear ; then as the hours passed he realized he was almost dead with hunger, so he nibbled at the wet grass as he lay. It was terrible stuff after the sweet oily seeds to which he had been accustomed before his escape, and he bitterly repented his folly as he cursed the black-hearted traitress who had let him down.

Dawn came at last and with it Samson noticed a number of sparrows flying overhead. He recognized one or two as the ' swine ' who used to feed at the bird-table and bath, outside his old flight.

A weary, repentant Samson shook the water from his body and flew after the sparrows—' He would fain have eaten the husks which the swine did eat '—but the sparrows were having none of him and his high-falutin' airs, so they set upon him and almost murdered him. They chased him round and round . . . few feathers were left upon his neck and back, when suddenly he heard a sound which was sweet music to his ears.

Samson had recognized the voice of his old father in the flight nearby. Pa had just filled his crop with delicious seed and was singing a song of praise and thankfulness. To a truly repentant Samson it was the sweetest sound he had ever heard. He exerted himself to the utmost, shook off the sparrows and made a bee-line to the flight, saying as he flew, " I will go to my father. . . ."

He had had enough of freedom and more luck than he deserved, for during the night he had been flying in circles and had dropped near to his flight. This final effort was almost his last, for a very exhausted Samson fell on to the netting, and he lay there gasping for breath.

Old Pa's joy was unbounded, and though he could not get his son back into the flight, he did the next best thing—he fed him through the wire netting. In his own fashion he killed ' the fatted calf ', much to the brother's disgust.

We found the ' Prodigal ' there in the early morn and easily netted him, but we did not return him to the flight ; we had noticed the danger signs—the pupils of his eyes were contracted, what feathers remained on the top of his skull were stood on end . . . exposure had done its worst, pneumonia was setting in.

The heat was switched on in the hospital cage (a wonderful gadget), and whilst the temperature was getting up a half-dead Samson was given a nip of brandy.

He was put into an electrically-heated, glass-fronted

35

compartment where he could be kept under observation. He was now too ill to eat and he huddled in a corner, wheezing and spluttering; a few drops of 'Valpine' in the vaporizer soon began to take effect and his breathing grew easier.

It was a tough battle to save his life. He was fed with 'liquid vitamins' from a fountain-pen filler every few hours. A fresh, palatable spray of millet was put to soak in water and chemical food, to be ready if his strength returned and he was able to eat by himself.

By the time he recovered his new feathers were beginning to grow. We had to watch over him carefully to prevent a relapse, and eventually a very subdued Samson was returned to the flight. If the door was left open it is doubtful if he would wander again, for Samson had been cured of wanderlust.

THE AMAZON

CHAPTER V

THE AMAZON

A Story of a Hen-pecked Husband

At 'Lintonholme' my friend Mr. W. W., a notable breeder and exhibitor of budgerigars, had rather a peculiar experience with a very estimable young lady whom we eventually named Gertie the Amazon.

As a very young lady, Gertie was a bit of a puzzle. It was quite a while before Mr. W. knew whether to call her Gertie or Bertie. She was so well developed, even to the extent of causing her features to appear rather masculine. However, in the end her wattle turned deep brown, and so finally established her as Gertie.

Reaching the age of maturity, Gertie adopted a very superior manner towards her sisters and one of aloofness to the young men in the next flight. Instead of hanging about the wires giving ' glad eyes ' to these gentlemen, she sat on her perch, prim and proper, yet she missed nothing of what went on around.

Gertie said that the young hens in her flight were ' fast ', and that they cheapened themselves in the eyes of the ' Don Juans ', who hung on the far side of the netting, calling to them and talking all manner of sentimental nonsense. She was very sedate and did not indulge in acrobatics. " It is most undignified," she said, " to hang upside down in the sight of gentlemen budgies."

37

She also scolded these young ladies of her domicile for their lack of cleanliness in the house. They scattered everything they could about the flight, in their haste to rush meals so that they might have more time to spend on the wire, flirting with their beaux.

Gertie stood primly on the edge of the pot eating her meals with proper decorum. She chose each seed with care, cracked it and then dropped the husk on to a neat little pile outside the pot; her sisters dropped theirs in the pot or wherever they could, much to her annoyance. Sometimes, they even stood in the pot, scattering the seed all over the place with their feet. The lectures she gave them about dirty feet in the food!—such things jarred upon her nerves and hurt her finer feelings.

Finding that her protests were either ignored or that the invariable reply was, "Oh yeah!" Gertie adopted a sterner attitude and gave these other young ladies a jolly good hiding, which sent them scurrying into the house to sulk. Later, after they had somewhat regained their dignity, we watched them preen their lovely feathers and powder their noses. Oh, yes! budgies do powder their noses, and it is quite a simple process —they just rub them up and down upon the white-washed walls.

Gertie was very meticulous in all that she did; rising with the dawn she sipped at the water-pot, bathed her face, replenished her crop and then took her exercise. She flew sedately round the flight, pausing now and then to pick up some piece of wood which her sisters had chewed from the woodwork of the flight, or perches. These splinters she carefully dropped into the water-pot, knowing that Albert, the aviary attendant, would empty it. In this way Gertie got rid of much of the litter her companions made.

These Amazons, the masculine type of females, are by no means dirty or slothful. Usually, they are just the opposite, which probably accounts for the hectic time they give to those around them.

Now, in the next flight was a young gentleman budgie who was rather timorous. He was beautifully marked, of a very excellent colour, and of the correct type. In fact, he possessed all the good qualities of the show bird excepting that he failed in one essential —size. He was a wee bit small.

Albert thought him a bit of a dandy, and so named him Bertie, probably thinking of the popular song, ' I'm Burlington Bertie from Bow '.

It was a pity that Bertie was small, otherwise he would have most likely become a very famous gentleman in budgie circles. His brothers used to twit him ; they soon picked up the name bestowed upon him and developed a nasty habit of singing, ' Here comes Bertie ' to the rhyme of a famous radio signature tune. This annoyed him, especially in the sight and hearing of the young ladies in the next pen.

Bertie, like his brothers, had seen prim and proper Gertie ; all had tried to win her affections but he. The continual leg-pulling had created in him an inferiority complex, and while Gertie refused to join in what she termed vulgar flirtations, Bertie was too timid and self-conscious to make any advances to the maid of his desire.

Gertie had noticed him, however, and like Penelope, she had made her choice. At last spring came, and with it the irresistible call of love. One day she was caught by Albert, giving a sly wink to Bertie.

This incident was at once reported to Mr. W., and a little discussion took place upon the merits or de-merits of letting such a courtship continue. In the end it was decided to allow the match to proceed. Bertie's general good qualities but lack of size might be well balanced by Gertie's similar good points and greater physical development ; so they were both moved

to a breeding compartment containing the usual ' villa '
as a nesting place.

Thus started the strangest courtship it has been my
lot to witness.

Bertie, out of sight of his leg-pulling companions,
plucked up courage to make the first advance ; he rushed
towards Gertie to rub noses. Biff ! a well-planted
foot caught him in the pants and he landed on the floor
of the flight, where, dazed, he remained for a while
gazing at his beloved, who sat serenely upon the perch
as though nothing had happened.

" Not so fast, young man ; we will begin as I in-
tend we shall continue. You may be my husband, but
you must learn to keep your place. Now you may
tickle my left ear ! " said Gertie.

Bertie was overjoyed at this favour ; he flew quickly
to her side to do her bidding. When he thought that
the left side had been ' tickled ' enough, he moved
over to the right side. Biff ! again he found himself
on the floor. He was amazed.

" Now, look here, young man ! le+'s get this straight.
When I say the left ear—I mean the left ear. Don't
be so impetuous. I'll do all the thinking in this es-
tablishment, and you will do just as you are told."
Gertie was most indignant. " Go, and fill your crop
with the choicest seeds, and perhaps I'll let you
feed me."

Any ' cave-man ' in Bertie died at that moment, but
he loved his G. ; also he had a sneaking regard for
that strong foot which she used so effectively. So
without comment he did as he was bid, under the
watchful eye of his bigger and better half.

Thus did Gertie establish her ascendancy over Bertie,
and he became her willing slave. Then came the day
when Gertie thought it time to investigate the inside
of her nest. One morning, she disappeared inside
the little villa and Bertie saw no more of her until late

afternoon when he was informed that she had laid her first egg. Bertie was very excited.

That evening, Bertie thought it a good plan to keep his beloved company in the nest. Gertie was now sitting tight. He was half-way through the entrance when he found himself projected backwards, and again he took a count. A head quickly followed him through the aperture.

" Young man ! haven't you heard that twin beds are the fashion to-day ? Your place is on the little perch outside ; there you will stay. At meal-times you will knock upon the door, but don't you dare to enter ! "

Poor Bertie, he was very curious to know what was going on inside the nest, but he never got another peep. At feeding times he would tap, tap, tap ! upon the wood by the hole with his strong beak. Out popped Gertie's head ; when she was satisfied that her husband was keeping up to his household duties, then, would she allow him to feed her.

One morning, about eighteen days later, Bertie heard a faint chirp inside the little villa—his firstborn son and heir had hatched. He could control himself no longer ; he shot to that hole like a bullet in flight. Gertie had anticipated his coming ; she met his headlong rush and bowled him over. This time she did not scold, but followed him down and proceeded to give him a sound drubbing.

" Will you never learn *not* to bring outside germs into my nursery ? Have you never heard of hygienics ? "

Bertie did so want to see his babies, but the first he did see of them was about five weeks later when the first chick left the nest. Bertie thought that here was a real pal to play with, and he proceeded to have a jolly game with his son. Gertie was soon on them like a wild cat, and gave them both a hiding.

" You'll do just as mother tells you, my son ! It will save a deal of trouble if you do."

Little Bertram soon found her words true; it *did* save a lot of trouble. Also he found that strict obedience meant that he could sit upon the perch much more comfortably—there was no ache under his tail.

So did Gertie the Amazon set her house in order. She set a very strict code for each of them. It was a most peculiar marriage, yet I'm sure that Bertie would not have had it otherwise; he had a silent and secret admiration for his loved one.

Later, when they were all moved to the large flights for exercise, other bigger fellows tried to ' get off ' with Gertie, but Bertie only smiled as they flew shrieking to the hut to nurse their wounds.

" No one can tame this shrew of mine, but me ! " he thought, but he was far too wise to say so. He had learnt that discretion was better than valour.

At eventide, when Gertie allowed her husband to caress her, Bertie found that sufficient recompense for the trying times of the day, and he was content.

BILLY THE BOY SCOUT

Chapter VI

BILLY THE BOY SCOUT

His Daily Good Deed

HERE is a story of a young yellow split white budgie. He was not a very desirable bird, for he was not pretty ; he was, in fact, a mongrel. His colour precluded him from being useful as an exhibition bird, but any dog lover who may read this story will know how faithful these mongrels, the throw-outs, can be. They make such pals.

While Billy, the unwanted, was quite a baby he was taken from the aviary into the house to be taught to talk. He soon won the affections of his master and mistress, Mr. and Mrs. General Dealer.

At first he was very shy and timorous, but he soon got over that. Much can be accomplished by patience and kindness, and eventually Billy lost his fear and once more became his perky little self.

He was a cocky little fellow, full of vitality and ingenuity. Full of mischief, quick on the uptake, he was happy the whole day long.

Each morning Billy woke the hous by ringing his bell. " Time to get up, you sluggards," said he. " Come on ! what about my daily dozen ? " he persisted. " Open that cage door ! "

He had learnt how to open the door by himself, so at nights it had to be securely fastened, or it would have been ' Good-bye, budgie '.

43

Once the cage door was opened Billy took his exercises. First a few times round the room to stretch his wings, then up and down the chandelier chains, mostly using his beak ; this was to take the kink out of his neck. Budgies sleep with their heads tucked up under their wings, which gives them a nasty kink in the neck ; if you don't believe it, try it yourself some night.

Then of course his legs were a wee bit cramped ; they must be straightened out.

If you slept with one leg tucked up into your tummy you might feel a little creaky in the joints. (All healthy birds sleep standing upon one leg. The lifting of one leg causes the other one to grip so that the bird does not lose its balance while dozing, and so fall off the perch.)

So upside down Billy swung on the chains, gripping with his claws and flapping his wings at a terrific rate meanwhile. This created a pull on his feet and so stretched his joints.

" Well, it's good to be alive ! " said Billy, his exercises over. " Now for a spot of breakfast." Down he came, to perch on the edge of Mrs. G.D.'s cup, and sipped the tea. " Not sweet enough," said Billy with a grimace, and he flew over to his master's cup. " Ah ! that's much better." Mr. G.D. possessed a sweet tooth. Having drunk his fill, Billy next perched upon his master's hand and nibbled a few crumbs of bread, chattering between each mouthful.

Exercises over, his hunger appeased, Billy thought it time to spruce up a little, so across to his cage he flew and splashed about in the water-pot for awhile, then to the mantle-shelf, where he carefully preened his feathers before the mirror. " There ! " he said, examining himself in the glass, " that should do. Every feather in its place, thanks to ' Aqua pura '."

About this time the *Yorkshire Observer* was pushed

through the letter-box. Mr. G.D. lingered over that last cup to scan the morning news. Billy loved to sit on the edge of the paper and read the news too; he chatted all the while, " I wonder what that fellow P.G.F. has to say this morning? Beauty, Penelope, Richard, Samson, Gertie? Bah! They know nothing. See that fly? Well, get a load of this!" and off he went like greased lightning after the fly.

The fly ducked; Billy swerved, did a half-loop, and —gotcher! Back he came and deposited a dead fly upon the paper. " Now, isn't that clever?" Billy is a dab at catching flies.

Mr. G.D. closed the paper and folded it. Billy suddenly found an overwhelming interest in the electric bulb. He made a great pretence of trying to find where the light goes when switched off, but this was merely a dodge, for he had one eye upon the door leading to the general hardware store at the front of the house.

With a sigh Mr. G.D. put the paper aside and moved towards the door, opened it and passed into the shop. Something else went through first; Billy had flown past his master like a flash. Then the fun began.

" I always believe in trying everything once," said Billy, as he somersaulted from a chandelier to the edge of a bucket, and then on to the handlebars of a bicycle. " Whoops a daisy! That's a slippy perch if you like." He had gone clean over the top and landed on a radio set.

" As dead as door-nails," he observed, disgustedly, noticing that the dial was not illuminated. " No jazz this morning." You should see Billy dance on the top of a radio, to the tunes of Henry Hall, and he can out-croon any crooner.

Finding that there was nothing doing on the wireless, and seeing Mr. G.D. making a bee-line towards him with the net, Billy dodged between the suspended rakes and spades into the window. " Bring that net in here and see what happens," he chuckled, as he proceeded to drop the price tickets from the goods to the bottom of the window, and knocked over a show-card or two.

In the heat of the moment, Mr. G.D. did so, but instantly regretted his hasty action. He missed Billy and hit a glass shade, which fell in tiny pieces. " Darn that bird ! " ejaculated Mr. G.D., and tried other methods.

It fairly ticked Billy to note the expressions on the faces of the school children when they pressed their noses to the glass in their excitement, as they watched with joy his merry antics in the window.

" Well, the window needed dressing again, anyhow," said Mr. G.D., after the struggle was over and Billy was safe in his cage—to stay, for being a naughty boy.

He did not stay long, however, for Mrs. G.D. soon forgave him and he was freed once more ; but this time the door leading to the shop was closed.

Billy then noticed some sparrows mopping up the crumbs on the window ledge outside. He tried to get at them. " You big stiffs," said he, but somehow he was held back by an invisible hand. He never knew what held him back. He knows that it's there, but he can't see it. The first time that he was let out of the cage, he made a perfect swallow dive for the garden ; he came to on the floor beneath the window, and thought he must have been dozing, for the stars were coming out, as well as a bump upon his head.

Just at that moment the sparrows flew away ; an April shower deferred till August sent little drops of water scurrying down the pane. Billy had a great game while it lasted, chasing the drops as they ran down the window. He tried to gobble them up but failed. " This is a dry job, licking up water that isn't even wet," he said, as he gave up in disgust.

Later, Billy saw a patrol of Boy Scouts in the garden, going through their tactics ; it amused him to see their evolutions with their poles. Down to the ash-tray he went, picked up a match-stick and flew back to the window, where he tried to follow their movements with his little pole.

He tried vaulting, but his match-stick went down the crevice between the two sashes and he bumped his nose upon the latch.

" Oh, shucks ! Did you see me make that pole disappear, Ma ? I'm a conjurer."

The Scouts had gathered around their leader to receive final instructions for the day before being dismissed. " Now don't forget, boys, you must do at least one good deed every day." This puzzled Billy ; what that meant he did not know, but he still listened with interest.

Two of the young ' Cubs ' paused before going home. " What are you going to do, Joe ? " said one.

" I think I'll go and get in the coals for Mrs. Murphy ; she's not so well to-day," replied Joe.

" Eureka ! " exclaimed Billy, " I'll get the coals in, too." Down to the coal scuttle he flew—and dirty work it was. Mrs. G.D. heard the scuffle in the scuttle and started to investigate.

" Pa, come here quick ; we have got a black budgie at last," she cried. In the excitement of the moment she had forgotten about Billy.

Mr. G.D. soon dispelled her joy, however. " Give the little devil a bath," he said. He was still sore about the episode of the shop window.

" Why. . . . Good heavens, it's Billy ! Oh, how could you ! " exclaimed Mrs. G.D., and she proceeded to give him a good tubbing. Like all other boys, Billy did not like soap and water, and when he was put in his cage near the fire to dry he just went into a corner to sulk.

While there he ruminated over that problem of the good deed ; those young cubs had let him down badly with that one about the coals.

47

Later that evening, the way's work done, Mr. G.D. settled down with his pipe and the *Telegraph & Argus*. He was immersed in the gossip of the day, when his wife put' down her knitting and said, " I'll let Billy have a fly round ; it will help to dry him thoroughly before he settles down for the night." So the cage door was opened and out flew the little scamp.

Totally ignoring Mrs. G.D., whom he hated for that scrubbing, Billy flew to the edge of the paper and commenced to tear tiny pieces from the edge with his sharp beak, much to the annoyance of Mr. G.D.

" Here, get up there out of the way," said Mr. G.D., as he pushed Billy on to his shoulder.

" Oh, all right, don't push," replied Billy, " I'll go on to the grand-stand." He had spotted some lessons in slimming by Margot Thinn in the paper in his master's hands, and thought he would have a better view, so he climbed on to his master's head. He was bending over in his excitement to see how Margot retained the perfect figure, when he slipped and landed fair and square in the ladies' beauty parlour.

" Now, who the heck pushed me ? " cried Billy, as he flew back to his stand to see what had tripped him up. There he noted for the first time a little bald patch on his master's head.

" Ye Gods ! how does he expect me to get a grip on that ? " he said. Then he glanced across to Mrs. G.D. " Well, she's got far too much." He paused ; a sudden inspiration had flashed into his mind. " I've got it ! A good deed every day." He flew to his mistress and took a great delight in pulling from her head some of the superfluous hairs.

Back to his master he flew, and then endeavoured to stick these on to the bald patch. Billy was doing his good deed for the day.

He did not quite succeed, and his transplanting efforts tickled Mr. G.D. so much—his pate, not his sense of humour—that Billy was once more relegated to his cage, where again he sulked.

Poor Billy, his ' good deed ' nearly proved to be his undoing, for next morning he failed to ring his bell. When Mrs. G.D. came down she found him in the bottom of the cage. Long hairs protruded from his beak. They had entered his crop ; he was crop-bound and had had a fit.

The hairs were gently withdrawn ; Billy was given a nip of brandy and he recovered. Well, he had done his best, and for a little man he had had a very busy day.

CHAPTER VII

THE GOOD SAMARITAN

A Story of feathered Heroes and Heroines

MR. DARBY and Mrs. Joan Green were, as their name denotes, a pair of light green budgerigars. They were only eleven months old when they commenced their ' honeymoon '.

Usually, we only give our consent and blessing to love matches which have a little variation in age. We like to have a little more age on one side, and thereby more experience. It matters not which side.

With Darby and Joan, however, we made an exception. They had entwined themselves round our hearts ; they were an ideal pair, and we had great expectations from them. They would surely produce winners for us—and they did.

We were delighted when we saw that they had fallen deeply in love. It was a beautiful romance ; Darby thought the world of Joan and she worshipped him.

He was a very handsome young man, tall and slender, of gorgeous colour and markings. His features were perfect, his manners beyond reproach. He must have come of a very good family ; we used to say, jokingly, that he was the perfect Oxford product ; we could hardly find any fault with him, and he lived up to his perfect training as a youth.

Joan was a replica of her husband, and must have been to a very high-class finishing school for young

THE GOOD SAMARITAN

ladies; her manners were perfect, and she was kindness and gentleness personified. She was the very antithesis of Gertie the Amazon, for she was both loving and gentle.

Darby was the man of her house, and as such she respected him. It was an ideal honeymoon; Darby waited upon Joan hand and foot. Her slightest wish was a command and he obeyed her every whim. He was passionately in love and not afraid to let her see it. Joan in return never abused this great gift.

Then came the time when they prepared their love nest, for Joan was expecting to lay her first egg. Darby was almost beside himself with anxiety, yet he never showed his feelings. He said to himself, " I must be brave ! I must set the example and so help Joan all I can." He knew that the first and third eggs were difficult ones to lay.

Egg-binding was a thing to be dreaded. Often young mothers were so ill that they died. The mere thought of such a catastrophe nearly drove him frantic. But if Joan had any fears she did not get them from her lover. Darby was splendid. He kept her spirits up as well as his own.

The day that Joan disappeared into her nest to lay that first egg Darby was a bundle of nerves; his control was taxed to the uttermost. All went well; one—two—three—four tiny white eggs were laid in turn, without any difficulty. Both Darby and Joan were delighted.

Joan sat her eggs quietly and without fuss. Darby kept her well supplied with food; between meals he sat with her in the nest and he crooned softly to her. He told her stories of beautiful romances and tickled her ears ever so gently. All the world loves a lover, and it was like a lovely dream to watch these two youngsters setting up house.

Soon four baby chicks pushed their way out of the shells. Pushed is hardly the proper word, for ' cut ' would have been better. This is one of the miracles of nature. These tiny chicks—puny things about half an inch long and much less in width, looking so helpless and fragile—have a tiny sharp point on the end of their beaks. It is a very minute projection, no bigger than that of a pin; yet they press this into the shell and turn completely round inside the egg, cutting the shell into two perfect halves—and out pops a tiny pink baby chick. It squeaks in a tremulous voice as the mother tucks it under her wing to dry.

Darby and Joan were in the seventh heaven of happiness when all the four tiny babies prospered; he was the proudest father in the whole aviary and she the fondest mother. We thought that Dame Fortune had indeed been kind, and we sighed with relief.

But Dame Fortune is a fickle wench. A tragedy was taking place under our very noses, and we were quite unaware of its coming until too late. Why these things do happen, just where everything seems so ideal, is a problem. Never had we experienced a more ideal pair of lovers, and they never deserved the calamity which followed their union.

It was entirely Darby's own fault; yet what could we say? We could only grieve for him and especially Joan.

One day we saw him fill his crop with seed and go into the nest; there was nothing extraordinary in that. Late that night, on going the round of the flights, Darby was nowhere to be seen. This did seem strange, for about this time he was usually to be found near the seed-pot, filling his crop for the last time that day.

He did not pop his head out of the little hole at my call, so I lifted the nest down. Joan flew out uttering a mournful cry. My heart felt like lead; I had a presentiment that all was not well. I opened the door of the box with Joan's sorrowful cries ringing in my ears the whole time, and my worst fears were confirmed. That dreaded ' Miss Fortune ' had blighted their love.

There in the nest was Darby—dead. The three-weeks-old babies were huddled on top of him as though to keep him warm. Poor little fatherless mites, I wondered if they realized what had really occurred. Their father had given his life that they might live. Darby had loved too well.

The very last thing that he had done just before he died had been to feed every seed in his crop to his babies ; so anxious had he been for the welfare of his family that he had starved himself. He had died in the midst of plenty. Now we knew why the chicks had grown so quickly.

There was no other nest available at the moment where we could foster the babies out, and thus be certain that their lives might be saved. We were at our wits' end to know what to do.

It was easily seen that Joan was beside herself with grief, but she was a heroine ; she decided to carry on. There seemed to be nothing that we could do to help, so we buried Darby under a rose-tree in the garden with all due honours. Each year as the roses bloom we allow the petals to fall on the grave of this hero, whom in our hearts we remember as a great lover.

But there was a Good Samaritan. He also was a hero, though of a different type.

We soon found that Joan was fighting a losing battle. The self-denial of Darby had made these four chicks grow exceptionally fast, and what with fretting over her loss and trying to feed these ever-hungry mouths there was a distinct danger that she might go the same way as her beloved. The strain was beginning to tell upon her.

Unable to bear it any longer, we decided to take a great risk. Joan badly needed a man about the house —that was the only solution that presented itself.

Now, in the outside flight was a young green budgie, by the name of William. He was an extraordinary big lad for his age, and, moreover, he was well-behaved. I believe that he must have been to the same public school as Darby, for his manners were similar. Would he take over Darby's responsibilities, or would he slaughter the babies if we put him into Joan's compartment?

Would Joan carry on? Or would she lose interest in her family if we gave her a new husband? This was the problem confronting us.

Having first made sure that William had had a good feed and that Joan was in the nest, we quietly put William into her pen. We stood by and watched.

Hearing Joan's sobs, William flew to the little perch outside her villa, but he did not enter. He just knocked on the wood with his beak. Out popped Joan's head. "What's wrong, my dear?" asked William kindly. "Can I be of service to you?"

Joan looked him over. He was big and strong, but nothing near so handsome as her late husband; yet he had a plain honest face, one that inspired trust. She told him all her troubles.

"You poor dear!" cried William. "This is a man's job. Why, you are half-starved yourself? Hold up your pretty head and let me feed you."

So Joan did hold up her head and William fed the seed from his crop to her. "Now to put your house in order—but first I must pop down to the larder."

Down to the food-pot he flew and soon filled his crop again. Back to the nest he went. "Now where are these hungry young rascals, Mrs. Green? May I come in?"

"Please do!" said Joan. "I'm afraid we're a lot of trouble to you."

"Don't mention it, my dear. Happy to oblige you," replied William as he stepped into the nest.

So did William the Good Samaritan save Joan and

rear her family. Later, when the babies were able to take care of themselves, William had a quiet talk with Joan.

" Well, I suppose they will take me away now my job's done," he said.

Joan looked alarmed ; she knew that she could never love anyone with that same affection she had had for Darby, but she had come to rely on William. " I hope not ! " she said.

At her words William flew quickly to her side. " My dear, I did not dare hope for that," he said. " I love you. Could you love me a little, dear ? "

" I do ! " replied Joan, snuggling close beside him. William bent over and tickled her ear with his beak.

We found them in that position, and were delighted at this turn of events.

So Joan married William, and they presented us with many babies which grew into beautiful adult budgies, winning many prizes.

Joan died early this year at a ripe old age ; we buried her by the rose-tree. Once more Darby and she were united, this time by death. William sighed when Joan died, but we think that he knew she had gone to join her first love, and he had no selfish regret. He was the Good Samaritan ; for him, a good deed done was its own reward.

Thus ends the story of two very gallant gentlemen and a very lovable little lady.

CHAPTER VIII

SATANELLA

The Demon Budgerigar

EVEN in ideal surroundings where every care is bestowed, one occasionally finds ' the odd man out '. In this case, however, it was one of the opposite sex. It takes many kinds of budgies to make budgie-dom, but there is much consolation in the knowledge that such stories as the one I am about to relate are rare, for Satanella, as I named her, was the most invidious personality it has been my misfortune to know.

Satanella was indeed a veritable disciple of his Satanic Majesty. She was a grey-wing mauve budgie, quite a beautiful specimen, having many good points which endeared her to her owner. She had been allowed to develop into a very handsome young lady before being joined in matrimony.

Her husband was a grey-wing cobalt, Harlequin, a close relation of Pierrot, who with Penelope were ' the perfect lovers '. Harlequin was just another Pierrot, of the same amiable disposition and an ideal hubby. No blame could be attached to him for the subsequent events, in fact we were all sorry for him. He had a very rough time for a while; it was no sinecure being tied to a temperamental young lady like Satanella.

People often don't realize the silent suffering that is the unhappy lot of these ' Harlequins '. They have no redress, no court of appeal, when they have taken ' for better or for worse '. They receive the full repercussions

56

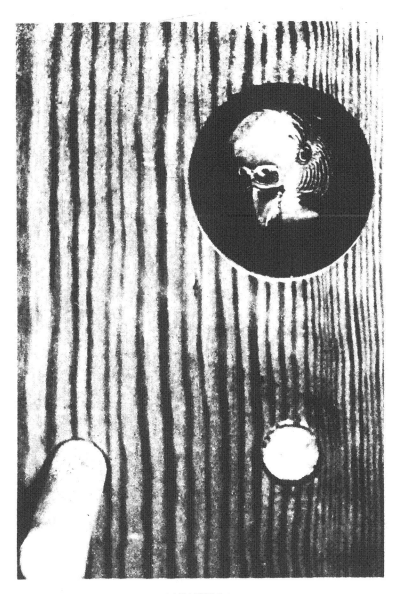

SATANELLA

of their partner's aggravating actions ; ostracized, lonely, they carry the cross with a bravery which must be admired.

It takes but mere trifles to start these unbalanced ' Satanellas ' on the downward path. It was but a little thing which upset this particular example.

Now Mr. S., her owner, believes in breeding budgies in large flights, where they may have plenty of room for exercise. This is quite a good plan and very ideal for the birds themselves, if only they have the common sense to agree together, like sensible people would. Mr. S. places four pairs of birds in each flight, their colours so arranged that should any promiscuous flirtations or infidelity take place, the pedigree of the offspring will not be impaired. They had the best of food and every attention.

Six little villas were hung in each flight so that they had a choice of residence, two more than necessary. Each of the four pairs had been previously married and had separate honeymoons, before being put into the communal breeding flight. Each had settled down as partners, and no infidelity had taken place ; so everything seemed to be destined to progress smoothly when Satanella went off the deep-end and ran amok.

Each wife had chosen her own cottage, and each husband had settled down to minister to his wife's needs. One day a young grey-wing olive hen disappeared into her nest, and to her fell the distinction of laying the first egg. This was an honour eagerly sought after by all the young hens.

Satanella was furious with jealousy ; she had wanted to be the first. She reviled Harlequin, though he was not to blame, and he pleaded with her to have patience ; but she brooded over this trifling matter until at last her distorted mind led to her undoing.

It must have been some devilish prompting that told her that she had been unfortunate in her choice of villas.

" There is a Hoodoo on this house," she said to Harlequin. " We are going to remove."

" Have your own way, then," replied her husband, greatly annoyed at her lack of patience. " There are two empty villas close by ; which do you prefer ? "

" Neither ! " cried Satanella with an ugly look upon her face. " To-day we move into Olive's flat. It is lucky, and I'll have no other."

Harlequin was astounded. He remonstrated with his wife, but she was adamant. He told her that he would have nothing to do with such evil designs. He warned Olive's husband, who was his friend, and that dreaded bogey—Fear—entered that little home for the first time.

Satanella, her unreasonable jealousy hounding her on, too obstinate to retract her wicked plan, took the law into her own hands. Like a fury let loose she flew at Olive's husband as he sat on guard. Taken by surprise at the sudden attack, he found himself bowled over before he could put up any effective resistance, and Satanella was in the nest where Olive was sitting on four tiny white eggs.

Olive, poor thing, put up a good fight for her home, as did her husband and Harlequin, who had rushed to her aid, but nothing could stop this bewitched demon once she had got started. It was a bloody battle ; all four suffered severely, but Satanella won the day. Half dead, Olive and her husband were driven from the nest to fall to the floor of the flight, where they were forced to remain in agony. The fiend had bitten their wings so that they could not fly.

Harlequin, himself hurt, flew down to them and tried to console them as best he could, while his pugnacious half proceeded to drop the eggs, which had been broken in the fight, from the nest-box to the floor.

Olive nearly went mad with grief as she saw her half-formed babies come tippling down. Had she been able to fly back to her nest-box she would have gone, and

Satanella

the next battle would have been to the death of one of them ; but Satanella in her cunning had done her dastardly work well, and all that Olive could do was to moan in her agony and sorrow.

When going his rounds of the flights, Mr. S. found them and was furious. He took Olive and her husband off to hospital to be cared for. Regarding Satanella, he was puzzled what to do. ' Now that she has got what she wants,' he thought, ' she will settle down.' Had he known that the slightest concession of victory usually makes such natures more pugnacious than ever, he would probably have executed her upon the spot, rather than take more risks.

Poor Harlequin, he had been very unfortunate in his choice of wives. But, like Darby and William, he too was a hero ; he never complained, but made the best of a bad job. He carried on with his duties and eventually Satanella was sitting on five eggs.

Mr. S., thinking that all was now well, replaced Olive and her husband with another pair, and they too were soon on eggs. Then the eggs of the two pairs which, by some streak of luck, had missed the unwelcome attentions of Satanella, began to hatch. This annoyed Satanella, but she made no move, and later her own eggs hatched out.

Both Mr. S. and Harlequin thought that things were looking up, but once that evil streak makes its appearance it can never be totally eradicated.

One afternoon, while out for a walk, Mr. S. had a presentiment that all was not well at the aviaries ; so persistent became this feeling that he returned home as fast as he could, got his keys and went to the garden. Ten yards from the house his worst fears were confirmed. The din was terrific. There was no need to seek where the noise came from, and he went straight to Satanella's flight.

The sight which met his eyes was terrible to behold.

59

HAPPY-GO-LUCKY-BOY

CHAPTER IX

HAPPY-GO-LUCKY BOY

The Hail Fellow Well Met Budgie

FOUR years ago we built our first large flight. Up to this time we had been keeping our birds in large cages or compartments in a hut in the garden. There was one drawback to this system, however. We could not go in among the birds, but could only admire them from the outside of the cages.

Now, one of the greatest pleasures one can have from bird-keeping is when one can go among them, tame them, or at least gain their confidence, so that they fly on to the shoulder or head, where they play about and do all manner of tricks. The extra flying-room develops the birds more, and is well worth the outlay.

One day a dark green budgie flew on to my shoulder, while I was in the flight filling the seed hoppers. He did not seem the least bit afraid, and commenced to chatter in my ear as though he had known me for ages.

I turned my head and looked at him, saying, " Hello, Boy ! What do you want ? " Either the sound of my voice or the interpretation he put on my words pleased him, for he tried ' rubbing noses ' with my ear, still chattering at a tremendous rate.

" You like the name, eh, Boy ? " I said. " Right then, ' Boy ' it shall be." He soon learnt to answer to the name, which stuck to him until his death.

He was real pal. He had the time of his life upon my Donegal tweed cap, which I kept exclusively for use in the aviaries. He must have been a regular ' Tory ', for he took great delight in pulling out the yellow flecking from my cap ; evidently he couldn't bear the sight of the opposition colours. It wasn't long before he had half a dozen chums helping him with the good work, and soon half the fifty birds were hanging on to the slightest vantage-point my body offered.

The cap was ruined in no time, but that did not worry Boy ; he had found another little trick which pleased him. He liked to hang from the lobe of my ear, suspended by his beak. He only gripped very lightly, as though aware that he must not nip. The other birds soon copied this trick, but were not so particular, and this became very embarrassing, especially if we had lady visitors in the flight. They sometimes hung on like grim death and would not let go.

Another little pleasure he got out of me was after I had visited the barbers and had my hair cut : he just loved trying to get hold of the very short hairs in my neck. This sport became quite a trial when half a dozen of them started the same trick together, and Boy fairly chuckled at my discomfiture.

It was a game of follow your leader, with Boy as the leader every time. He was the shining light in that aviary, and none disputed his kingship. He was friendly with all, and by keeping them in a good mood there were no fights.

Most of the time when he was not showing them new tricks, Boy spent in feeding all and sundry. The quantity of seed he cracked, gobbled up and then passed on to them in one single day was enormous.

He was absolutely brimful of vitality, consistently good-natured—in fact, Boy was a hail-fellow-well-met sort of a chap.

Sometimes he would fly on to the dividing partition

and flirt shamelessly with the hens at the other side, in front of their own particular beaux, too. The hens encouraged him, and vied with each other to attract his attention. Yet their own fiances never seemed to take exception at Boy's flirtations, whereas they would have soon resented interference from any of the other young men. None ever took Boy seriously.

A likeable sort of chap, he held the esteem of all the birds in the aviary. We thought that Boy would do well for us, both on the show-bench and in the breeding-pen—" he will make an ideal parent," we said. Both of these surmises were destined to be wrong, however.

We had noticed that Boy had taken over a duty on his own initiative. Very young or ailing birds he took into his charge, and fed them and cared for them until they were again well or able to feed themselves.

Young babies are inclined to be either very wild or to fret when taken from their parents and placed in the large flights. Boy would immediately make friends with these youngsters, and many a backward baby was put on a sound footing by his careful attention and happy-go-lucky ways.

Eventually the show season came round, and Boy was sprayed and then put into a show cage and sent to a show. Boy will stand well for the judge and prob-ably catch his eye, we said. But things did not pan out as we thought. He was not himself when alone; he missed the companionship of other birds. True he got into the lower cards, but he spent most of his time at the show on the wires calling to the other birds in the class.

The joy seemed to have gone out of his life. Boy lived in the crowd. In a show cage, he was like a leader of community singing stranded on a desert isle.

We tried him out several times to see if he would become accustomed to that kind of thing, but he wilted and, afraid of losing him, we returned him to the flight. Back in the aviary, Boy soon picked up and seemed more vivacious than ever. So there he stayed until breeding time came along in the Spring. "They are not all good show birds," I told my wife. "Perhaps he will make a better stock bird; these are at a premium."

The spring sunshine came, and with it the call of love. The whole of the aviaries were agog with excitement; there was much billing and cooing through the wires which divided the young men and the maidens. Boy seemed to be in his element at this time; he flirted with all and sundry and pulled the legs of his love-sick companions in his flight.

We chose a very smart young lady for Boy, put them both into a breeding compartment, and hung the little villa on the wall. Now, we thought, this is where Boy will prove his worth and fulfil his destiny. But once again our plans misfired; our calculations seemed to have a nasty habit of going wrong where he was concerned.

Apart from a preliminary "How do you do?" and a rubbing of noses, which in budgie-land is comparable with our kissing a sweet young thing, Boy absolutely ignored his now *bitter* half. His wife became cross-tempered; no lady likes to be treated with such indifference. True, he fed her, he was no sluggard, and he was far too good-tempered to be brazenly unkind, but that was as far as he would let himself go.

Really, I don't think that Boy was aware of the little villa on the wall; if he had noticed it he did not show it. His sparkle gone, he spent his time again on the wires, calling to his chums who were now in the other breeding compartments, pursuing their matrimonial duties with vigour.

Thinking that he did not like our choice of wife for him, we changed her, and later still for yet another. Each failure was simply a repetition of the first. Boy liked the opposite sex; he was kind to them and did not mind a harmless flirtation with one of them; but he would not settle down—he was no family man.

We noticed that again he began to wilt. He was a puzzle to us, and we began to wonder if he was worth his keep. Yet we could not honestly sell him in these circumstances, and he was too much of a pal for us to give him away, so back he went into the flight.

He was soon his old sweet self, and would come on to my shoulder and chatter away as though trying to explain something to me. Boy was now with some young men that we had decided were worth ' running over ', so that they might develop unchecked and make good showbirds for the following season. He had the time of his life with them; after the evening meal he would stand on the edge of the pot with others grouped around him and then he told them the tale. What he told them no one will ever know, but it must have been interesting, for they all were deeply attentive to his chatter.

Soon the babies began to be ready for separation from their parents. This is always a worrying time, for we do sometimes lose a good chick through fretting or fright, yet it is not advisable to put them back to their mothers. They often bolt straight back to the nest, where they are chased out by the mother, who may damage her next round of eggs in the scrap.

It was then that we found the real value of Boy. We put him into the young bird flight with the babies. He loved children and doted on them, even though it seemed too much trouble to him to acquire some of his own. Here he was worth his weight in gold to us; he took them all under his care and we never lost a youngster in his flight, either by accident or decline. Boy was a star turn at fostering babies.

For three years he served us well and truly; we

doubt if ever we shall find his equal in this job, but one day he caught a chill and died. We grieved over him as we buried him in our little cemetery.

We never doubted his fertility; in colony breeding he might have been in his element, but we did not practise such methods, and Boy was certainly not monogamous. He lived in the crowd. He was the Jovial Monk, a Beloved Vagabond, and many other characters rolled into one.

He strolled the gay highway of life, shedding sunshine and happiness around him; he lived for the day—the morrow could well take care of itself. He won no medals, he left no dependants to mourn his passing, he left no trail of broken hearts behind him, yet he had been loved and respected by all.

That was ' Happy-Go-Lucky Boy '.

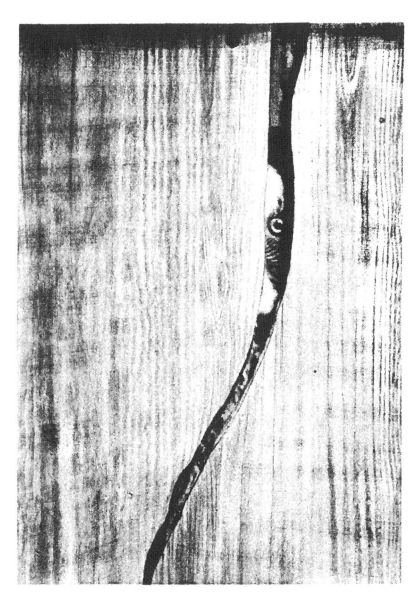

A FEMALE PEEPING TOM

CHAPTER X

A FEMALE PEEPING TOM

" 'Twas Curiosity That Killed the Cat "

ONE day while feeding the birds in one of the aviaries I suddenly became conscious of a feeling that I was being watched. It is a peculiar sensation, one which most people have experienced at some time or other, and which is very annoying. It is not exactly a feeling of fear, but more of a creepy sensation down the spine; one feels very uncomfortable.

I looked around but could see nothing; there was certainly no one but myself and the birds in that particular part of our aviaries. A glance through the window showed that no one was in the garden, so I shrugged my shoulders and proceeded with the job on hand, that of replenishing the food-pots and hoppers.

It was no use, however, the feeling persisted; I could not shake it off. I looked minutely along the back of the hut, searching for knot holes; there were none, each tongue fitted perfectly into the grove of the next board, so that ruled out the thought of anyone peeping in from the next garden.

The top half of the front was fitted with glass windows and no one could peep in there without me seeing them first. The side of the hut where I had entered the flight was composed of double boarding with a space of two inches between. The door fitted into a rebate to prevent draughts penetrating into the interior. That side was solid enough.

67

The roof was of thick T. & G. boards, covered with felt and tarred ; there was no peep-hole there. The floor was made similarly and covered with lino, so that presented no loophole.

There remained but one more side. This was made of a partition of three-ply boards fixed on a light frame work, with a door in the centre leading to another flight which housed another lot of budgies. There was no entrance into that portion except through the flight in which I stood. No one could be in there ; besides, the birds would soon have warned me if a stranger was about, but all seemed normal and quiet.

Still, as the strange feeling of being overlooked would not go, I thought there could be no harm in looking that partition over. When examining this I noticed for the first time a tiny crack in the plywood close to the roof. It was about 6 in. in length and about one-eighth of an inch in width. I almost passed this over when a more careful inspection revealed an eye pressed close to the crack on the other side.

I nearly jumped out of my shoes. A very tiny pupil turned and followed my every movement ; it was weird. I opened the door leading to that section quickly, but a flutter of wings told me that it was useless to try to find the culprit. In there, were forty yellow hens, and they were very much alike.

Having finished my feeding operations, I stole to the front of that portion very quietly and peered in at the window. There, clinging with the tips of her claws to the niche where the partition joined the roof, was a yellow young lady.

Her back was towards me and her body covered the coloured ring on her leg, so I had no means of discovering at least to which family she belonged. Her left eye was pressed close up to the crack, and she was following with great interest every movement of the birds in the next flight. When I knocked on the window,

all the birds rose in flight and I lost her. Try as I might
I could not identify her; she was shrouded in mystery
—just one of forty. But, except for feeding times and
night-time, she was ever at that peep-hole with her
eye to the crack.

Whenever I was in that first section that tiny pupil
twisted and turned to see everything I did. I could
hardly take my eyes from it; it was uncanny.

She never made the slightest sound or called to the
other birds whom she watched, and as she was doing no
harm we took no notice of her for some time, but named
her Miss Pry.

Unfortunately, the uncomfortable feeling that I had
before discovering her did not wear off, but grew in
intensity. When feeding the birds I could not resist
watching that pupil twist and turn, and I found that I
was wasting much time, so it was decided to put an end
to her prying. A piece of stout board was nailed over
the crack on her side of the partition; but this was soon
eaten through, and she was back at her tricks once more.

I could not remove forty birds from that flight for
the sake of one, so another piece of wood was nailed on
the inside; I would not admit defeat. "That will stop
her little game," I said to my wife.

Every time my back was turned, however, Miss Pry
attacked that new obstruction and ate at the wood. It
was her turn to be persistent.

One day I discovered that operations had ceased;
there were no more tiny chips of wood lying about, so
I thought that at last I had tired her. For two days no
yellow hen clung to that woodwork, and I was now
certain I had won the day. But on going to feed the
yellow hens I found that one was sickening. Her eye
was puffed up and her cheek was swelling fast.

She was taken into the house and put in the hospital
cage to be treated. I wondered if it was Miss Pry—it
was! Yet I had misnamed her, for she was an old bird

and had bred us some winners ; I should have called her Mistress Pry.

A close examination of her injury showed a tiny scratch on the cheek near the eye. An inspection of the peep-hole revealed the point of a rusty nail, which she had bared during her process of eating through the wood.

Her insatiable curiosity urging her on, too stubborn to heed the danger of that point, she had in a moment of carelessness scratched her cheek ; the rust had entered the wound and blood-poisoning had set in. It was septic.

Under skilful treatment the wound was healed and she was pronounced fit to go outside again, but not to that same flight. She was put with some coloured hens in another place, where there was no possibility of the performance being repeated.

Unfortunately Madam Pry's temper had been rather upset by this change into fresh quarters. Peeved at the frustration of her plans, she allowed her temper to get the whip hand ; she quarrelled with her companions and they fought.

It was a terrific battle, and in the mêlée her old wound was re-opened. Back to hospital she went. This time it proved to be a more serious job. A tumorous growth began to form ; she was operated upon, but the wound being too close to the eye, we were not able to cut all the growth away, and it grew and spread until at last death mercifully put an end to her suffering.

We were really sorry to lose her. She had been the best of mothers and had produced some of the most valuable birds which we have bred, but she had one failing—an overpowering curiosity which had proved her undoing.

Life is full of such ' idiosyncrasies '. We human beings are just the same.

Often, when going the rounds, I look unconsciously at that partition, and I can still see that tiny pupil turning to follow my movements. It was the most weird experience I had known.

CHAPTER XI

THE GOOD COMPANIONS

A Story of a Strange Companionship

THE story of 'The Good Companions' is one of a strange friendship which sprang up between a parrot and a budgie, a bird much smaller than himself and one you would have thought greatly below his dignity.

This story always reminds me of that of the convict who saved crumbs to feed the stray mouse which wandered into his cell and which he tamed, becoming very attached to it : the parrot representing the convict and the budgie the mouse.

A friend of mine owned the parrot, a big bird, and getting on in years, which had learnt to talk a little. Pluto by name, he was rather an autocrat and very dignified.

One day his master, who was passionately fond of all kinds of birds and who had heard much about talking budgies, thought that it would be fun to bring one into contact with Pluto and see what the two would do if allowed to fraternize.

He was rather sceptical of the results, but thought that Pluto might teach the budgie more quickly than he could. So a beautiful young budgie was brought into the house when only about seven weeks old ; he very quickly became tame and had the name Dido bestowed upon him.

When Dido had become amenable, he was given his

liberty in the room and so he soon made the acquaintance of Pluto. The parrot was a veritable giant to him, and presented a rather fearsome appearance.

" What a terrible beak—I must keep clear of that ! " he said.

Being rather timid at first, Dido kept well clear of Pluto's cage during his flights around the room, and he stood on the mantel-shelf and surveyed this monster with awe.

But Pluto was really a very harmless sort of fellow, and he tried to make friends with the little stranger. He addressed him in parrot language, but this sounded mere gibberish to Dido. Australian bush slang was the only language he knew ; that of the African jungles was unknown to him.

One day Pluto found that he could have great fun at Dido's expense. Their master had begun Dido's education and was teaching him to answer to his call. Pluto soon copied this call ; and, when Dido was flying about during their master's absence he would whistle loudly, whereupon Dido at once stopped in his flight and looked around for his master.

Pluto got much pleasure from hoaxing Dido, who once he had solved the mystery, would take his stance upon the standard lamp and cheek Pluto, occasionally adding one or two bush oaths to his abuse.

This outburst of vituperation simply left Pluto cold. " Oh yeah ! Kiss pretty Pluto," he would reply.

It was great fun to watch them at it. They reminded one of a couple of boys slanging each other because they were doubtful of the result should they slug one another.

Then Dido began to pick up words from Pluto. It seemed easier for him to learn from his bigger brother than from his master.

By this time Dido had begun to lose his fear of Pluto, and he would perch on the ring of the parrot's cage and chatter to him in his cocky manner. The conversation was very amusing; it went something like this:

Pluto : " Kiss Pretty Pluto ! "
Didc : " Pretty Pluto."
Pluto : " Oh yeah ! "
Dido : " Yeah ! "
Pluto : " Mammy's pretty darling."
Dido : " Darling ! "
Pluto : " Give us a kiss ! "
Dido : " Kiss ! "
Pluto : " Oh, Boy ! "
Dido : " Boy ! "

So it went on. Dido chattered away, then tap, tap, tap went his beak in quick succession on the ring of the cage. Pluto showed no sign of embarrassment as he replied, " Come in ! " This, of course was Dutch to Dido, who remained where he was.

As the time passed, and finding that Pluto made no attempt to get at him, Dido grew bolder and clung to the wires of the parrot's cage. His wings were braced, ready to fly away if the big fellow moved. But Pluto had no intention of scaring his new friend, so he just remained still and said, " Show a leg ! "

Dido must have liked that for by the way of a peace offering he regurgitated some millet seed from his crop and dropped it into Pluto's cage. Pluto looked at the tiny seeds. " Mere chicken food," he said scornfully; and then, taking a large peanut out of his own food-pot, he pushed it through the bars to Dido, saying, " Here, have some man's food ! "

Dido immediately flew down to investigate this object which had fallen to the table. For the next half-hour he was busy peeling the shell off this new delicacy and gobbling up the nuts which were inside. Both having made gifts to each other, their friendship had been founded.

It was only a matter of days after that before Dido

cautiously put his head between the wires of Pluto's
cage. Finding that his action was not resented he picked
a sunfllower seed from the parrot's dish, and gobbled
that up.

One day Dido plucked up courage and slipped between the wires into Pluto's cage. He was trembling
with fear, but Pluto was a wise old bird, and did not
move, but just murmured, " How do, Cocky ! "

Confidence grew with mutual understanding, and
soon Dido was allowed to stand upon Pluto's shoulder
and tickle the parrot's head with his beak. He looked
for all the world like a tiny child standing on the arm of
Daddy's chair, trying to part Daddy's hair, to make
him look pretty.

It is really funny how we all pass through these
transitional stages, whether beast, bird or man.

Dido spent a greater portion of his liberty each passing day with his new-found chum. They ate together
regularly now ; thus the prisoner in his cell made
friends with the tiny ' mouse' who had ventured into
his domain. It was a beautiful friendship.

But unfortunately the cold nights were approaching,
and Dido had been a late-hatched chick ; Pluto, himself
an old bird, knew what this meant. He had noticed a
change taking place in his young pal. Dido was beginning to moult.

At night Mistress let the fire go out, and the room
became decidedly chilly before morning. He wondered
how the young budgie would stand this without catching
a chill ; moulting time was early Autumn, and it was a
trying time to all birds. He certainly did not want anything to happen to his little friend, and he pondered
over the problem.

Once he had seen a lady visitor wrap her baby in a
warm shawl before putting her into her pram. Well,
he had no shawl in which to wrap Dido. He cast his
mind back to those far-distant days in the jungles of

Africa, when he had been a child. It had been very hot during the daytime, but at night, when the sun had gone down and the chill night air had blown across the tree-tops, his mother had tucked him away under her wing, where he had remained snug until the sun had again warmed the air.

It was years since he had been in that nest, for shortly afterwards he had been captured by a trapper, whilst quite a youngster, tamed, placed in a cage and taken over the seas. He had passed from hand to hand until at last he had come into the possession of his present master.

He had never been allowed to take a wife, so his experience of family life was limited to that faint knowledge of a nest in Darkest Africa, somewhere in the recesses of his memory. That makes this story all the more remarkable.

Here was the only solution to the problem. Dido had been sleeping in his cage for some time now, so that night before he and his little chum settled down Pluto whispered something into Dido's ear.

Dido was perfectly willing, and delighted to find that his big pal was so concerned about his welfare, so he did as he was bid. He climbed up under the wing of the parrot and clung to his thigh. Pluto then lowered his wing and closed it tightly round his small friend.

It was a strange picture, to see Dido climbing into bed as it were, and being tucked in by his nurse. His little head alone peeking out, he was as snug as could be and perfectly shielded from any draught which might come along.

Though he weathered the trying period of moulting, he still slept with his big brother. They were indeed a lovable pair and ' Good Companions '.

Owing to the death of Dido we were unable to get a photograph of ' The Good Companions ', so we substituted other ' Good Companions '.

Chapter XII

CARRYING ON

A Story of Devotion to Duty

HERE is another story of an incident which happened in the aviaries of my friend, Mr. S. of B., the same aviaries where Satanella ran amok with such dire results. The budgie in this story, however, is of a totally differing nature, of a much sweeter character.

The custom of Mr. S., you will remember, is to put four pair of birds in each flight arranged so that should any infidelity take place the pedigrees of the progeny would not be impaired. It is this fact that makes the story all the more remarkable; for after the acident 'Old Faithful', as we afterwards named him, did not look round for another wife or cause the slightest trouble to the other three pairs, but 'carried on'. In other words he minded his own business.

Early in the spring four pairs of budgies who had previously been joined in matrimony were placed in one of the flights, the villas had been hung on the walls, and for a time everything went according to plan. As in the majority of cases, they were sensible couples and minded their own business. They did not squabble over the choice of villas, nor were they jealous of each other.

Soon eggs were laid, and, after the usual period of incubation, began to hatch. Dame Fortune seemed to be in a happy mood. Four little hens had gone to nest, four families had appeared and all were doing well.

76

CARRYING ON

It was a delightful scene to watch these four happy fathers, standing in a circle on the edge of the seed-pot, filling their crops for the last time, the toil of the day over. They chatted and gossiped to each other as they extolled the virtues of their respective wives and families.

Each was intensely proud of his responsibilities.

The reminded one of the groups of old men seated in the shelters of the parks, telling the tale with pardonable pride of their achievements and those of their children.

Old Faithful's family of four varied in ages of four to ten days old, when a terrible tragedy happened which gained him his proud title.

One night after dusk some mischievous boys began to throw stones over the wall, hitting the roofs of the aviaries. It seems to be a failing of some wicked boys to take a special delight in frightening any animals and birds whenever they can.

With a terrific crash, a stone hit the back of the hut just where the villa of Old Faithful and his wife was hung. It must have been like a thunderbolt to Mrs. O.F. as she sat in the dark, nursing her four tiny babies.

The nest lurched and wobbled perilously for a few seconds. Old Faithful almost lost his balance, but by closing his claws round the perch and gripping, he managed to hang on.

His wife, however, did not meet with the same good fortune. Unnerved by the crash of the stone, not stopping to think, she shot out of the entrance hole in sheer terror. Had the nest been facing the netting covering the windows, she might have been saved ; but opposite was a hard, solid-boarded wall. Unable to see the danger in that pitch black darkness, she continued her mad flight, hit the side of the hut with a thud and dropped to the floor. Not a sound or movement did she make— her neck was broken.

Old Faithful, clinging to his little perch, heard her

77

fall ; his first instinct was to go to his wife's aid. That awful crash and then the dull thud of the falling body told him that something terrible had happened.

He knew who had fallen, even though the hut was in darkness, for it had been a miracle that he had not been swept from his perch as he had felt her rush past him. Had the nest not wobbled and thrown him backwards he would have been bowled over.

The tenseness of those next few seconds must have been agony to his tortured mind. Of course he had never read that wonderful poem ' If ', yet he was conscious of a feeling that ' the things he gave his life to ' were broken !

The frightened clamouring of the other birds in the flight and on their nests filled his heart with despair. He wavered ! That tiny pause saved his life and that of his family.

Just at the critical moment one of his babies, missing the warmth of the mother's body, gave a pitiful cry. The parental instinct was immediately aroused within him. This was the lead he needed. Had he flown after his wife into that darkness he, too, would have suffered the same fate.

He felt for the hole with his beak, and climbed through into the nest. There was a sob in his voice as he comforted the startled chicks who snuggled to him. With his heart well nigh breaking he settled down to wait the dawn. The danger was past.

During the night he fed the youngsters with the food in his crop. This should have been his, it was all that he had had during the previous day, but Old Faithful did not mind that.

As the first streak of dawn lighted the aviary he peeped from his nest and looked around. A terrible sight met his eyes. There, where she had fallen the night before, was the one he loved ; all crumpled and broken. Her head lay twisted under her body, which had now assumed ' rigor mortis '.

Carrying On

Did you know that budgies mated for life, that they do not believe in divorce? Once mated they remain faithful to each other till death. But here death had intervened —would this mean the breaking up of that little home?

Mr. S. found him sorrowing by the side of the dead body, which he gently removed. Now, a problem had arisen what to do with the babies. They had been fed by someone since the mother had died. By whom?

There was no other nest available to which he could transfer these motherless mites ; dare he risk leaving them to the mercy of the father? He decided that Old Faithful should have the opportunity to prove his true worth. He would give him the chance to carry on. Would he take it?

Should you have visited that aviary a month or two later and seen those chicks, you would have been given the answer to that question.

What it cost Old Faithful to carry on, ' to stoop and build again with worn-out tools '—in this case, a broken heart—only those who have experienced similar circumstances can tell.

He ' carried on ' in spite of the fact that in the same flight were three other couples whose course of love ran smooth. He minded his own business and reared all his babies. The only difference it had made was that he had had no time for confabs round the seed-pot after the day's work was done. He had to work the whole twenty-four hours of the day, until his task was accomplished.

Some day round the seed-pot when tongues are wagging the story of this ' hero ' will be told and re-told, but not by Old Faithful. As he gazes proudly at his four sons, now big, strong, healthy young men, he can hear his wife's voice saying to him, ' Well done ! ' and those five weeks of slavery seem of no consequence.

Old Faithful is a modest budgie ; he should have been a Rotarian, for had he not practised ' service before self ' ?

CHAPTER XIII

THE MIRACLE

A Story of a Great Heroine

DURING the breeding season the birds in our aviaries lose their names and are known by numbers. Our breeding pens are numbered 1 to 31, and we never refer to John and Mary, but to pen 25, or whichever pen they happen to occupy.

One day this summer, while busily feeding pens 23 to 31, I noticed the peculiar behaviour of a skyblue cock in pen 24. He sat upon the little perch outside his ' Villa ' with his eye glued on something upon the floor of his pen. His head was cocked partly to one side, his whole attitude one of fixed intentness.

I looked at the floor of the pen, but could see nothing, and was about to walk away when the lady of the villa popped her head out of the tiny hole—and she, too, gazed at the same spot as her husband.

I felt piqued ! Whatever could they be looking at ? Feeling bound to investigate the mystery, I put my hand into the pen and scooped up a handful of the chaff which the birds were so intently watching.

" Great Scot ! " I exclaimed as I saw what was in my hand. There in the chaff was a newly-hatched chick ! It must have become entangled in the claws of the hen as she came out of the nest, and so must have been dropped into the chaff. Its struggles had been noticed by the parents, who, however, had no idea how it had come to be there.

My wife, who was feeding pens 12 to 22 in the next compartment, heard my cry and rushed to see what was amiss.

THE MIRACLE

"Look," I said, and I showed her the tiny baby. It was quite cold and apparently dead. I held it to my cheek as a further test. Yes, it was quite cold. I was about to throw it into the refuse bin when, for some unknown reason, my fingers closed around it, and I held it to my mouth and breathed upon it.

"Whatever are you trying to do?" asked my wife. "Are you trying to raise the dead? The days of miracles are past!"

I laughed and, though feeling rather silly, persisted. Presently I felt the tiny body move in my hand, and I almost dropped it in my excitement.

"Now then, scoff!" I cried, as I rushed into the house, followed by my wife. "Get a piece of flannel, quick! and light the griller!" It was the work of a few seconds to do this, and the chick was laid upon the flannel under the gentle heat of the toaster. In a few moments it began to kick and squeak vigorously; 'the miracle' had happened! The dead *had* been raised to life!

"Are you going to risk it again with that careless mother?" asked my wife.

I thought hard and fast. "Not I! I feel inclined to take a much greater risk than that!" said I.

"How?" queried my wife.

"You know the light green hen in pen 30. All her eggs are infertile. It is quite a puzzle to me, for she has all the appearances of being quite a good mother. I am going to put this baby under her!" I said.

"Then you are asking for trouble!" retorted my wife.

When we thought that the chick was 'roasted' enough, we wrapped it in the warm flannel and returned to the aviary. My wife held the tiny bundle while I carefully opened the door of the villa in pen 30. The green hen flew off her eggs. So I took one of the useless, infertile eggs away and put the tiny baby in the centre of the remainder.

The nest was returned and we stole quietly to the

end of the aviary and waited. Now what should we see
—murder ?

Like a stroke of greased lightning the green hen had
shot back to her nest. A low clucking sound came to
us. She had found the baby, and in the dark too. Her
husband, a big light green cock called Ferdinand, soon
followed her into the nest.

" What is the matter, dear ? " we heard Ferdy ask
his wife.

" See, one of our eggs has hatched," she replied.
" What does it feel like to be a proud father ? "

Ferdinand scratched his head. He had examined
those eggs himself a few days before, and I had noticed
a look of disappointment upon his features. He said
nothing, but sat down in the nest by the side of his
wife and tickled her ear with his beak. Ferdy was a
sensible kind of fellow, who knew better than to argue
with his wife. We heard the sound of rejoicing—of
budgie love ; and we went away.

Next day I peeped into that nest with a feeling of
nervous dread. I wondered what I should find. My
hand trembled as I opened the door and the hen flew
out. Then my heart sang as I beheld that the babe still
lived. Its little crop stood out like a tiny patch of white
matter against the pinky skin. It bulged to the size
of a small sweet pea, for it had been fed !

" Now then, where is the trouble ? " I crowed triumphantly to my wife.

" That green hen is a marvel ! She puts Florence
Nightingale into the shade as a nurse. Florence Nightingale——" I paused. " We will call her Florence," I
said ; and Florence she became from that moment.

Two days later I found another tiny chick, this time
a greywing, which was being neglected by its parents.
Another journey to Florence's villa and she had another
baby. We heard her call to Ferdy to see the second
miracle which had happened. Again he scratched his

head. "I must be a doddering old fool," we heard him say. "But carry on!"

Florence was terribly excited. She had two eggs less, but two babies in their place. We chuckled as we saw the way she sent her hubby rushing about his household duties. Ferdinand did not worry, all he wished was to see his wife happy and contented. He was a lover of peace, but I am sure that we saw a smirk upon his face. His beak curved into the semblance of a smile and he winked at me several times when I replenished the food-pots.

On alternate days, when we went the rounds of the nests, we found yet other chicks sadly in need of Florence's ministrations. There was a skyblue in a nest of seven. Its elder brothers and sisters were grown much bigger, and they liked to rest their feet on the neck of this insignificant relative, so he was transferred.

Two baby greens followed. As I took the last of the tiny babies to pen 30, which I had now re-named the hospital, my wife spotted me.

"You will take the pitcher to the well once too often, young man!" she cried.

I laughed again. "Not I! You don't know Florence, she will rear them all. 'The more the merrier' seems to be her motto!" Nevertheless, I did not put any more babies under her. I had seen Ferdy give me quite a look. As a matter of fact I had forgotten for the moment that he had to do all the housework and take the seed up to his wife and family.

"It's all right, old man," I said to him; "we will call that a day." He did not reply, but just solemnly winked. I returned that wink.

We were all happy, but Florence most of all. She, too, had worked a miracle; and if you have any doubts about this, just try feeding a tiny baby budgie that has just been hatched—if you can hold it.

Florence reared her motley family; one cobalt, one skyblue, one greywing and two greens. She was a wonder nurse!

CHAPTER XIV

"SHE LOVES ME, SHE LOVES ME NOT"

A Story of a Budgie and a Monkey

THE mere mention of the word intelligence, whether of human beings or of animals, is often enough to start an argument.

In humans it is very easy to apportion the degree of intelligence a person happens to have acquired. The man who is loquacious, we say has little, because he talks too much; the man who says 'nowt', we say knows 'nowt', and so covers up his ignorance by keeping his mouth shut. So, you see, human beings present no problem whatever.

Birds and animals, however, will keep any company arguing all night as to whether they really know what certain actions which they copy, mean. I have heard dogs often given credit for being the most intelligent of animals.

The poor monkey is badly libelled. You know the old saying that monkeys like to imitate; that is sufficient to damn whatever pretensions they may have to learning. The talking budgerigar had been often labelled 'copy-cat', for the only reason that he is like his big brother the parrot, who picks up oft-repeated sayings.

Now I would like to tell you a story about a dentist, a dog, a monkey, a budgie and some little children. This story is true, so perhaps it will serve to start a further series of debates.

84

" SHE LOVES ME, SHE LOVES ME NOT !"

" *She Loves Me, She Loves Me Not!* "

Mr. H.P., a friend of mine, is a little versatile in his hobbies. Besides being a breeder of budgies, he keeps a small dog, a monkey and several species of foreign birds.

Now in one of Mr. P.'s aviaries the flights are arranged on either side of a centre aisle. Down one side are budgies, and down the other cockatiels, and in one compartment a monkey.

It was the habit of the little dog to follow his master into the aviary at feeding times. He was told many times that he must not alarm the birds, and he must certainly not try to harm them. The dog soon learnt what these instructions meant, and he would cock his little head on one side as he gazed at the birds perched above him as much as to say, " Come on down, you fellows and play with me. I'm a sport ; won't you be sports, too ? "

He followed his master into the flight, and gradually the budgies learnt to trust him. They are obliging little fellows. Budgerigars don't mind whom they play with as long as they can have fun with someone. As they lost their fear, they came lower and lower until at last one flew on to the dog's head. Others quickly followed, and soon they were all good pals.

The birds would run between his legs, look up at the dog, and say, " Hello, big boy ! Is it cold up there ? " The pup towered above them.

The dog would put his paw upon their backs and hold them, but so gently that they were never hurt. The budgies thought it great fun. Jacko, the monkey, watched from his cage and wondered why he could not play with the funny little birds also.

Later the dog found yet another little trick which pleased his feathered chums. He would pick them up in his mouth and carry them proudly round the aviary.

This certainly amused the budgies ; they were

like little children, who like to be carried pick-a-back ; they cried, " Again ! Again ! "

Jacko, from his cage, saw this and he smacked his lips ; but finding that he could not participate in this game he went off to the window at the back of his pen, wiped the mist from the glass with his paw, and sat watching the children playing in the garden nearby. He just loved to watch the children at play.

Now Mr. P. had the good fortune to breed a beautiful young yellow hen budgerigar. She was a little peach ! Visions of diplomas and trophies at forthcoming shows flashed into his mind. She was such a splendid colour that he called her Marigold.

Now Marigold was one of the birds which the little dog carried in his mouth. Many times Mr. P. felt his heart thump quite uncomfortably as he watched. He never believed in pampering the best, but he would often admonish the dog to be very careful of this tiny gem.

" Be careful with Marigold."

Jacko heard the words and turned up his nose. " Marigold, indeed ! What a lot of fuss over Marigold ! " he said.

It was on Friday the thirteenth that Marigold had been born. It must have been, for one black day she escaped into the corridor. Jacko saw her and licked his lips in anticipation.

Marigold also saw the monkey. She thought he must be a brother of her friend the pup who played with her, so she flew straight between the bars of his cage, to a spot in front of his paws.

" Give me a ride, please ! " she exclaimed ; but the words were scarcely out of her mouth, before a paw descended upon her and closed.

" Don't be so rough ! " she tried to shout ; but the words choked in her throat—she had died ! Jacko had no intention of ever letting this beautifully coloured creature fly away.

He put the body in his mouth and ran round the cage. Up and down the bars he swung. " The pup could not do this ! " he cried. Then he put her down, but Marigold never moved. He touched her with his paw, but of no avail. Then the monkey proceeded to do a strange thing.

Mr. P. had just come on the scene. He stood and watched, a sadness in his heart as he thought of those prizes.

Jacko sat in the middle of the floor of his cage and began to pull the feathers from the wings of the dead bird ; some of them he allowed to flutter to the floor, some he blew from the palm of his hand. The whole time he muttered some gibberish, of which no one could have made head or tail.

When the body had been absolutely denuded of feathers Jacko gave a sigh, and then, pulling the head from the body, flung it over his shoulder through the bars of his cage. The game had ended !

Mr. P. related the story to me, and asked me what I thought the monkey had been playing at. I must confess I was puzzled. The action of putting his paw on the bird and then carrying her round in his mouth, we were pretty certain he had picked up from watching the dog do the same. The pulling out of the feathers —No !

" I wonder if he can have seen into your surgery and seen you extracting teeth ? " I said. " Perhaps he thought he was pulling teeth ! "

" He might have seen, for I do fasten him to the garden seat beneath the surgery window, sometimes," said Mr. P.

" No ! It cannot be that," I cried. " Monkeys only imitate,"—the old saying running through my mind. " You do not toss the teeth over your shoulder, do you ? "

My friend laughed. " Of course not ! "

" Then that is no solution ! " As I spoke I watched the monkey. His nose was pressed against the glass of the window at the back of his pen. He was observing something which had him totally engrossed. " Come ! " I said to Mr. P. " Let us see what is at the other side of that window ! " We went to the rear of the aviary and looked into the next garden. Some little children were playing there.

" Get a marigold," said one. " See what your luck is."

The children each plucked a flower and began to pluck the petals, saying as they did so, " She loves me ! She loves me not ! "

" There is the solution ! " I cried triumphantly. " Watch ! "

The children had almost stripped the flowers ; one little fellow finished first. " She loves me not ! " he exclaimed in disgust, as he screwed the round knob from the stalk in his hand and threw it over his shoulder. " Marigold loves me not ! "

The names and the colours were synonymous ; I wonder . . . but then, what do you think ? Do animals and birds know what they are doing, or do they only imitate ? When our tiny budgies talk, do they know what they are saying ?

THE MERRY WIDOW

CHAPTER XV

THE MERRY WIDOW

A Story of Strange Motherhood

A FRIEND of mine had an aviary in which were several pairs of birds ; he believed in colony breeding. Each of these pairs had been properly married, and all were busily engaged in rearing their first round of babies.

One of these pairs, a dark green gentleman by the name of Augustus, and his beautiful wife Fiffinella, were the favourites of the owner. He expected great things as a result of this union.

Fiffinella was a cobalt budgie—and what a beauty ! Like most pretty girls, she knew how to make the most of her looks. She was a perfect peach. I watched her as she performed her toilet and powdered her nose, which she did by rubbing it up and down the white-washed wall of the aviary. Her snow-white blaze extended well over her forehead. She reminded one of a platinum blonde.

Her dress from throat to tail was the colour of powder-blue. Her wings were black with clear white lacings. Her zebra markings on her neck looked for all the world like a Marcel wave. Her four black spots were as clear as a necklace of jet upon a snow-white background.

This vivacious little witch was the possessor of a pair of large black eyes, ever flashing in the direction of any male who happened to be near. The other husbands in that flight called her ' Fiffy ', but only when Gussy, her husband, was out of hearing.

Gussy was rather sedate, and resented all familiarity. However, when her husband was not looking, Fiffy managed to get home one or two glad eyes, setting the hearts of the other gentlemen all of a flutter.

That was as far as the flirtation went while Gussy was alive. He was a big, strong, handsome bird quite capable of asserting himself. In fact, he was not such a ' Gussy ' as his name implied.

One day, unfortunately, he caught a chill. His strong constitution, temporarily weakened by the feeding of a fast-growing family, had failed him. Gussy was at once moved to the hospital and given the best treament possible, but in two days he died.

Fiffy was now a widow with a large family to rear.

My friend was sorely puzzled what to do for the best. I went along with him to inspect the nest. As we entered the aviary, Fiffy flew out of the nest. She still looked as pretty as fresh paint.

"Fiffy is taking her loss very philosophically!" I said to my friend.

"Yes! She says that she is ultra-modern. To-day, people believe that what has to be will be—so why worry over spilt milk?" remarked my friend.

"I see!" I had taken down the nest and was busily engaged examining the babies. I gave a low whistle of surprise! "Look here!" I cried. "These youngsters seem to be better fed than when Gussy was alive!"

"She seems to manage very well," said my companion. "I wonder how she does it, and yet keep herself and her home so spick and span."

As I came out of the aviary a big sky-blue gentleman looked at me from his perch on his little villa. I could have sworn that he winked at me.

"Well! If you take my advice you will leave well alone!" I said later. "The youngsters seem to be progressing."

My friend agreed to adopt this course, but he kept his eye upon the birds in that particular nest.

He sent for me about ten days later. I could see that he was very excited. "Don't tell me that Fiffy has deserted her family!" I said. Somehow one ever distrusts these *too* efficient housewives. One always has the desire to peep into the corners to see if things are really clean. I was rather doubtful of Fiffy.

"My dear boy! she has done nothing of the sort! Do you know that Fiffy is laying again, and her family is doing splendidly. They will be leaving the nest shortly." My friend seemed to be delighted at the way things were panning out.

"You may leave the eggs with her, but they will be of no use!" I said. "Wait until the babies have left the nest, and then you can throw them away."

"But I have also something else to tell you!" said my enthusiastic companion.

"Well?"

"Fiffinella is the best mother in this aviary. She has carried on perfectly. You with your doubting were badly out!"

"Hum! We shall see!" I would not commit myself to reply further.

Later I again visited this aviary. Fiffy's first babies were fully fledged and had been removed to the big flight to grow into adults. The youngsters from the other nests had been removed too. All the hens were busy sitting their second clutches.

"Why! I see you haven't removed Fiffy's nest!" I exclaimed.

"Not likely!" replied my friend. "You were wrong again; there are six *good* eggs in there!"

"I think that we had better look!" I said.

We examined the nest. My friend was right. The eggs were all fertile. I gazed round the flight. Three young gentlemen sat sedately upon their doorsteps.

The sky-blue looked at the mauve, and a very slight smile curbed on his beak. I said nothing, but went for a camera, which I fixed where it could not be seen by the birds, and waited.

When they thought that the coast was clear the three young husbands went over to Fiffy's nest and tapped upon the woodwork. They each took a share in her welfare. They each fed her. Click! They cast a look in the direction where I was hidden, but they were too late. I had the evidence which I required.

We developed the photograph reproduced here. "Now," I said to my friend, "I think I was right in my estimation of Fiffy's character!"

All went well until the babies were out of the nests. Fiffy proudly watched her second six babes leave that nest. She was pleased.

"You're a 'Merry Widow' indeed," said I, but she took no notice.

A few days later my friend sent for me, and there was a look of dismay upon his face.

"Well, what's gone wrong?" I asked.

"I came in just in time to prevent the other youngsters wiping Fiffy's babies off the map," he said.

It seems that there had been a real dust-up, and fortunately my friend had arrived in the nick of time, or there would have been a tragedy. We were at a loss to understand why these other babies from the various nests had turned upon Fiffy's family.

Later, one of Fiffy's babies was taught to talk. Then we got the whole story. One day the children had been swanking about their parents and their virtues. One of sky-blue's babies had said to the baby of Fiffinella, "My Pop's better'n yours."

"Oh!" replied Fiffy's prodigy. "There's my Pop! Just you look at him and then tell me!" He pointed at the sky-blue cock.

Sky-blue's baby gasped! "That's *my* Pop! You have got a cheek!"

Well, you know what children are. Complications were bound to follow after that.

That is the story of the Merry Widow. You might say that this story could not be true, but I assure you that it is.

CHAPTER XVI

HIDE AND SEEK

A Story of a Budgie and a Policeman

HERE is a story as told by Boy to his confederates round the seed-pot. You will remember ' Happy-Go-Lucky ' Boy '. He was the budgerigar who would not settle down to matrimony, but who loved to be amongst ' the lads '.

Each evening he would sit upon the edge of the seed-pot and jabber away to his particular cronies as he regaled them with his yarns. Here you see him caught in the act. Note the attitude of rapt attention of his three chums. I knew that the story must be interesting, so I listened myself.

How Boy got hold of this story is a mystery to me. It is perfectly true, and I will tell it to you just as I heard it myself.

" Did I ever tell you the story of young Joey and the detective ? " said Boy as he split open a juicy canary seed.

" No ! " came a chorus of voices from the three eager budgies on the opposite side of the seed-dish. " Please tell it to us ! "

" In our city police force is a detective known as Alec Smart ! No ! he is not what is facetiously termed a ' smart Alec ', but a very conscientious officer, one who does his duty well, and whose home is run in the same punctilious regulation style by his better half, Betty. They have one child, a chip off the old block—Jimmy, the

94

HIDE AND SEEK

apple of his father's eye. Detective-Sergeant Smart has great hopes of his young prodigy following in his footsteps someday, and also becoming a member of the City's force.

" After the great *Yorkshire Observer* Show last year, Alec Smart thought that it would be a fine idea to give his son a young budgie so that he might teach it to talk. It would teach the boy to have patience and to persevere when puzzled with abstruse problems later, he said to his wife.

" So Jimmy found himself the owner of a pet budgie whom he named Joey.

" Unknown to his father, Jimmy endeavoured to say, ' Hush ! here comes the bogey-man ! ' each time his father entered the room. Joey, unfortunately, had only learnt to say, ' Bogey-man ' when a series of incidents occurred which almost shook the Smart household to its very foundations.

" Betty Smart was a very careful housekeeper. She had been trained by her husband to be very meticulous in all things," said Boy, as he picked up a dainty piece of white millet and rolled it round his tongue prior to cracking the husk.

" Yes ! Betty was a very capable woman, and her share of the upkeep of the home proceeded like clockwork. The exchequer was in her hands, all bills were paid regularly and there were no debts.

" One day Alec noticed that his wife was not looking too well. She had a worried, anxious look. Alec enquired about her health, but to his surprise his wife burst into tears. She was perfectly fit. The whole story was coaxed from her. ' There is a thief in the house ! ' she said.

" Detective Smart was astonished ; he could not believe it. No ! it could not be Jimmy, his son. The thought was absurd. Betty explained. Each Saturday morning she put upon the mantel-shelf little piles of coins—so much for the milkman, the insurance money, the laundry money, and so forth.

"For some weeks past coins had been disappearing with regularity. She had done all she could to catch the thief, without result.

"'That's my job,' said Alec to his wife. 'We'll soon get him!' So the following Saturday morning, being off duty, he set his trap. He and Betty carefully marked the coins and placed the usual piles upon the shelf. 'Now you go to the matinee and take Jimmy with you. I'll solve this.' So Betty went to the pictures and took her boy.

"Alec set about the job with precision. He locked the door at the front of the house, fastened all the windows, took his spade into the garden and commenced to dig—where he could keep an eye upon the back door.

"It was a sunny afternoon, and Alec thoroughly enjoyed himself. Not a thing happened as far as he could tell. Betty and Jimmy found him still busy in the garden on their return.

"'Seen anything, my dear?' asked Betty.

"'Not a thing,' replied Alec, 'But come, we'll go in and look.'

"They opened the dining-room door and trooped in. They were immediately met with cries of 'Bogeyman!' from Joey, who was perched upon the top of his cage. Alec's heart sank to his shoes as he counted the money. Two shillings were missing! He looked at his wife, and she looked at him.

"'Now you see, dear, what I've had to put up with for some weeks.'

"'Please leave the room! I'll get to the bottom of this!'

Alec searched the room. Not a single strange fingerprint. Not a solitary clue rewarded his efforts. At last he gave up in disgust. He was worried more than he liked to say.

Hide and Seek

" The week that followed was purgatory to Detective Smart. His chief noticed that his mind was not upon his work and tackled him about it. ' Oh, it's just a spot of bother which I've got to settle at home. I would like next Saturday free if you could arrange it, sir,' replied Alec. The chief was amazed ; he had believed that the Smart household ran on oiled wheels, but he thought it wise not to ask too much, and he granted Alec the day off.

" The following Friday afternoon, as Betty was cleaning out the dining-room, the sky suddenly became overcast ; it went dark, a thunder-storm was brewing. Betty switched on the light. Unconsciously, she looked at the shade, and then gave a start ! Then she laughed happily. Now she would have a huge joke with her detective husband. She went on with her work and said nothing.

" The next morning she chuckled to herself as she watched her husband make his preparations. The coins were carefully marked again, the shelf was thoroughly cleaned and polished to clear it of marks, the window fastening was checked and a lock fixed to the dining-room door.

" After dinner Alec prepared for his vigil, but Betty laughed. ' Aren't you going to see Avenue play Barnsley ? ' she said sweetly.

" Alec gave her a withering look. ' What about this sneak-thief ? Don't you realize I must catch him ? I'll lose my job if I don't.'

" ' I'll catch him for you, if you'll take me to the match. But if I do you buy me a new hat ! Is it a bet ? '

" Alec was about to say something very cutting, when he stopped. Betty was rather a shrewd woman —right, she should have her chance, on condition that if she failed she bought him a new pipe.

" ' Right ! Mrs. Sherlock Holmes, it is a bet—

97   G

you catch him. Let me see your wonderful powers of elucidation.'

" Betty laughed. She laid her trap, which was simple—she just dusted the mantle-shelf with face powder. ' No need to lock the door, Alec. The thief won't get away this time ! '

" ' Powder won't give you as good finger-prints as will polish, my dear,' sugggested Alec.

" ' I know that. I'm not after finger-prints, darling ! Well, come along and see the match.'

" Alec insisted upon locking the door to the room. He did not like to see his efforts wasted. So the dining-room door was made secure, and they all went to see Avenue win a hard-fought game.

" On their return, Alec could hardly wait to open the door.

" ' Bogey-man ! ' shouted Joey, as they entered the room.

Alec rushed in, and a voice behind him said sweetly, ' Look at the lovely FOOT-PRINTS, darling. Do I win my hat ? '

" Alec looked upon the shelf. Money had gone —but he was not looking at the depleted piles of coins, but at the little trident marks upon the whitened shelf.

" ' You win, my dear, but where has the little villain hidden the money ? I thought of Joey, too. I searched his cage without result.'

" Betty laughed and switched on the light. Alec, too, unconsciously looked at the shade—then he, too, laughed ! There in the bottom of the bowl be-neath the light, were many round shadows. They were *not* dead flies, but shillings, sixpences, pennies —the secret of the bogey-man was out.

" Alec laughed heartily. ' The washleather has not been in there lately, eh ? '

" Betty chuckled and glanced at the villain of the play.

" ' Bogey-man, bogey-man ! ' said Joey the budgie.
" ' You little darling ! ' breathed Betty.
" ' You little scamp ! ' said Alec, fondling him.
Then he brought the steps from the kitchen and lifted
down the bowl. ' I shall require to take this as evidence,' he said, as he counted the money in the bottom
of the shade. Not a penny missing. ' Hum ! Just
enough to pay for three seats at the Nig-nog Revue.
The verdict of the court, my dear, is that you are fined
the price of three seats for your laxity in your household duties. We find that there was no reasonable
excuse.'

" ' Thank you, my lord ! ' said Betty humbly, though
her eyes twinkled.

" That," said Boy to his three companions perched
on the opposite side of the seed-pot, " is the story of
the budgie and the policeman. Joey had a fine joke
at their expense. Look out, here comes P.G.F. ; let's
be off ! "

The four birds flew away, but I had heard the
story.

PART TWO

FULL INSTRUCTIONS FOR TRAINING AND TEACHING THE
BIRDS TO TALK, TOGETHER WITH FULL DETAILS OF
HOW TO BUILD UP A STRAIN. ALSO ADVICE AS TO
PURCHASING, HOUSING, BREEDING, REARING, EXHIBIT-
ING, AND DOCTORING.

CHAPTER XVII

THE BUDGERIGAR AS A PET

And How to Train and Teach Him to Talk

ALMOST everyone, whether of high or low degree, loves to possess something upon which to bestow affection. Down through the ages, men, women and even tiny children have been attracted towards all manner of living creatures, and have found a great delight in 'Adopting' them as pets. In this way they have found a new outlet for their innermost feelings of love and kindness. Many people who are shy and self-conscious in the presence of their fellow human beings have become voluble, and have come out of their 'shells' all because they have been able to express themselves to their new pets without that dreaded bogey, ridicule, resurrecting that inferiority complex which held them in subjection.

Living creatures have the power to dispel loneliness, and so prevent the solitary mind from becoming morbid or subject to melancholia. The lonely shepherd with his dog, and the loveless spinster with her cat, are striking examples. But these pets, though very faithful and responsive to affection, are rather inclined only to react to one's own feelings for them; they do not usually display 'initiative' in enlivening the companionship.

The budgerigar, on the other hand, can claim to be in a class quite to himself as a pet, and few people

103

can dispute this assertion. Why? Firstly, being small, he takes up little room; he is clean, free from lice, has no unpleasant odours connected with him, and he is inexpensive to keep. One penny per week will cover the cost of the whole of his housekeeping budget.

Secondly, he is a born mimic and as mischievous as a monkey. He is almost always on the go. Unlike the canary, who is dull company when not singing, the budgie is entertaining with the tricks he is ever doing. He is perky and curious. A tame budgie flying round the room will investigate every nook and corner, and then poke his nose into whatever you are about.

He loves to be near a mirror, and many an hour's amusement is afforded one watching his merry antics with the fellow at the other side.

On the inception of the parrot ban, which debarred the importation of parrots to this country, many people found this restriction very irksome; the resultant rise in price for birds already here precluded them from possessing a bird which could be taught to copy speech.

That first pioneer who taught the budgie to talk deserves some honour, for he surely solved a great problem and at the same time rendered a great service to the fancier and the general public as a whole.

The fancier found a new outlet for those birds which were not quite good enough for exhibition purposes, or even as good stock birds. These ' surplus ' birds, the ' mongrels ', soon found a ready market awaiting them; they seem to make the best talkers, and are usually very healthy, strong specimens.

The public found a new craze. They had found a perfect substitute for the parrot, yet a cheaper one, and one which did not emit that piercing shriek of its larger brother. The budgie's melodious chattering is not unmusical, and it is certainly not annoying.

Moreover, budgie's gorgeous colouring, displayed in the artistic cages which the enterprising manufacturer soon placed upon the market, added yet another touch of colour to the home.

Thus our 'fascinating little fellow' has become quite the vogue.

TAMING.

It is not generally known to the public that to be of use in the aviary the budgerigar should be kept wild, but as a pet in the home or as a companion he must be tamed.

All the budgies in this country are naturally wild. They have to be tamed to become tractable before they can be trained and taught to talk.

One fallacy which quickly gained ground was that, to be most successful, the bird should be taken from the nest and hand-reared for the last week or so before he became proficient at feeding himself. This was to ensure that he became perfectly tame. This is not only in-correct but cruel to the bird.

A young budgie leaves the nest fully fledged, i.e. fully feathered, at about five weeks old. Within two days of leaving the nest he will have been taught by his father to crack seed and thereby look after himself. Allowing a good safety margin of say one week, from the time he leaves the nest, it is soon enough to take him away from his parents.

A youngster of six weeks which is feeding himself soon becomes tractable and easily tames. The first two days it should be left alone to get used to his cage and to find his different food and water pots. On the third day a long thin stick may be gently inserted through the wires, and the birds will soon commence to perch upon it, when he can be gently moved about in the cage to start with.

As soon as he shows signs of settling down and not being afraid, the hand may be inserted, and the bird allowed to jump on and off the finger at will, without being brought out of the cage.

The secret of taming a young bird is in gaining his confidence. The bird should never be startled. It is here where the utmost patience counts. If you haven't that, you are bound to fail.

Many people have the wrong impression that birds and animals which appear on the stage, doing all manner of tricks, are taught by cruel methods. Such talk is rot! Their well-fed bodies, the sheen on their coats, prove otherwise. Fear has no part in the taming and training of live creatures; it never succeeds. Kindness and patience can work miracles.

EXERCISE

As soon as the bird becomes steady, he may be allowed out of the cage to fly round the room to exercise. Birds must have exercise, just as humans, if they are to be kept fit. One should never run away with the idea that a bird can never be kept tame unless he is kept cooped up in his cage the whole time. Such methods are cruel, and if you are not prepared to allow the bird liberty in the room each day, then don't keep one as a pet at all.

Here, a timely warning would not be out of place. Never let a bird out of his cage into a strange room unless you first draw the net curtains across the windows. Many a poor bird has received a nasty cracked skull, sometimes a broken neck, through darting as he thought for the open garden, and suddenly coming into contact with the glass which he cannot see.

Once a bird has got thoroughly tame he gets used to the glass, and will play about on the woodwork of the window-frames without coming to harm; but one should be most careful at first.

The fire should also be guarded until the bird is

TEACHING HIM TO TALK

used to it; cases of birds flying into the fire have been known. A triangular, folding guard may be bought cheaply, and will answer the purpose admirably.

If the room opens straight on to the road or garden, one should guard against the door being suddenly opened by someone on the outside who is unaware that the bird is loose, or the chances are that your pet will be through the opening and away before a warning can be given.

Many young birds are lost annually through carelessness with doors and windows. If they were able to find suitable food and withstand the rigours of an English winter, it would not matter so much; but these poor truants, unless they are again caught, meet with a slow death from starvation.

TRAINING.

When Master Budgie has become what is known as 'finger-tame', he may commence his education as a talker. A good method of teaching him to talk is to leave this tuition in the hands of one person only, a lady preferably. Women seem to have the knack of teaching birds to talk quicker and better than men; one theory advanced to explain this is that the lighter tone of voice which the fairer sex possess, is easier to copy by the bird. Whether this be true or not, the ladies seem to possess more patience and time to spend upon the young tyro.

Confusion of voices is detrimental in teaching the youngster the articulation of human speech.

It is well to bestow upon the bird a short simple name such as Billy, Bobby, Peter, etc.; he will soon learn to know this, and will answer to the call, eventually repeating it himself.

Hold the bird upon the finger about one foot from the mouth, and repeat the word or sentence several times clearly and distinctly; let the bird go, and when he has flown round bring him back and repeat the performance again.

A small mirror is a great help in teaching the bird to talk. All budgies like mirrors ; they will chatter away to the fellow on the other side, and regurgitate seed which they will endeavour to pass on to their image in the glass.

Never keep two birds together or within hearing of one another if you wish to teach one to speak ; they will simply chatter to each other in their native tongue, and your best efforts will be in vain.

HOUSING.

In purchasing your cage, err on the large side ; give the bird room to move about in it when you do not desire to have him loose about the house. Many people buy a small cage, fill it with a multiplicity of ladders, bells, balls, Kellys, food-pots, etc., until there is hardly room for the bird.

A better plan is to keep the cage clear of these articles, save perhaps one small bell ; and then buy or build a ' play-pen ', which is composed of a flat tray fitted with ladders, perches, swings, etc. ; this may be placed upon the table or sideboard, and Master Budgie will soon learn to take his daily dozen on this contraption. Many hours of amusement may be had watching him go through his acrobatics.

Those cages with the deep glass sides are the best for your pet. The glass slides will prevent the husks of the seed being scattered about the room. The cage should be kept clean both for the bird's health and your own. Sand should never be sprinkled upon the floor of a cage, but be given in a small dish or pot, so that it does not become fouled by the excreta.

An excellent plan is to cover the bottom of the cage with white paper, which can be changed every two days.

This saves the enamelled bottom of the cage from having to be scraped, and so becoming unsightly when the paint has disappeared. The paper also absorbs the moisture from the excreta, which quickly dries, and so does not soil the tail of the bird as he runs about the cage.

FEEDING.

To keep your pet perfectly healthy his diet should be varied, yet not be too overheating, or he will become too fat and lose his activity.

Plain seed, a mixture of canary, white millet and Indian millet in the proportions of 2-2-1 in the order as quoted is the main diet of budgerigars. Your pet must have sand, and the best is sea-sand. Rough pieces of flint and oyster shell are not good for him, and may lead to his death.

Cuttle-fish bone or iodine nibbles hung on wires in the cage will not only help to keep him in condition, but provide him with something with which to manicure his beak. A small piece of old dried mortar or builder's lime will also answer the same purpose.

Lime is, indeed, essential to budgies, especially when moulting.

A millet spray occasionally is good. This can be varied by soaking it in a basin containing water to which a teaspoonful of Parish's chemical food has been added, for twelve to twenty-four hours.

Once a month it will do your bird no harm, but probably a great deal of good, to soak the millet spray in a basin containing water to which a teaspoonful of Glauber salts has been added. Always give a millet spray which has been soaked, wet. Just shake off the superfluous water. He will enjoy it.

A little green food may be given once or twice a week; lettuce, dandelion, chickweed and groundsel are all safe foodstuffs, but should be given sparingly, and never to a bird whose droppings are loose.

CONDITION.

One of the secrets of keeping the bird healthy is to keep him free from draughts and extreme changes of temperature. Never leave a bird in a bay window overnight, especially in the winter months. Here, the temperature drops very low after the fire has gone out. The better way is to bring him into the room and cover over three sides and the top of the cage at night-time, so that he may sleep comfortably but out of draughts. Try to keep the bird in even conditions of temperature, and he won't ail much, but live a long life.

To keep your bird clean and sprucy, tight in feather and active, he should bathe. Unfortunately budgies don't bathe in the ordinary way in their native haunts—they just shuffle and roll in the wet grass. In captivity, however, some budgies will bathe in a shallow dish of water, placed in the bottom of the cage. If he won't, he should be sprayed occasionally. To do this, run him into an old wire cage, place it upon the board by the sink, and spray him by means of a bottle spray. This will not only keep him clean and tight in feather, but it will be greatly appreciated by the bird himself.

Use cold water in summer and warm water in the winter months ; allow him to dry away from draughts before returning him to his cage.

The budgerigar's worst enemy is draught ; cold he can stand. Perhaps you don't know that a bird catches cold in the back and not in the chest as in humans. His anatomical construction is the opposite to ours.

SEX.

You will have probably noticed that the budgie advocated as a pet is—Master Budgie.

Though hens can be taught to talk, they are never as amiable and easy to tame as the male. The cock can be distinguished easily at maturity, as the fleshy cere or wattle over his beak is blue, while that of the hen is brown.

At six weeks of age it is very difficult even for the expert to tell with certainty the difference of sex. In buying your potential talker it is advisable to go to a reliable breeder, tell him what you want and rely upon *his* choice.

By way of a guide, in the early stages, the cere of the male is of a fleshy colour with a purplish tint showing beneath the skin, whereas that of the female is usually of a pale, whitish blue ; this often leads to the confusion of sexing young birds.

A talking budgie is worth his weight in gold, for he is indeed a fascinating little fellow.

Chapter XVIII

THE BUDGERIGAR AS A HOBBY

The Right Way to Commence

It is often the case that people, having purchased a new pet, solely as a pet, without the slightest intention of ever indulging further, succumb to the fascination of the bird or animal and, before they are aware of the fact, it has got a hold on them and has become their hobby.

This applies to budgerigars particularly; for in the wonderful range of colourings there is almost bound to be one which, in the minds of all who are fanciers at heart, stimulates the desire to possess more of them.

If facilities are favourable, then the new enthusiast can hardly control his patience, but needs must rush into an orgy of purchasing, sometimes with excellent results, more often with consequences that are dire.

This book is primarily written to interest new people to the taking up of this charming cult, and then to endeavour to show them the difference between the right way and the wrong way of commencing the building up of a small stud, or the establishing of a strain.

Each succeeding year new fanciers join the ranks of budgerigar keepers. For a while they often flourish with the rapidity of mushroom growth; then comes disappointment or disillusionment, and they quietly fade out of the picture. The causes of their failure are manifold. Mostly it is the old story of acting in haste and repenting at leisure; the fascination of a new hobby is usually such that the preliminary step of ascertaining the pros and cons is sometimes skipped altogether, or only casually studied. Sometimes it may be that the beginner has fallen the prey of some unscrupulous individual who has seized the opportunity to get rid of his ' dud ' stock at the expense of his customer's ignorance. Happily, such cases are fewer than one might suppose.

A little time spent in reflection on the causes of these failures might well be the means of profiting by the mistakes of others, and so avoiding the pitfalls of precipitancy.

WRONG METHODS.

One of the most common errors which the beginner makes is that of wanting to start at the top. This can only result in a decline in both results and satisfaction. It is far better to start in a modest way and climb gradually as one learns the lessons of experience.

How many people have succumbed to the glamour of the ' Red Ticket ' !

They go to a show, see the winning birds—their interest, perhaps, has been already aroused beforehand —and, suddenly, before they realize what is happening to them, the craving to become the possessor of ' a winner ' seizes them—and they are lost.

If they have the means with which to purchase the bird that caught their eye, they endeavour to do so ; most probably they do purchase it, and pay far more than the bird is really worth. Away home they go, the proud owners of a beautiful bird, with visions of prizes, trophies and diplomas galore running riot in their minds.

Probably they have never made any preparation for the housing of their stock. There is a hectic rush of buying cages, the spare bedroom or a corner of the tool-house or garage is commandeered as temporary quarters, and then the seeds of folly and disappointment are sown.

At the earliest possible moment the bird is entered at another show. Again it may win : the thrill of that first win on their own account is fatal, they never really recover from the disease. More and more birds are bought, usually without any thought of ascertaining the pedigree or with any fixed plan of procedure in their minds. If the purse is really deep, it is amazing how far one can go in this respect before the new-born passion burns itself out.

As the show season draws to a close the mind turns toward a proper aviary, and one is hastily purchased or built to accommodate the stock, which is now becoming a bit of a nuisance in its temporary quarters. Again money is poured out ; far too elaborate an affair is put up without due thought to the conditions prevailing. The mind, flattered and deluded by those false honours, is not functioning as sanely as it might.

The words ‘false honours’ may hurt the tender feelings of some who have been guilty of this method of starting in their new hobby, but remember the story of the man who called in his friend to see the wonderful roses which he proudly claimed to have grown in his new garden the very first year. The friend looked round the wonderful blooms and then replied, “ Yes ! they are indeed glorious, but *you* did not grow these ! The man from whom you bought them and who grafted those tiny shoots grew those roses. I will come round in a couple of years’ time and then see what *you* have grown.”

Thus it is with the man who starts by purchasing winners ; he is simply reaping the reward of the brains of the actual breeder, and when disillusionment come he usually takes the knock very hard, and either blames the men from whom he bought the original stock, or the birds themselves.

This 'short cut to success' fancier usually finds that he has indiscriminately purchased cocks, and is now faced with the problem of buying hens to mate to them. So occupied has been his mind whilst exhibiting these birds that he finds that the good hens have all been picked up and he has to be satisfied with whatever inferior stock he can get. Thus the business of buying hens is but a foolish repetition of that of the acquiring of the winning cocks.

Perhaps our ' slick ' fancier thought of this beforehand and has purchased a similar number of winning hens. He pats himself on the back for his astuteness, and thinks the matter of breeding winners is now simplified to the extent of turning them out like peas from a pod.

No thought has been given to consanguinity, i.e. blood relationship. Whether the birds are suitable mates, he never stopped to consider ; the bogey of the ' red ticket ' had him spell-bound.

The birds, tired out by continual travelling to and from shows, are mated and are expected to perform miracles. They do their best, but probably the result is dismal failure. Even if youngsters are produced, they are often of a very inferior standard.

After that, the rot quickly sets in, and another fancier is lost—one who might well have proved himself an asset to his fellow-members in the hobby.

.   .   .   .   .

Another foolish beginner is the man who also errs, but differently. He, too, seeks trouble and quickly finds it.

This man thinks that he is blessed with an abundance of wisdom ; he says the price of the good bird is totally out of all reason. He does not realize what

it might have cost the breeder to produce that one
' stormer '. He is not going to be had; so he too,
expends much money on equipment and so-called
' cheap ' bargains. He buys and buys, and then, with
aviaries full of birds of a very mediocre quality, he
commences to mass-produce. The fecundity of inferior stock of any kind of living creature is notoriously
abnormally high. In his ignorance he thinks that a
certain percentage of winners must necessarily be bred
from numbers.

Later he realizes that the trouble and hard work
entailed is not worthy of the results, and he is landed
with a multitude of worthless birds which he cannot
sell.

So another disgruntled fancier is lost. Another
bubble has burst.

.   .   .   .   .

Then we sometimes meet another kind of fancier
who is keen but has only limited finances. He commences to build palatial aviaries suitable to house a
big stud. When these are finished he finds that he
has exhausted his money and has to purchase inferior
stock, with the same disappointing results. He, too,
usually fades out.

.   .   .   .   .

Another kind of enthusiast in the fancy is the man
who is not a real fancier at heart, but simply craze-
mad. This man rushes at everything with a fervour
that is not in the least inspiring, and no one is greatly
surprised when the fire of his zeal burns out and he,
too, packs up the hobby—but not with feelings of
disappointment, for has he not found his new and
true love in some other sphere?

These are but a few of the wrong ways of commencing a new hobby.

These examples are not peculiar to budgerigar keepers, they are to be found in the followers of every pastime. But it is to save the time and money of the people who are about to take up this fascinating cult that these remarks are written.

THE RIGHT WAY.

No builder would ever dream of building a house without first making his plans; no gardener would ever think of planting out a new garden without first plotting out his new land; so it should be with the man who is embarking upon a new hobby. The first thing that he should do is to sit down quietly by his fireside and talk the thing over with his wife, if he is married. If he be a single young man, he should talk the project over with his friend or parents. This is the finest brake one can apply to that overpowering impulse to spend money without due thought, and so it prevents wastage.

The first thing to decide is how much one can afford to spend; and, having decided that, then how to lay it out to the best advantage. Some of the most successful studs have had very modest beginnings; it is far better to 'feel' your way.

If the hobby is to be purely an ornamentation to the backyard or garden—a flight and sleeping compartment wherein a few budgies are to be kept for pleasure—then the problem is simple. All one has to do is to decide the amount to be expended and apportion it out—what shall be spent upon the aviary, and what shall be left for the purchasing of the stock.

In this case the accommodation should be artistic or ornamental, and many firms supply catalogues containing beautiful illustrations of the very aviary you need. If one gets pleasure from building one's own structures, then it is only necessary to draw the plan, buy the requisites and carry on with the work.

On the opposite page a suggestion of such an aviary appears. Specifications are dealt with in a later chapter.

Having erected the building, all that remains is to purchase the stock.

The wisest plan is to go to a well-known breeder, tell him what you require and leave him to choose good, strong, healthy stock for you of the colours which you like best. In an aviary of this description only cocks should be housed, for no breeding should be contemplated. To run both sexes together would mean trouble and fighting when the spring months came round, or the cocks would feed the hens until they became fat and sluggish.

The flight composed of males would agree together and still keep lively. They could be added to or losses replenished at will and with little expense. So much for the garden aviary.

If, however, one wishes to take up the hobby with a view to breeding winners and establishing a small stud or strain, then one has to approach the matter differently. There are a few people who fit out a bird-room and keep a few exhibition birds, probably in a spare bedroom; but as the breeding of budgerigars is not very successful in these circumstances, that phase of the hobby may be skipped, as anyone keeping such a small stud will find in these pages all the information necessary for the welfare of their birds.

The man who wishes to pursue the cult of the budgerigar with the idea of building up a strain should first of all decide what accommodation he can spare, either in his garden or backyard or wherever he intends to keep them. The wise man then estimates the quantity of birds a certain area of ground will comfortably take, allowing for some place where birds can be trained and prepared for exhibition.

Rough Suggestion of outside Aviary and flight for those who do not wish to breed Budgerigars but keep them for a hobby and as an ornamentation to garden.

There are three ways in which a stud of budgerigars can be housed.

1. In a bird-room, where the procedure is purely cage-breeding, and which has been already dismissed as unsatisfactory.

2. In outside aviaries or flights, providing space for cages in which to train and prepare birds for shows.

3. In outside aviaries or flights where the birds are just bred and developed to maturity, and then an inside bird-room where birds are trained and prepared for exhibiting. This is the ideal method, but cannot always be conveniently arranged.

The ideal way of breeding budgerigars in building up a strain is to do so in single compartments, when the parentage of the progeny can be guaranteed, and where the chances of pairs quarrelling or fighting is totally eliminated, thus preventing many losses.

A single compartment may mean either a glorified cage alone, or a large cage with an outside flight attached. If the former is used then provision for turning the youngsters out into large flights when they have left the nest should be made, to ensure that they have plenty of flying room for exercise. Exercise is the secret of ' size '.

Before the exhibition birds can be sent to the show bench, they must be steadied and tamed, they must be cleaned and conditioned, therefore a place must be set apart for this purpose. Also there is storage room for show-cases and spare appliances to be taken into account. All these points should be carefully studied and planned out before starting to build, thereby saving alterations having to be made afterwards and also to create compactness and an air of tidiness about the place.

By planning things out beforehand labour is minimized and wasteful repetition of effort can be cut out.

Having suitably planned your aviaries according to the ground and capital at your disposal, the next job is to erect them and proof them against the elements, and then one is ready to commence purchasing the initial stock with which to build the strain.

This is the most important job, and should never be done until one had thoroughly settled in one's mind the variety or varieties one wishes to keep. It is far better to specialize on one or two colours to begin with, and add as one progresses, than to start buying all manner of odd pairs the first year and be landed with a conglomeration of colours which will need much more space in succeeding years, or which cannot be safely followed up by the beginner.

Just as it is important to specialize on few colours, it is of utmost value to start with the right kind of stock. It is far better to commence with a limited number of *good* pairs than to fill the aviary to capacity with mediocre stock birds. If possible, it is best to try to get hold of the idea of what a good bird looks like before purchasing your stock. If this is too hard to grasp at the beginning, then endeavour to get some friend to go with you who understands a typy bird ; he will help to ensure that you get the right kind at once.

If you are unable to acquire the services of someone with that knowledge, then go to a reliable breeder of standing, tell him exactly how you are placed and what you desire, and trust him to put you on the right lines. With very few exceptions one may safely trust the old breeder to do the right thing by you, in fact, he will be delighted to help you all he can.

Even though his advice may not coincide with your own views, take it and keep to it ; remember he is giving you the benefit of his experience, which you haven't. Many beginners have failed through not following out the instructions so kindly and freely given them. Don't be suspicious of the breeder ; his reputation may be at stake, and this is of greater value to him than the profit on your purchase.

The Budgerigar as a Hobby

Having made your purchases, don't rush headlong into exhibiting the birds, even though there may be one or two likely winners among them. The first season it would be well to keep them at home to let them get acclimatized to their new surroundings ; and, above all, let them have plenty of exercise before starting to breed.

Meanwhile, you are gaining experience at bird-keeping, and are laying the foundations of a successful season when mating time comes along. Each step you take is being firmly planted, and there should be little or no sliding back—and thereby no serious disappointment in store for you, which is so disheartening.

Until it is the season for breeding operations to begin, spend the time studying your birds, gaining all the knowledge that you can, not only about breeding, but about type, colour, show points, and how to tell the good bird from the poor one. A good reliable book dealing with the technical side of breeding budgerigars can be digested at this period.

Above all, gain the confidence and trust of your birds ; talk to them and let them know you—that is the secret of success at breeding time. The birds are far more intelligent than you think, and they will soon have you summed up, whether you know it or not. They should never be afraid of you. Fear has no place in the aviary during the breeding season. The birds must trust you ; they can still be wild and fit for breeding, and still keep faith with the hand that feeds them.

CHAPTER XIX

AVIARIES AND THEIR EQUIPMENT

ON page 124 you will see the ground-plan of the suggested garden aviary illustrated previously. This aviary is designed purely for those people desirous of keeping twenty or thirty budgerigars as a hobby, or to add to the amenities of the garden. No provision is made for breeding compartments or for the training of the birds for shows.

Some people might try to breed in such an aviary by what is known as the colony system, but this is not a proposition wherein one might hope to have even a modicum of success. If anyone who has such an aviary, or contemplated the building of one, did desire to breed a few budgies, then the most feasible plan would be to partition the indoor flight, keeping the section nearest the outside flight for the birds using that to roost in at night-time, and using the division by the small window as a breeding compartment.

Wire netting as a partition in this case is not suitable; the cocks would be ever hanging to it and calling to the birds on the opposite side, thus neglecting their household duties. A partition of light three-ply boards would give better results.

Aviaries similar to the one illustrated are always available, built in sections ready for easy erection; or it is not beyond the abilities of the handy-man to make one by himself, which often adds to the pleasure of the hobby.

Ground Plan of Garden Aviary and flight.

Outside Flight.

Slide

Indoor Flight.

Corridor.

D.

D

W.

W. W. W.

W.

D.

The one shown is on a concrete base ; not only does this make the aviary vermin-proof, but it also tends to keep the general appearance of the garden neater. Weeds will not grow round the base of the walls and it simplifies the question of paths if the concrete base is made a little larger than the hut dimensions. Your visitors can view the inmates in bad weather without soiling their shoes. All garden aviaries should be lifted above the level of the surrounding soil ; damp is detrimental to the condition of your feathered pets.

HOUSE.

The house portion could be about eight feet square, and the flight ten by eight feet, or in accordance with the space at your disposal. After the main building has been erected, a good idea, in an aviary of this description, is to re-board the inside of the house portion with thin matchboards, covering all spars and leaving a flush finish. This not only cuts out all ledges whereon dust and filth is apt to collect, making the work of keeping the aviary clean much lighter, but it prevents the birds from running along these projections and thus ruining their tails. Your birds would keep a much smarter appearance.

WINDOWS.

All the windows should be fitted with hinged frames, covered with ½-in. netting on the inside. This will allow the windows to be opened in good weather without the birds escaping, and it also keeps out marauding cats. This applies to the windows in the corridor also.

Nest Box as used by Author most successfully.

Entrance Hole I½

Front View.

6″

8″

1″ Wooden Concave hollowed to ¼″.

Thin Copper Sheet.

Perch

Side cut away

6″

Stepping Block 1⅛″ high × 1¾″.

Hinged Door.

Back Cut away.

6″

Wood Concave 5½″ × 4¾″ × 1″.

PARTITIONS.

Having got the house double-boarded and the windows fitted with the netted frames, the partition forming the corridor can be erected. This is composed of ½-in. wire netting stretched upon light spars, and placed 5 ft. from the back of the hut, allowing 3 ft. of room for the owner to move about in, which is quite ample. The door (netted) from the corridor to the flight need be only 4 ft. 6 in. to 5 ft. high; the lower, comparable with comfort of entrance and exit, the better. The birds will usually fly upwards on fright, and so will hit the netting over the door, thus the chance of the birds continually escaping into the corridor is minimized.

If this flight be sub-divided for breeding purposes, then two doors should be fitted from the corridor, one into each division. If the netted front is taken to about a foot from the concrete floor and the bottom portion boarded, husks will not be wafted from the birds' flight into the corridor, thus keeping the place tidy.

HATCH.

Next, an aperture must be cut in the side of the wall next to the outside flight, and fitted with a sliding door so that the birds may be confined to the house at will. This hatch should be at least 18 in. square. The larger the exit the better for the quick passage of the birds in case of sudden fright. It should be placed as high as possible, but care should be taken to see that it is clear of perches on the inside, or broken necks may be experienced.

PERCHES.

The perches, round or oval (not square), should be high and across the narrowest sides of the flight, giving the birds the longest flight possible from one to the other. Never fix one perch directly over a lower one, or the droppings from the birds on the top perch may fall on to the backs of those on the lower one. If several perches are put at the end opposite to the hatch they should recede in gaps of about six inches, the top one being nearest to the wall of the flight.

A small table or buffet should be placed in the flight upon which the seed-dish might be placed. The husks will then be wafted to the floor by the flapping of the bird's wings, thus saving the labour of blowing the seed to keep it free of husks. Many good seed hoppers holding sufficient seed to last the birds for many days are on the market, and which hang upon the walls. If you use these, and you are not sure whether the birds you have bought are accustomed to them, always play for safety by placing a dish of seed in a prominent position until the birds have got the run of their new quarters.

The water-dish or fountain and the sand-tray are better placed on shelves, and not on the floor to become contaminated with husks and droppings.

A glass panel should be placed in the door leading to the outside flight. This will prevent them from being startled when you open the door to go into that portion of the building : they will see you beforehand. But it is advisable to cover this with netting on the bird's side if you don't wish to have accidents.

A SECTION OF THE AUTHOR'S 80 FEET OF AVIARIES

THE OUTSIDE FLIGHT.

You will notice in the illustration of the aviary that the roof extends over the outside flight for about one third of its length. This allows the birds to have somewhere to shelter from the strong rays of the sun in very hot weather, and it also protects the door to the house from driving rain.

The flight should be netted with $\frac{1}{2}$-in. netting on both sides of the framework, leaving the width of the spars between the double netting. The idea of double netting the flight is to prevent cats from striking at the birds with their claws when on the netting. A door may be fitted in one of the panels of the flight to facilitate the swilling of the concrete floor when necessary, but care should be taken to see that the birds are safely enclosed in the inner flight before using this door.

If the builder desired, the two open panels on either side of the roof of the open flight could be enclosed during the winter months by glass frames similar to those used in the cold frame in the garden. These could be replaced by loose, netted frames in the very hot weather. This same system [1] has been used successfully at 'Duchy Aviaries' on the windows at the front of the huts. In this case the inside should be permanently netted to prevent escapes when changing the frames and to keep out unwelcome visitors at night.

The back and end of the flight could be either netted or boarded, as the owner wished, and according to the position of the aviary. In very exposed places it would certainly be advisable to board in these sides.

The flight should be provided with perches and twigs, keeping these to the sides and end so that the birds have plenty of clear space in which to fly. No food, however, should be placed in the outside flight;

[1] *See illustration of Author's aviaries opposite*

it is better to train the birds to feed inside. Nothing is more messy and hard to clean up than wet husks in an outside flight.

The netting exposed to the elements will last much longer if treated with a quick-drying enamel, but ask your dealer if it is non-poisonous. Whereas the inside flight is lime-washed or painted white according to the means of the owner, the outside flight is better creosoted, or it could be painted a nice shade of green as long as you use non-poisonous paint. No paint where the birds can have access to it should contain white lead.

THE CORRIDOR.

A long narrow cupboard fitted with doors might be conveniently placed under the long window in the corridor. Here, seed and utensils could be kept out of sight and dust. The top of the cupboard, if covered with lino, would make an excellent table, one that could be easily kept clean.

The floor of the corridor might be covered with lino, and would add to the smartness of the interior as well as be easily mopped over. Lino should never be put on to new concrete, however, until the water has sweated out. Newly concreted floors do sweat.

From the foregoing the reader should be able to gather sufficient information on the erecting and equipping of a garden aviary. The pointers offered are merely suggestions and as a guide ; most people like to plan these matters to suit themselves. Such an aviary, with its complement of brightly coloured budgerigars, would not only be an improvement to the garden, but a source of great pleasure to its owner.

HOUSING A STRAIN.

Now to cater for the man who wishes to take up the keeping of budgerigars in all its phases : the keeping and building up of a strain of prize-winning bugerigars as a hobby, or possibly as a means of augmenting his income. In this case the procedure is different, for there are many things to be considered.

Space must be provided for controlled pedigree breeding ; flights for exercising and growing the young stock ; training cages for steadying and preparing the birds for shows ; indoor flights where the birds can be moulted and kept clean in the process— all these matters have to be taken into consideration.

The tyro just commencing a hobby often has to pay dearly for his experience, and frequently has to change his methods. This can well prove expensive, entailing much wasted labour and capital, if one has to re-construct and start again.

THE IDEAL HOME IN WHICH TO BUILD UP A STRAIN OF BUDGERIGARS.

The Author, in describing what he has termed " The Ideal Home in which to build up a strain of Budgerigars ", lays no stress on " *The* " as though this were the only ideal way. There are many ways a man may house his stock successfully, but the aviary herewith described is the result of many years of experience, both by the author himself and from his close attention to the methods of others.

Such an aviary would however be an ' ideal home ' for a stud of high-class budgerigars. The outside is neat and businesslike in appearance. The inside is divided into compartments catering for every sphere of the cult, and will comfortably house from 100 to

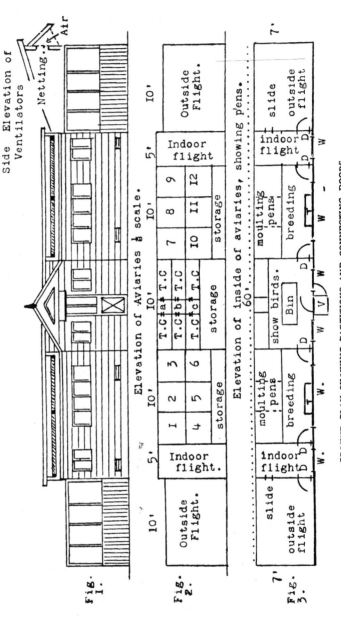

"AN IDEAL HOME IN WHICH TO BUILD UP A STRAIN OF BUDGERIGARS."

Fig. I.

Side Elevation of Ventilators

Netting. Air

Elevation of Aviaries ½ scale.

Fig. 2.

5'	10'	10'	10'	5'	10'
Indoor flight.	1	2	3	T.C=a T.C	Indoor flight	Outside Flight.
	4	5	6	T.C=b T.C		
Outside Flight.				T.C=c T.C	7	8	9
	storage	storage		10	11	12	storage
					storage	

Elevation of inside of aviaries, showing pens.

Fig. 3.

7'   60'   7'

indoor flight	moulting pens	show birds.	moulting pens	indoor flight	slide
breeding	Bin	breeding		outside flight
slide				
outside flight				

D   W.   T   W.   D   W   V   W   D   W   T   W   D

GROUND PLAN SHOWING PARTITIONS AND CONNECTING DOORS.

200 birds. Not one inch of space has been wasted; it has been so planned to cut down labour to a minimum and be not difficult to keep clean, yet every care has been taken to ensure the health of the occupants.

The comfort of the attendant during bad weather has been taken into account; all work to be done is under cover, and every point accessible from the central compartment. During hot weather the aviary can be turned into a very airy place, yet in the worst of weather remain quite snug. In fact, with such a building and the right kind of stock to start with one should succeed with the very minimum of effort.

The fancier who wished to follow out the whole scheme, but who perhaps thought the entire range too much for him to tackle at the commencement, might start with one of the 15-feet huts and the outside flight attached, and then extend as he progressed with the hobby. He might possibly pay for the extensions out of the profits on the sales of his first surplus stock. In that case he should plan his ground for the whole range beforehand.

BASE.

The whole lot might be built upon a concrete base if the owner could afford the cost, or the buildings could be raised above the ground upon substantial spars or brick pillars and the outside flights alone be concreted. The complete scheme could be modified or elaborated according to the pocket or ideas of the owner.

SITE.

The ideal position of the aviaries would of course be facing south or south-west, but unfortunately one has to build according to the site of the land one possesses. Whether in an exposed position or not, with aviaries, it is always policy to make preparation for bolting the houses down to the concrete bed or to strong posts let into the ground, so that they cannot be overturned by gusts of wind.

HOUSES.

All three huts are of the lean-to type, the false span on the centre hut being added for ornamentation. If this was painted white or any colour to match that of the window-frames, and continued in the form of a flat plinth along the fronts of the other two huts, a note of distinction would be added, and it would create a pleasant break in the severity of the fronts of lean-to type buildings.

The centre hut, 10 ft. × 7 ft., you will note by reference to the ground plan, is used solely as training quarters ; first for the young stock leaving their parents, and later for the exhibition birds. Thus this compartment serves a dual purpose. The thought foremost in the mind when planning this section was to place the birds to be trained where there was likely to be most traffic, and so accustom them to the sight of people and to noise. Also, as training cages need not be so deep as the breeding cages, more room could be gained in the most central position for the seed-bin and storage places for the utensils ; and if water and a sink could be laid on here, all the more convenient for the owner.

The ' wag ' who persists in coming in on Sunday mornings to stop you working could be safely left in this compartment to supply the noise necessary in the training of the birds, and he would be kept out of the way of the breeders, who want quietude.

DIMENSIONS.

The height of the lean-to huts is 9 ft. 6 in. at the front and 8 ft. at the back. This would allow for three shelves 18 in. deep and 1 in. thick being run right across the back, as in Figure 2. The first one to be 3 ft. from the floor, the second 19 in. above, and the third 19 in. above that one. The space between the bottom shelf and the floor could be enclosed by cupboard doors providing fine storage place for tackle. A large seed-bin [1] in the centre of the room, and covered with lino, would provide a useful table.

On the front elevation plan you will see six places marked T.C. These are the training cages, the dimensions of which are approximately 48 in. × 18 in. × 18 in. Some people might prefer to build these cages in, to save costs, but the best plan is to make loose cages which may be lifted down periodically for thorough washing and cleaning, a feature which is most important when training the birds for shows.

The spaces represented by the letters a-b-c are for specially made show cages—the standard cage, but having a slide door at *each* end instead of the regulation hinged door at one end. If these slides are placed to correspond with slide doors in the ends of the training cages, the birds can be run into the smaller cage at will, for transfer to the show cage proper or to the flights. This obviates the handling of exhibition birds just before going to a show.

There is a small projection on the ground plan of the centre hut marked V. This is a small vestibule, glazed for light, and which makes a useful safety door should any birds have escaped from the cages. By looking through a glass panel in the door of the hut, one can see at a glance if all is well. This vestibule also precludes the possibility of cold draughts striking

[1] Seed bins should be of wood—metal sweats.

135

directly on to the birds in bad weather, when the door is opened.

Two doors, one on either hand, lead from this central hut to the two larger huts, 15 ft. × 7 ft., the same height as the central hut. These two huts are each divided by a partition (three-ply boarded) into two compartments, the first 10 ft. × 7 ft., and the farthest one 5 ft. × 7 ft. This latter becomes an indoor flight, used as sleeping quarters for the birds using the 10 ft × 7 ft. outside flights at the extreme ends of the buildings.

These flights will accommodate 50 to 75 birds, and are first used as growing pens for the young stock and afterwards as segregating pens for the adults between breeding seasons. The cocks can be kept at one end, and the hens at the other. In these flights they will exercise and regain their strength and vitality before the next season. Thus these flights, too, serve a dual purpose.

If you again turn to the front elevation you will see that the remaining 10 ft. of the 15-ft. huts is divided into 6 compartments separated by sliding ply partititions. The size of these pens is approximately 3 ft. × 3 ft. × 3 ft. each. A space of 2 ft. at the bottom is enclosed for more storage room, where the nest-boxes may be kept when not in use.

These 6 pens in each hut, making 12 in all, are first used as breeding pens for controlled pedigree breeding, one pair to each pen. By removing the slides, these pens can be thrown into four 10-ft. indoor flights in which the potential show birds may be housed when brought in to be moulted. After birds have been for some months in the open flights they become wild again, and these pens form gradual steadying places before the birds are removed to the training cages proper.

Afterwards, these pens may be used to house the

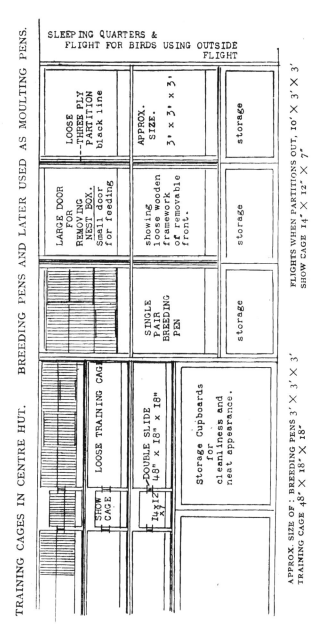

TRAINING CAGES IN CENTRE HUT.   BREEDING PENS AND LATER USED AS MOULTING PENS.

SLEEPING QUARTERS &
FLIGHT FOR BIRDS USING OUTSIDE
FLIGHT

LOOSE
--THREE PLY PARTITION
black line

APPROX.
SIZE.
3' × 3' × 3'

storage

LARGE DOOR
FOR
REMOVING
NEST BOX.
Small door
for feeding

showing
loose wooden
framework
of removable
front.

storage

SINGLE
PAIR
BREEDING
PEN

storage

LOOSE TRAINING CAGE

DOUBLE SLIDE
48" × 18" × 18"

Storage Cupboards
for
cleanliness and
neat appearance.

SHOW
CAGE

14×12
×7

FLIGHTS WHEN PARTITIONS OUT, 10' × 3' × 3'
SHOW CAGE 14" × 12" × 7"

APPROX. SIZE OF : BREEDING PENS 3' × 3' × 3'
TRAINING CAGE 48" × 18" × 18"

using both sides with a central aisle, this could be made to accommodate the same number of pairs "—the Author says : " The best results are not obtained in double-sided huts. Keep your breeding pairs in *hearing* of one another. Yes ! In *sight* of one another. No ! unless you wish the cocks to spend most of their time upon the wires."

Wire netted partitions are usually the precursors of a run of bad luck, and this applies to double-sided huts. About three years ago a double-sided hut with separate outside flights to each pen was boomed, but shortly afterwards one of the largest breeders in the country replied to this by building a hut, single-sided, of forty separate compartments in length; it was about forty yards long. This breeder had evidently gained much experience, or he would never have gone to that additional cost.

CAGE BREEDING OR FLIGHTS?

Some people have a misguided impression that budgerigars *cannot* be bred in cage compartments only, and still have the same stamina as those bred in cage-and-flight combined compartments. This is pure fallacy, for the hen spends most of her time in the nest, and the cock is either busy attending to her wants or seated on guard on his tiny perch outside the nest; thus the flight to the breeding compartment seems to be an unused luxury.

How many fanciers have considered the possibility of the cocks stopping out in the flights, clinging to the netting and chattering to each other for hours on end, thus neglecting their household duties.

The Author remembers once visiting such an aviary which had been greatly boomed as the ideal. The inside breeding cages were approximately eight cubic feet in size, yet each had a narrow outside flight attached. The exit from the cage to the flight was by means of a small hole about 3 in. square. On the day the Author went round this aviary there was a mild wind blowing, but the draught through those small exit holes was such that it was definitely bad for the health of the birds in those small compartments. They could not get away from it. In some cases the nests had been lifted down and placed upon the floor of the cage to escape the draught. It cannot really be a good plan to place nest-boxes on the floor of a cage under the hole, especially when budgies do like to nest in high places.

Thus the suggested compartment of twenty-seven cubic feet as used by the Author, and which is free from all injurious draughts, is strongly recommended. The chicks may be put into flights immediately after they have been somewhat steadied.

One should not confuse this with the indoor *flight* compartment. If one could afford the cost and the space, the really ideal controlled breeding compartment would be, a long hut with a corridor down the whole length, by the windows. The other portion divided into breeding compartments say 3 ft. wide, 6 ft. deep, and 7 ft. to 8 ft. in height ; each separated by three-ply partitions, each housing one pair of birds. But this would be a most expensive lay-out.

VENTILATION.

The reader will note that little has been said about this subject ; as a matter of fact, no one plan of ventilation will suit all aviaries. Conditions vary so much according to site and country that no standard details could possibly be applicable. One should aim at having an abundant supply of fresh air passing through the aviaries without direct draughts playing upon the inmates while they sleep. Endeavour to have small slides near the bottom of the hut to admit cool air, and then nearer the top, others to let out the fouled and heated atmosphere. All such ventilation holes should be covered with gauze to keep the vermin out. Mice soon find these inlets, and once in the aviaries are difficult pests to get rid of.

The individual fancier should use his own discretion about such matters according to the position of his accommodation. If the aviary smells sweet and clean after being closed up for the night, and your stock is healthy, then your ventilation is not far out.

After much thought and experience of other people's methods, the Author has no hesitation in recommending the aviary illustrated as " An Ideal Home in which to build up a Strain of Budgerigars."

Chapter XX

PURCHASING THE STOCK

Varieties, Colour and Type

BEFORE the beginner can purchase his initial stock with confidence, he should endeavour to learn something about the bird ; the different varieties, the colour matings, and—most especially—type. It is most essential in the building up of a stud to have the right shape of bird to commence with.

Type is paramount to all other exhibition properties. In exhibition livestock of any description the right type is of utmost value, yet it seems to be the last thing the new fancier usually grasps. One of the reasons for this difficulty is perhaps ' the subtilty ' of type. Type is built up of fine curves, delicately constructed, and which seem very hard to define by the new beginner. Were type composed of angles and harsh lines he would quickly grasp the outline because of the definite shape. Another little path upon which the beginner strays has for its sign-post ' colour '. At the commencement of things he usually gets a fancy for a certain colour, and then in his first passion of buying he lays too much stress upon this feature.

Type represents the bird—the construction of the article, the framework upon which is placed the attributes : colour, markings and condition. Still, before this vital question of the right type is considered, the beginner must have cleared up in his mind some of the lesser important matters. For instance, it would be of no use him setting out to buy his stock, even if he had mastered the problem of type, unless he knew for certain what he intended to purchase.

The beginner should first decide what colours he likes best and which he intends to propagate. It is far better to commence with a few colours than to fill the aviaries with a large assortment of oddments. Remember it is wise to specialize.

By varieties we mean ' groups '. These groups are then split up into different colours. Then, again, the colours are sub-divided into shades. These varying shades have an extraordinary action upon each other when mated together, and do not mix together in the same way as colours do when mixing paint ; yet breeding is by no means a haphazard mating of various colours ; a definite expectation can be anticipated.[1]

Not being desirous of confusing the beginner with a mass of scientific material which he would not understand, it is not proposed to delve into the problems of genetics or Mendelism, but in very simple language tell the tyro just those things which he should know before he commences to build up his strain.

VARIETIES.

The groups which will command the beginner's attention at the start are : the Normals, or straight colours, as they are often termed ; the Greywings ; the Cinnamonwings ; and the Red-eyed Varieties.

The normals are divided up as follows—
(sub-divided into shades)

The Greens,	light ; dark ; olive.
The Yellows,	light ; dark ; olive.
The Blues,	sky ; cobalt ; mauve.
The Whites,	sky ; cobalt ; mauve.

[1] *See the Budgerigar Society Matings List. It contains 2,000 different matings, and gives expectations.*

The greywings (at present) are divided up into—
             (sub-divided into shades)
Greywing Greens,   light; dark; olive.
Greywing Blues,   sky; cobalt; mauve.
The greywing yellow may soon appear upon the scene, and who will be the first to breed a greywing white?

The cinnamonwings are divided into—
             (sub-divided into shades)
Cinnamon Greens,   light; dark; olive.
Cinnamon Blues,   sky: cobalt; mauve.
Cinnamon Whites,   these are of practically a pure white body colour.
Cinnamon Yellows,   similar to the normal light yellow, but with a total absence of green suffusion.

The red-eyed varieties are divided into—
The Red-eyed White or Albino;
The Red-eyed Clear Yellow or Lutino;
The Red-eyed Fallow. Of varying shades.

A *brief* description of the colouring of the various birds would be of assistance to the beginner; but there are even finer points, such as density of mask colouring, which he would have to pick up by experience. The following will, however, suffice during the initial stages of purchasing his stock—

LIGHT GREEN (the original wild parrakeet from which the first mutation came).
      The body or breast and rump colour of a rich, brilliant, grassy green. It should neither be a dull bluey nor a light yellowish green.
DARK GREEN, of a dark laurel green body colour.
OLIVE GREEN, of a deep, even, olive green body colour; free from mottling by dark green or blue feathers.

All the above have similar characteristics : Jonquil yellow mask, four black throat spots, violet cheek patches ; black zebra markings on cheeks, back of head, neck, scalloping of scapulars, and lacing of wing coverts—on a bright YELLOW ground.

LIGHT YELLOW. The body colour varies on different birds from clear lemon yellow to daffodil or even a buttercup shade.

DARK YELLOW, of a dark yellow or orange body colour.

YELLOW OLIVE, of a cloudy, mustard yellow body colour.

These three varieties should have light yellow masks. A total absence of green suffusion on wings, neck and rump is most desirable for perfection.

SKYBLUE. Body colour of a pure sky blue, carrying no trace o cobalt shading.

COBALT. Body colour of a rich cobalt blue ; powder blue as used for washing purposes is a good comparison.

MAUVE. Body colour of a purplish grey, carrying a pinkish tint ; the dull leaden hue should be avoided.

The above shades each have white masks ; four black throat spots ; violet cheek patches ; and the zebra markings or wavings are on a WHITE ground.

WHITES. As stated, the white group is sub-divided into the White Skyblue ; the White Cobalt ; the White Mauve. Yet these are again sub-divided into two further groups—those of light suffusion and of deep suffusion. As the colours imply, the body colour is of the same shade as the normal black-winged varieties described above.

In the deep suffused birds the aim should be to get the body colour as deep or near the normal bird as possible in contrast to the light suffused, where it should be as pale as possible.

In both cases, however, the total absence of markings on the head, neck and wings is most desirable. These birds have black eyes, and should not be confused with Red-eyed Whites.

THE GREYWINGS.

As stated, the greywing group is composed of : the Greywing Light Green ; the Greywing Dark Green ; the Greywing Olive Green ; the Greywing Skyblue ; the Greywing Cobalt ; and the Greywing Mauve.

The characteristics of these birds are similar to those of the normal colours, with the exception of the DENSITY of WING and SPOT colour.

Whereas the normals have black wing markings, the Greywings, as their name implies, have half-tone wings and spots of a smoky brownish GREY.

The Greywings are really some of the most handsome of the Budgerigar family. Their delicate pastel shades, so pleasing to the eye, make a very charming picture.

At one time, and not very long ago, greywings were the rage, and some beautiful specimens were seen upon the show-bench, but of late they have dwindled in popularity. This is possibly because newer varieties have come to the fore, but more likely because both judges and exhibitors have had a tendency to ignore the writing on the wall. In such birds as half-tones there is bound to be an outcrop of bad-coloured birds which are reverting back to normal—in this case, heavily wing-marked birds.

It is really surprising how few people know the difference between a greywing of light suffusion and one of deep suffusion, yet the same people are very definite about the difference between light and dark greens. The name Greywing provides the clue. Any suffusion of greywing must have G R E Y wings, the difference of suffusion being in the body colour only. The light Greywing Green should have an apple-green coloured body and the Greywing Dark Green a laurel-green body colour.

These throw-outs of dark-winged birds have been passed off and even accepted by some judges as Dark Greywings, and this has, in the opinion of the Author, had more to do than anything else to cause the decline in the popularity of the greywing. The beginner should avoid these birds ; they are not handsome, but to the scientific breeder these dark-winged birds have their uses.

THE CINNAMONWINGS.

In the last few years this new colour has been added to the list of varieties. They have a beautiful, warm, cinnamon-brown marking in their wings. They are to be had in the normal body colours and whites. The cinnamon factor is sex-linked, and it has the advantage of some hidden power in cleansing the body colour of undesirable flecking. They are a lovely, pleasing bird, and should enjoy a long run of popularity.

THE RARER VARIETIES.

There are a few varieties which as yet are not within the reach of the multitude of fanciers, owing to the high price they command—

The Red-eyed White. The Albino is a wonderful bird : snow-white, without the slightest trace of suffusion and a pink eye. There are very few real Albinos about. In some of the teams of red-eyed whites the Author has seen at recent shows very few of the birds were genuine Albinos ; most of them showed a trace of suffusion.

The Red-eyed Clear Yellow, or Lutino is another splendid bird. Clear Yellow without the slightest

148

trace of green suffusion ; these birds are coming to the front line with rapidity.

Fallows. These are birds similar to the Cinnamon-wing, but having less density of body colouring and RED eyes. They are to be had in a variety of shades.

Opalines. These are multi-coloured or mottled birds ; some are pleasing to the eye, but their value is mostly based upon their rarity.

The Whitewings and Yellowwings. These are the latest creation, and when more of them have been bred and they begin to get that elusive factor of type which seems to be lacking at the commencement with all new varieties, they will command the admiration of all budgerigar fanciers. They are a most handsome bird.

The Yellow-masked Cobalt. These are described as a pleasing bird. They take the form of the normal cobalt, but having a bright yellow mask instead of the white of the normal variety.

From the foregoing, the beginner will have a rather comprehensive knowledge to commence with of the different colours. But most probably by the time this book is published newer varieties still will have been propagated. The scope of the breeder seems to be absolutely unlimited, hence one reason why they are so fascinating.

Having stated that the beginner would be wise not to purchase too many different colours to begin with, it would be as well to give him some idea of the combinations of colours which should be mated together and those which should be kept distinct. The tyro should have this firmly fixed in his mind before he sets out to purchase his stock.

Light Greens should be kept pure ; faults should be rectified by elimination or by introduction of fresh blood.

Light Yellows ; the same as in light greens. So

the beginner desirous of keeping two colours only might well make a start with these very popular varieties. One colour could be accommodated in one half of ' The Ideal Home ', and the other colour in the second half.

The man who likes to have a variety of colours, but who wishes to specialize, might try the blues plus olive greens. Skyblues, Cobalts, Mauves and Olive Greens all may be crossed in matings together without fear of deterioration of colour. Someone might say, " But you have missed one important colour here ! "

Quite ! One of the best birds in the aviary which should be used with the Blues is the Dark Green/blue type II. That to the beginner seems a mouthful, but later this is more fully explained.

There is no point in breeding greywings to the normal colours, though some people did think at one time that by doing so they could improve the wing markings of the normals, but greywings and whites go well together ; in fact, this is the best way to breed greywings, for the whites have the tendency to tone down the grey of the wings. So the beginner might well try these two varieties together.

The Cinnamonwings should be kept together. Now that there is a goodly supply of both sexes, there seems to be no point in breeding from ' split ' birds.

The mention of the word ' split ' brings us to the point where the Dark Green/blue was left out. The beginner always feels rather apprehensive of his ignorance at the start, and sometimes is afraid of asking others what these things mean. To keep to simple language, a split bird is one which resembles the normal in outside appearance, but which has the hidden factor of being able to produce the colour to which it is split when mated to another bird possessing the same factor.

For example : the pure light green mated to pure

light green will go on producing light greens *ad infinitum* until a mutation takes place, in which case the ' odd ' progeny is usually called a ' sport ' i.e. it came by chance. But if one mated a light green to a skyblue, we should not get, as most novices at the beginning would suppose, half light greens and half skyblues, but a batch of youngsters which would all resemble the light-green parent in outside or visible appearance, yet having a hidden factor of being able to produce skyblues under certain conditions. These youngsters would be called light green split blue—written, for the' sake of brevity, Lt. green/blue ; the oblique stroke denoting the word ' split '.

SPLIT COLOURS.

Now the condition under which these birds will produce skyblues is this : if you mate Lt. green/blue to Lt. green/blue the progeny produced will be 75 per cent. pure Lt. greens and Lt. green/blue, which will look exactly alike in outside appearance and which can only be distinguished by proving, i.e. by mating to suitable birds to find which of them is split and which is not ; and 25 per cent. of skyblues.

The beginner will require to know why this happens to be so before he commences to purchase his initial stock. Now, certain of the colours of budgerigars are DOMINANT over others which are termed RECESSIVE. Green is dominant to the paler colours yellow, blue and white ; that is the reason the chicks from Lt. green skyblue were all green in appearance. Yellow and Blue are dominant to white, and ' normals ' to greywings. Thus the recessive becomes the ' split ' factor. There is a perfect scientific reason for this.

A few examples to help the beginner to become more familiar with the term ; Lt. green/white, skyblue/white, Lt. green/yellow, Lt. green/greywing, cobalt/cinnamon-wing, yellow/white. These are but a few of the split colours, and in the next chapter we sha'l show the beginner how these split colours may be sometimes used to great advantage. At the moment all the beginner, who desires to build up a strain, wants to know is the presence of these factors, so that in purchasing his first stock he will be careful to ensure the pedigree of the birds he buys so that he may mate them correctly.

After he has gained practical experience the beginner might wish to delve further into the scientific side of the cult ; in that case he will find plenty of material at his disposal.

TYPE.

Now comes that most important of all things the beginner has to learn before he can go out to purchase his stock with which to build his strain : Type.

It is always very difficult at first to grasp the real qualities which go to the making of type. The beginner can certainly go to a show and see the winners, and come to the conclusion that they are the typy birds, because a man with more knowledge than he has judged them and classified them. He can even compare them with the also rans, or yet get someone to point out to him where certain birds have failed. After a long and minute inspection he may feel that he has got hold of the idea, and for the next few hours feel bucked with the progress he has made ; and then comes the snag.

The following day he might go along to an aviary or a large breeder and see about fifty or a hundred birds together in a flight ; then his heart feels like lead. The birds all look the same to him. Here, they are not labelled with red tickets, and dolefully he remembers that memory was ever a fickle jade. He hesitates . . . if he does he is lost, for that perverse craving for colour, that something which he can definitely value, comes to the surface, and he will usually end up by buying the

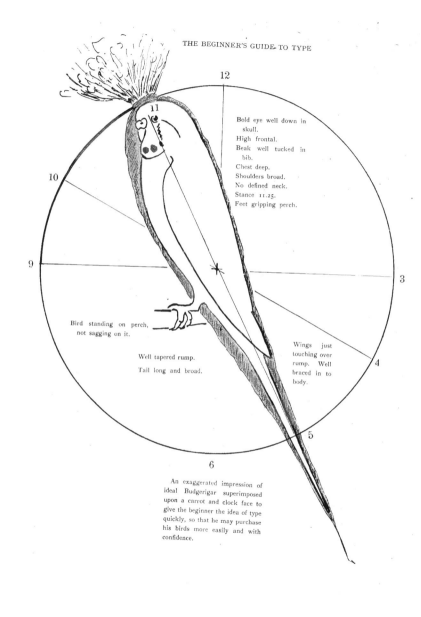

Bold eye well down in
  skull.
High frontal.
Beak well tucked in
  bib.
Chest deep.
Shoulders broad.
No defined neck.
Stance 11.25.
Feet gripping perch.

Bird standing on perch,
  not sagging on it.

Well tapered rump.

Tail long and broad.

Wings just
touching over
rump. Well
braced in to
body.

An exaggerated impression of
ideal Budgerigar superimposed
upon a carrot and clock face to
give the beginner the idea of type
quickly, so that he may purchase
his birds more easily and with
confidence.

brightest coloured bird. Henceforth he tries to cover his errors by exclaiming to his critics, " Quite ! but look at the colour ! " He has joined the ranks of the colour fiends—the men who cannot grasp type.

THE BUDGERIGAR SOCIETY STANDARD

CONDITION is essential. If any bird is not in condition it should never be considered for any award.

TYPE. Straight from nape of neck to tip of tail and gracefully tapered from the same point. Back and breast rounded and free from hollowness or from fat (lumpiness). The bird should be perfectly balanced, and convey the impression of being well proportioned.

HEAD. Rounded ; eye bold and set well away from top of skull.

WINGS. Approximately two-fifths total length of bird, well braced and not crossed at the tips.

TAIL. To be straight and tight, with two long feathers.

POSITION. Standing on perch at an angle of 30 degrees from the vertical, looking fearless.

MASK. Well-defined, with cheek patches large.

SPOTS. Clear, large, and symmetrical.

MARKINGS. Wavy markings on cheeks, head, neck, back, and wings to stand out clearly.

COLOUR. Clear and level in shade.

N.B.—In whites and yellows, face spots and wavy markings to be as faint as possible.

The old hand knows that the expert is the man with ' an eye for a bird '. He would never let such a man at large in his aviary with the net. The expert would not be side-tracked by colour or spots ; his eye would rove round the birds, no matter if there were two hundred, and swish ! would go the net, and at the same time the old hand's heart, for he would know that in that net would be the best bird—the best typy bird.

Now if it were possible to give the beginner something, some familiar similarity which he could carry in his mind because of its common knowledge, with which he could compare the birds he sees, then he might be able to buy the right type of bird without outside help, and not be side-tracked by things of lesser importance.

The most familiar object of which everyone knows the shape, and which compares well with the exhibition type budgerigar, is an exhibition carrot. That nice, smooth, stream-lined vegetable with the tops cut off. Big and round at the top and tapering away to a fine point at the other extremity. Think of a carrot when you go to buy your birds, and you will soon grasp the idea of a good bird.

Look at the illustration on the opposite page, and you will see a good type budgie superimposed on a rough sketch of this commodity.

HEAD.

A good-shaped or typy budgie should possess a good big, bold head. It should *appear* to have a high crown or dome and be wide in the skull. The eye should appear well down from the top. It should not go away quickly at the back, but in a good broad sweep.

Faults.—The beginner should avoid birds with *narrow* flat heads with the eye seemingly placed on the edge of the top portion of the skull.

CHEST.

The bird should be broad across the back and deep in the chest without being pigeon-chested. The bulk, if it can be termed so, should be all at the top end, and tapering away gracefully to the rump. Reject birds which are flat-chested in adults (this does not apply to young stock about six months old, they will probably continue to develop for another eighteen months) and birds which are thick at the wrong end.

NECK.

There should be no definition of a neck in the good bird, unless one could term it ' bull necked '. The head should be joined to the body at the back and chest in a sort of bulging way, but with pleasing lines and without appearing humpy at the back. Avoid long scraggy necks.

MASK AND SPOTS.

The mask should be clean, clear coloured, i.e. free from coloured edging to feathers ; the white mask should be snow white, the yellow mask of a good deep yellow.

Spots should be even in size and well placed. The extra large spot has a tendency to give an unwieldy heavy appearance to a show bird. The bird with moderately large spots well placed looks better.

TAIL.

The tail should be long and broad, the two feathers fitting one on top of the other so closely so that it appears almost impossible to tell whether there are one or two feathers. It should be carried in a straight line from the centre of the eye to the tip of the tail. Avoid birds with drooping tails. There are no angles in the ideal budgie.

WINGS.

The wings should be carried close up to the shoulders and the sides of the body, and just touch over the rump. Crossed wing-tips is a fault, though birds which have been flying out in large flights have a tendency to carry their wings high and cross them over the rump. This fault usually corrects itself after the birds have been in the training cages for a while. The beginner should reject birds with drooping wings, which is a sign of poor condition.

FEET.

An odd claw lost in a fight or by accident is no detriment to a good bird for breeding purposes, though it may mean loss of points on the show bench. The bird should grip the perch firmly with his feet and claws. Avoid birds with deformed or splayed feet.

BEAK.

Here is a little detail which is often overlooked. The beak should be rounded and smooth, short, broad at the top and tapering gently to the point, where it should be well tucked into the bib, or lower mask.

The long protruding beak like a miniature elephant's trunk is a deformity, and should be no more tolerated than an undershot, or a narrow, sharply-pointed beak.

At quite a number of shows lately the Author has noticed a few birds with beaks out of all proportion to the size of their heads; this is not good breeding. A bad-shaped beak is as much an eyesore as the long nose in humans. It detracts from the elegance of the bird, while a good-shaped beak adds charm and dignity to the good bird.

SIZE.

One of the most important factors is size, yet if one is not careful it becomes a craze which can be very detrimental in the building up of a strain. Everyone admires a big bird, but how often does one find a really big one which is a good one ? A good medium-sized bird is far better than a bad big one. A big bird is not judged so because of width, which may be a
, misnomer for fat, but by height from perch to top of head and then to tip of tail, with width in proportion. Nature is most symmetrical ; why should fanciers be less so ?

STANCE.

Stance or carriage is of vital importance. The bird should stand upon the perch in a position similar to the hands of a clock pointing to 11.25. The crouching bird, or the 10.20 bird, is not a good shower. The Budgerigar Society standard says : bold and fearless in carriage. The crouching bird is afraid—he is ready to bolt.

ACTION.

No bird should be sluggish whether in show-cage, pen or flight. He should have action—in other words, be perky. He should hop from perch to perch in the show-cage without being wild. In the pen he should always be on the alert when not resting.

Action is greatly dependent on condition, and type and condition are always synonymous, for without condition the true type of a bird cannot be seen.

BALANCE.

In choosing your birds you should aim at preserving balance. The well-balanced bird will always stand out amongst its fellows, even though it appears so unconsciously to the beholder, and he could not state why. Never let one particular feature sway you more than its value should. This is one of the secrets of the winners; they are so well balanced. That is why the novice sees them at shows, admires them, and then cannot carry the impression with him long.

Having given the beginner some idea of colour and type, now for a moment let us consider two features which are often forgotten until one gets the mania for details.

WING MARKINGS.

Except on the question of the wing markings of greywings, little has been said. Usually the attention becomes riveted on one feature, such as spots, in such a manner that one forgets the minor points. Clearly-defined wing markings add to the appearance of a good bird. The white on the blues should *be* white and not a smudgy grey; the yellow on the greens should be bright yellow and not greenish; the black in the zebra markings should be what is known to rabbit breeders as ' blue-black '. It should not have a rusty appearance, i.e. a brownish-black.

FEATHER.

The quality of feather is very important; it should be short and silky, not long and coarse and dull.

Budgerigar fanciers do not lay so much stress upon this as do the canary men, probably because they have

THE SKULLS OF TWO FAMOUS WINNERS

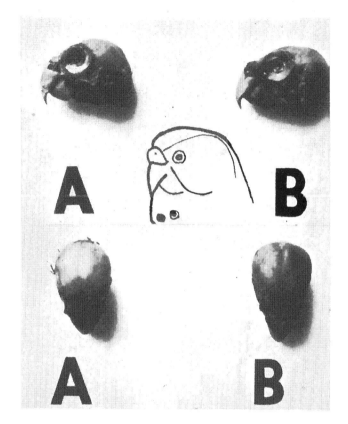

A. FRUDD'S FAMOUS YELLOW HEN No. 1. (THE HARTLEY HEN.)

B. A YOUNG GREEN COCK WHICH THE AUTHOR BRED AND EXHIBITED WITH SUCCESS. *Note*—-This youngster was not twelve months old when it died. The hen was four years old. Compare development.

The photographs are as near actual size as it is humanly possible to get them. The measurements were checked by means of calipers during the taking of the negative and the taking of the print, with the actual skull.

A. The hen was noted for her good head and the extra width between the eyes and across the skull.

In the photo, it looks as though she was actually broader than the cock. At lectures where I have exhibited these skulls in the bottles of spirit, I have asked, " Which is the Yellow hen's head ? "

(continued overleaf

The invariable reply was, " A ", which is correct. The reason given that it was the broader of the two, and these people knew the hen in question, as a very broad-headed hen.

Actually :

B. The skull of a young green cock, not fully developed, is the broader. It is about 1/32" broader. This skull is also 1/8" longer, from beak to back of skull.

This proves that it is an optical illusion. The cere is badly shrunk in both cases owing to long immersion in spirits,. Had this not been so, the flatness of the skull from the cere to the brainbox at the back would have been more pronounced. There is no FLESH on the top of the skull between the skin and the bone, the skin has to be cut off ; it is so firmly attached to the bone it will not tear off as on fleshy places. What, then, gives this rounded appearance ? There can be only one answer " Feather ! "

The side views were both taken on the same plate, focused at the same time, and were placed as near as possible in the natural position that the skull is when the bird is sitting on the perch. Note, when a bird is seated naturally on perch, the centre of eye and cere seem to be in a dead level.

so many other details to think about, yet it has a lot to do with the shape of the bird. A bird may look thick at the rump when it is not really fat at that point, but has a preponderance of long feather or under-down. The vent of the bird should be almost obscured by close-fitting feathers, so that no white patch of under-colour appears.

Look for short silky feather upon the breast; this greatly enhances the chances of the exhibition bird. It tends to create type and evenness in colour, since the under-colour does not show through.

How often does one hear the remarks ' bulging frontals ', ' high domes ' and ' breadth of skull between the eyes ' ? How many fanciers have stopped to consider how much feather has to do with those qualifications ? Dr. Armour, that great Scottish expert, unconsciously (that may not be quite true, for he may have taken feather into his calculations) upset many of the theorists when he pressed for a broader and flatter head upon the hen than that of the cock. Probably he thought like the Author, but from a slightly varying angle.

If the hair on females is finer and softer than that of males in humans, is it not possible that the feather on hens is softer and silkier than that of the cocks ? Now on the opposite page you will see actual photographs of the skulls of two famous winners exhibited by the Author. Both were said by the critics to have ideal heads for their sexes.

A is the skull of the first of Frudd's famous yellow hens (the Hartley Hen). Every fancier in the North remembers this bird.

B is the skull of a noted young green cock which did quite a lot of winning for its owner-breeder until it happened to break its neck in a regrettable accident.

Where is the bulging frontal and the width between the eyes which the hen was famous for ?

Where is the high dome of the green?—and how did the eyes of both these birds appear to be well down in the side of the head?

When Dr. Armour spoke for the broader, flatter head of the hen, was he not pressing for a finer, silkier feather in this bird, which would not stand so erect, but *fluff* out, giving the impression of breadth and flatness compared with the stronger feather of the cock, which *would* stand more erect, giving the appearance of height in dome?

The Author respectfully suggests that those people who talk so glibly of high domes are really thinking of the ' bulge of the brain-box '. Anyone who has children knows what that means; take hold of the head of a child and feel for this, it lies more to the back of the head and extends to the base of the skull.

A large ' brain-box ' on a budgerigar will obviate that ' falling away quick ' from the top of the head, and give that nice sweep which holds the feathers in such a graceful curve to the shoulders, giving the ' bull-neck ' appearance which puts so many birds amongst the ' Diplomas '.

Even the beginner should commence early to learn to look for this quality of feather.

.   .   .   .   .

One more word to the tyro before he sets out to purchase his birds: don't buy all young birds. The old breeder usually tries to put a little age on one side of the mating; not only does this help to improve stamina and size, but it helps to regulate the breeding of the sexes.

Take a note from the books of the poultrymen who breed for a preponderance of pullets. A two-year-old cock mated to a young hen will usually breed more hens than cocks, while a young cock and a hen having the greater age will produce good cocks. Two youngsters together will often produce more cocks than the breeder desires.

The wise beginner will first purchase his hens. In the opinion of the Author, the hen is by far the more valuable of the pair. Get the best type of hen that you can buy, and then get the best cocks that your purse will allow. The good stock hen is one which is a little shorter than the cock, yet more stockily built, having as much width across the shoulders and breadth across the rump as one can get. Her neck should be definitely ' bull-necked ' if you wish to breed good, big-boned cocks. The thick-set stock hens make good breeders and good mothers, usually. Avoid the masculine type of hen, the big raw-boned bird ; these are rarely good feeders.

If livestock is worth keeping at all it is worth keeping well. Just as we said ' balance ' is of importance in type, so is ' balance of mind ' vitally important in breeding. Don't be temperamental; you are the responsible person, the birds have to fit in with your whims.

When to Commence Breeding?

Assuming that the aviaries have been built and the initial stock has been satisfactorily purchased, the question arises—when to make a start?

The usual impatience gets everyone at the beginning, but this impulse should be curbed until the right time presents itself. Budgerigars will breed all year round if the nest-boxes are left in the pens, in fact they would continue till death took a hand in the game.

The correct time to start breeding in this country is about the beginning of March, though many people do begin much earlier. The Author has mated his birds as early as December 17th, the first egg being laid a week later on Xmas Eve, the first chicken being hatched on January 11th; and has successfully reared a large percentage of the youngsters hatched without heat. This is, however, exceptional, and should not be taken as a guide. The experimental breeder does many things which the average breeder would never attempt.

One would never advise a beginner to start so early ; only those with great experience should attempt such a feat, and only then if they are prepared to risk the whole of that stock, without complaint, should it be lost.

The first week in February, if the climate is mild and the aviary not too exposed, would be a reasonably *early* time. This would allow plenty of time for the young bird to moult and still be ready for the Autumn shows.

Cold Winds.

It is not so much a matter of cold weather—the birds seem to make themselves very snug in the nests—but a question of cold drying winds and sneaky draughts. These are the source of most of the troubles of early breeding.

If you can do something to counteract the ill effects of the cold north and east winds, and stop all draughts striking on to the birds and the nest-boxes, then there is no reason why you should not try a little early breeding *if* you are prepared to take risks. The cold drying winds have the effect of drying the inner membranes of the eggs and the chick cannot cut its way out of the leathery stuff, thus causing a preponderance of ' dead in shell '.

Lack of Moisture.

Thus we find that lack of moisture is the bug-bear of early breeding ; to get these chicks out of the eggs successfully, they must have moisture in the right proportion and at the right time. That is the secret of good hatching. Have you ever wondered why the bird in the tree builds of twigs and begins to sit in the early spring ? The nests which they build are porous ; at the time they are sitting the nights are filled with heavy dews, and the heat of the bird's body causes that moisture to be drawn into the twig nest, to supply the necessary humidity. In early breeding this is lacking, for with frosts and cold winds the humidity is dried up. This can be counteracted, as explained later.

Preparations for Breeding.

As March is the proper time, all such times before that must be of an artificial nature, therefore if you want to commence early you must use artificial methods to accomplish the job.

One of the things which incite the wild birds to nest in the spring is the lengthening days; then to breed early you must first of all 'bring your stock forward' as we do with summer-time. By installing electric light this may be achieved; the birds are deluded into thinking that the longer days have arrived. They keep active, and so come into breeding condition. Unless you have this light you will lose your chicks, even though you get the birds sitting; the adults can last twelve hours without food, but not the newly-hatched babies. At 'Duchy Aviaries', when early breeding is in progress, the aviaries are lighted from 6 p.m. till 12 p.m., and then again at 7 a.m.

Now all breeding compartments should be thoroughly cleaned out to prevent the unwelcome advent of lice. Nest-boxes have to be prepared, sand, lime, cuttle-fish bone, millet sprays, and seed treated with cod liver oil —all must be ready to hand.

As previously stated, there is no one fixed way of doing things; fanciers may think differently about slight details, but the general procedure is much the same on the whole. So in describing the methods used at 'Duchy Aviaries' no claim is made that this is the only correct way, but it has certainly proved very successful each year.

Nest-boxes.

Illustrated on page 126 is the nest-box used at these aviaries. The size is 6 in. × 6 in. × 8 in. The entrance hole is 1½ in. in diameter, and placed near the top right-hand corner. A small perch is let into the front about 2 in. below the hole; this perch should not project into the box or the youngsters will be out before they are ready.

The inside of the box is creosoted and allowed to dry. Next, a stepping block is placed across the bottom of the box inside and under the entrance hole; this prevents the birds from cracking or bulging the eggs should they be frightened and rush into the nest hurriedly. Then a concaved wooden bottom approximately 5½ in. × 4¾ in. × 1 in. is placed in the remaining space. The concave, in which the hen will lay her eggs, is hollowed out to a depth of ¾ in., leaving but ¼ in. of wood at the bottom.

The concaves are soaked in water and then allowed to drain, but not to become totally dry, before being placed in the nest-box. They are *not* creosoted.

Moisture : *Providing it Artificially.*

Many writers have recommended the spraying of the eggs with warm water a day or so before hatching; some have even gone so far as to advocate dipping the eggs in water. These methods might be right if one knew which egg was about to hatch without having marked each egg when laid. As budgerigars lay every other day, the first egg is due to hatch a good week before the last, so this method does not seem very helpful. Of course, these writers do not say exactly how much water and how hot it should be. They say nothing about how many times it is policy to disturb a wild bird when sitting. (Budgies are not domesticated poultry.) All these methods entail messing about with the nest and eggs.

None of these methods appealed to the Author, who desired to ensure that the eggs should have moisture but without disturbing the hen; so experiments were started with this idea in mind. The first idea was a small tube let into the side of the box, which could be filled with water from the outside of the nest, and which would allow water to dribble under the concave. It was unsuccessful; the water soon soaked into the wood, which then began to dry under the heat of the hen. Too much water made the concave wet all over; this was not ideal, the moisture being needed only beneath the eggs.

Then a tip was taken from nature, from the wild bird's nest, and the humidity caused by condensation. A thin sheet of copper was procured and slipped under the concave bottom. It was soon apparent that the heat of the hen when sitting percolated the thin wood left in the concave and warmed the top side of the metal. The temperature in the pens was below freezing-point at the time (the water-pots being frozen two or three times a day), so the bottom woodwork of the nest was decidedly cold, and so was the bottom side of the copper; the natural laws of science did the rest —condensation took place on the top of the metal directly under the concave where were the eggs. The water began to soak into the concave, which had become very dry during the period of incubation.

Every egg was fertile, and every one hatched and the chicks were reared. The necessary amount of humidity had been automatically supplied without one recourse to the nest. It was the ideal method— 'Dead in Shell' during early breeding was no longer a 'bogey' at these aviaries. Any breeder will tell you that the last egg is usually the most difficult to hatch because, as the other chicks grow, they throw out heat; and this together with the droppings which become caked on that last egg tend to dry the membrane, giving the tiny baby inside a task beyond its strength when it attempts to get out.

Here is a summary of the good and bad points of the box—

Good.   The nest has not to be touched once it has been hung. It is slow in action, almost thermostatically controlled ; the greater the heat on the concave, the more condensation. It is simple. It is fool-proof.

Bad.   It does not act in hot weather, as the metal becomes warm on both sides. (The heavy dews will do its work then ; the hens sweat.) It tends to make the nest sloppy when five or six growing chicks are each throwing out heat. (Slip the copper out after the last chick has hatched.)

It adds another 4d. to the cost of the box. (The loss through ' dead in shell ' might well be pounds, but the fancier usually thinks in pence—' overheads ' !)

So much for the copper sheet invented by the Author. By the way, many people have enquired, ' Why copper ? '—with an eye on that 4d. The reply is, because it does not rust like tin would, and won't need replenishing for years.

After the copper has been put in the nest-box, a little dry sawdust is rubbed into the cracks around the edges of the concave—two tiny chicks lost through getting their heads down the crevice taught us that wrinkle ; then the box is hung.

The dishes are filled with seed, to which a teaspoonful of cod liver oil to the pint of seed has been added, the water-pots are filled with water with a touch of chemical food included, the sand-pot has sea-sand and crumbled builders' lime (old lime which had gone hard and to waste), a piece of cuttle-fish is hung on a wire, and the pens are ready for mating up the birds.

Mating.

Hens are caught up from the flight, those which are down on the list previously prepared for that year's matings, and one is put into each pen and given five minutes to settle down. If she is in breeding condition, she will soon display active interest in the tiny hole in the nest-box.

The cock which has been chosen for her is then introduced to the pen. The mating should take place at once; if it does not take place in the five minutes allowed, they come out and another pair is put in their place.

The whole of the matings are not put up the same day, but in blocks with a few days' break in between, so that all don't strike the bad patches of weather at hatching time.

Breeding Condition.

People often ask, "Is breeding condition show condition?" The condition of a show bird just reaching his form, BEFORE being sent to shows, might be right for fertilizing the eggs, but not for a prolonged period of feeding—only exercise will fit him for that. A show-bird has usually been caged up for awhile, and that is definitely not breeding condition.

Quite a lot of people bemoan the fact that they had a bad start, and say, ' But look at the stuff I mated, all winners; they won all over the country, so they must be good birds." Quite! and probably almost physical wrecks, the cocks mentally too apathetic to look twice at the best of hens. Week after week of travelling in a show-cage, in hot rooms, gaped at and poked by thousands of people, tonic put into them time and time again to keep them going, having a pair of wings which have been merely ornaments from September to February—are these the birds which are to breed strong, healthy youngsters ? The whole proposition is ridiculous—except from a birth control point of view.

Breeding condition in the cock is when he stands upon the perch as though he owns it, and ruffles his neck feathers to every other male and wants to feed him ; when he is continually tapping everything with his beak and warbling his serenade ; when he is ever darting to the wires and back to the perch ; when he is bubbling over with vitality and can't keep still ; when he is vigorous and aggressive ; when his tail is broken and he is soiled from head to foot with fighting his rivals ; when he feels ' that he hasn't seen a girl for eighteen months '—in other words, when he's wild and as fit as a fiddle, no matter how dirty he might be. The cere then is full of colour.

Breeding condition in the hen, is when she is as wild as a March Hare when you go into the flight to feed ; when she, too, is full of energy and vigour ; when her cere is full and deep brown ; when she is either on the wires calling to the cocks or chewing the woodwork to bits ; when she struggles fiercely and bites hard when you catch her—a regular little shrew.

Some hens will go a pale, whitish blue in the cere just before coming into breeding condition, and also will sit upon the perch with their heads tilted back as though gazing skywards. This is a good sign.

Exercise.

What brings birds into this condition ? Exercise, plenty of it, and hard tack. The poultry man who wants eggs buries his seed and says, " Now scratch for your living!" Budgerigars who are too richly fed get fat and sluggish, and are useless as breeders. Fat and lack of exercise is at the root of egg-binding.

Last year, in the depth of winter in our aviaries, we had young hens dropping eggs from the perches in the worst of weather, without damage or egg-binding, and no stimulants or cod liver oil. Why? Because they were in big flights, fed on hard seed, and were wild to breed.

Give your hens as much exercise as you can before breeding, and you will have no trouble with egg-binding; it is the most natural thing on earth for a hen to lay an egg.

Pairing.

Does it not make you smile when you hear of people pairing up their cocks and hens in small cages for ten to fourteen days before putting out into the breeding compartments. When did nature in the raw start to observe the laws of convention? When did the birds and beasts of the field take to becoming engaged? There are no match-making mothers in the wilds. If the birds have been segregated and are fit, mating should take place on sight.

Once this has taken place there is no need to wait to place the nests in position, the hen is better in the nest biting wood until she is ready for laying, than being harried by the cock. All their energy should be conserved for the trying times of feeding ahead.

Pairing in small cages is undoing what you put them into the big flights to gain. Even if four pairs to the flight were our method, the better plan would be to put the hens in first for a day to agree and to find the nests, and then introduce the cocks together; one has no guarantee that they will not fight or that infidelity will not take place even if they are, so-called,

paired together first. The simplest plan is to let them
fight it out quickly. We once did pair four pairs of
birds together, and then after the due period put them
into a flight. One cock did all the treading, the others
fed, the hens seemed to enjoy the joke, three cocks were
miserable, and results were none too good.

Reference.

The ring numbers of each mating should be placed
upon a card on the front of the pen for reference, and
those of the chicks added in due course.

Laying and Incubation.

The hen will begin to thicken at the rump about
five or six days after mating, and usually on the seventh
or eighth day the first egg will be laid. Our practice
is to look in the nests each day until the first egg has
been laid, when we book the date, and then the nest
is not touched again until after the fourth chick is
hatched. Some would say that this is not a good policy ;
we think it the only one. The argument against is,
" What about a hen which is egg-bound ?—you will
miss her." No, we should not !

There is a very simple way by which the newest
beginner can tell if all is going on well. When a hen
is laying, her droppings are black and turned out in
great quantities. Cultivate the habit of looking round
all the breeding pens every morning, watch for the
latest droppings of the hen—she will usually go to the
same place upon the perch each morning, after daylight,
to do this. The man who might be afraid that he would
not be able to tell the fresh droppings could take up
the old ones each night with a scraper and then he would
have nothing to fear.

Hens which are egg-bound usually come out of the

nest into the air and crouch in a corner looking very ill; you may even find them dead. The losses in this respect are much smaller than that caused by too much interference with the nest.

If the droppings are very loose and grey the hen is chilled. Look in the nest to see that she has not dropped some excreta there, soiling the eggs. Then warm the place a little, or the hens might die.

The incubation period is about eighteen days.

Hatching.

Restrain your curiosity to peep when hatching is in progress. You will hear the whistling squeak of the hatching chicks—then stuff your ears with cotton wool or go away and leave them to it. After the fourth egg should have hatched you might look in the nest, and if very dirty, clean it out.

A good plan is to scratch upon the side of the box before lifting it down; the hen will then come out. They soon learn that this is the signal that you are going to remove the box, and anticipate it.

In the nests where you have heard least squeaking you generally find fat chicks doing well; they don't chirp much after hatching if the mother is a good feeder.

With young hens go carefully; they are very fussy, and you will supply sufficient fussing for a dozen aviaries. Learn their little idiosyncrasies—each hen behaves in a different way—and you soon will know how to treat each one.

Cleaning the nests

The nests don't often want cleaning until about ten days after the first chick has hatched, but as the chicks grow the nests will require cleaning every other day. We put a little sawdust in after ten days to keep the droppings dry. Some people put in fresh concaves each time they clean the nest, washing the others in readiness to go back. This is taking cleanliness to faddiness ; if the fresh concaves were warmed it might be feasible, but to put young chicks on a cold concave is asking for trouble. Ring the chicks at about ten days.

Removing the babies

When the chicks are about five weeks old they leave the nest fully feathered but with barred heads. They should be left with their parents for a few days to learn to crack seed for themselves. They soon get this habit ; when they are eating, and their beaks are turning yellow, they should then be put into the training cages for about ten to fourteen days.

Young birds are very wild and timid, but a short period in the steadying cages soon teaches them not to put their heads under the food-pots, but to perch and not be afraid. As soon as they are steadied they may be turned into the indoor flight and allowed to go into the open flight the first warm day afterwards.

They need flight to develop to maturity ; plenty of exercise will broaden them out.

Food

The best mixture for breeding purposes is, one third mazagan canary seed (not too large, but of a good quality), one-third best white millet and one-third Indian millet. In cold weather a few groats may be given separately, but as the season advances this heating food should be cut out and green food substituted.

A millet spray when the first chick is due to hatch,

and one to the youngsters when they leave their parents, is advisable.

Plenty of clean water during breeding season is essential. This is the only time when budgies do drink a lot; they need it to help to digest their seed for feeding.

Never forget to give some form of lime; the hen requires it for shelling her eggs and the youngsters for feather and quill-making

INBREEDING.

Inbreeding is really a misnomer, for it often develops into *out*breeding, i.e. the breeding out of the blood that has been introduced. If birds were bi-sexual, then when one was fortunate enough to get hold of a ' stormer ' one would expect to be able to reproduce that almost ' ad infinitum '; but unfortunately one has to introduce fresh blood to reproduce at all. Immediately a mating has taken place the blood of the progeny has taken the proportion of 50 per cent. of each of the parents. Now, supposing that the hen was the wonderful specimen, the breeder has mated her to the best cock that he could find and which he thought would be most suitable for her. But at the back of his mind is the fact that he wishes to reproduce as many birds as he can, each as good as the hen, or better if possible.

So he takes the best son, the one which shows most *visibly* the features of his mother, and he mates them together. The 100 per cent. blood of the hen plus the 50 per cent. of her blood in her son brings the proportion of the hen's blood in her grandchildren to 75 per cent. In this way he tries to breed out the blood of that cock in the first mating, and strives to ensure that his subsequent matings turn out birds having the features of that first hen; thus he is fixing

Now, this question of how steady a show bird should be is a debatable point. Some people still imagine that the steady bird is the one who just sits and looks at the judge and won't budge.

These birds are perfectly tame, in fact look bored to death with everything that is going on about them. A ' wag ', speaking of a noted bird once said, " He simply sits and asks for the prize." As a matter of fact, had he had action he would never have won half as many prizes as he did, for when he moved he showed a distinct falling away of the head. You might think that that was a good point, his refusing to budge ; but. that is not the ideal show bird, and in the keen competition of to-day he would not have won—birds must show themselves.

The ideal show bird should have action. By action, we mean that it must move about and show himself to advantage ; surely there are two sides to a bird, and the judge must see them both. One can have action without wildness ; no judge will look twice at a bird who goes mad in the cage. So get them steady, but not still. The good show bird hops from perch to perch, he neither crouches nor stretches his neck in curiosity.

TRAINING CAGES.

This is where the need for proper training cages comes in, such as those depicted in the illustration. Then the more you can keep your show birds in contact with humans the better. This is where the aviary attendant comes in very handy ; he is knocking about the place all day. That, too, was the reason for putting the training cages where there was likely to be most traffic. The show bird must not be afraid of the sound of voices and try to hide on hearing visitors speak.

In your training cages have two perches only ;

place them as far apart as possible taking care that the birds do not scrape their tails against the wood each time they rest. If one perch is slightly lower than the others the birds will swoop and not flutter across. This will give them action and wing carriage, especially if you can teach them to go about without getting wild. Training cages should be spotless.

On alternate days open the double sides into the show cage and let the birds have every other day to move about at their leisure in and out of the show cage, which you will note is situated between the two blocks of training cages. The birds will get then the feeling of being in a confined space without fear. Children don't like being shut up by themselves in small rooms, neither do budgies at first. If they are afraid of the small cage they will spend most of their time trying to get out, and so damage themselves and their tails.

Another good training plan is to run two birds at first into the small cage and leave them in together for half an hour. Then try them singly ; as they get used to this gradually lengthen the periods. Then walk about with the cage in your hand ; the stewards will do this, and if your birds are not used to it they are not ready for the judge.

One great advantage of having your show cage in close proximity to the training cage is that there is no need to handle your birds in getting them out for the show ; they soon learn to hop into the show cage, then they are easily transferred.

Get your birds used to a pencil. Carry one in your hand when you are examining your birds, rest it on the wires, put it inside and stroke the birds with it if they will allow you, tap the cage with it, move it gently across the wires—in fact, get them to know it, then you will have no fears about the judge, who uses a small cane when judging.

SHOW CONDITION.

No bird should ever be sent to a show that is not in condition, no matter how good a budgerigar he may be. He should be all there ; in perfect feather, each one held tight to his body, and showing that silky sheen denoting fitness. He should be clean ; dirty tails and wings do much to peg a bird back. He should be alert and perky, carrying himself properly, neither drooping his wings nor dropping his tail. He should not develop that annoying habit of dropping his pinion feathers.

If your birds were brought inside to complete their moult, they should be fairly clean and not need hand washing. In stating that they should be fairly clean after moulting, we do so to draw the attention of the beginner to the fact that budgerigars don't usually moult all their feathers at one period of changing their coat. It is rather an annoying habit, but one which we have to put up with ; for instance, they might moult their heads and bodies, but not the primary flights of their wings. These are the long feathers. It is no uncommon thing to see a budgerigar practically moulted out and then for him to drop these long wing feathers—not all of them, but enough to spoil his chances at a show—or even drop his tail.

On the light-coloured varieties, these wing flights which have not moulted look very dirty indeed against the snow-white background of the show cage. That is why we state they might be comparatively clean. If they have not moulted these feathers and they are dirty, they should be washed on the edge of a bowl with warm soapy water and the lather thoroughly sprayed off, so that not the slightest trace of soap be left in the feathers. If the soap is left in it dries like rats' tails. There is no need to hand-wash the whole of the bird in a case like this. Hand-washing is not good for budgies ; we never do this unless absolutely forced to do so. It takes far too much out of the bird and is not natural. The beginner would be well advised not to attempt to hand-wash a bird without experience ; he might lose the bird, for they have been known to die during the process. If the bird is too dirty to be got clean by spraying, then the best plan is to get to know a canary exhibitor, who are past-masters at this feat, and ask him to help you out. They are a most obliging lot of men, and will probably be very pleased to do the job for you.

SPRAYING.

Now spraying the birds is a pastime which both the bird and you yourself will enjoy very much. They love a good spraying with water. It is quite a simple job, and makes a wonderful difference to the condition of the bird. Bottle sprays can be bought very cheaply or where a lot of birds have to be sprayed quickly, large metal pressure sprays can be obtained.

Place the birds to be sprayed in an all-wire cage such as the canary men use, stand it on a tray or sink, gently spray the birds and leave them for a few moments for the first lot of water to soak into the feathers and soften the dirt. Then go back and give the birds a really good drenching. A hole in the bottom of the cage allows the water to drain away.

We are often asked, how often we spray ?—whether the water should be hot or cold ?—when is the best time to spray the birds ? As a matter of fact, this is a job where one should use his discretion, for there can be no set plan, conditions prevailing at the aviary may not be the same in each case. The best way is to consider whether you yourself would like it on the day in question. It would not be advisable to drench the best birds through on a very cold bleak day in an outside aviary during the late afternoon. The birds should never be allowed to settle down for the night in cold weather, or even in summer, when wet.

In hot weather, the birds will dry very quickly, and the afternoon would be quite all right, for the evenings are long and the birds would be dry long before dark. In cold weather it is best done in the morning, so that the birds can keep active until they are thoroughly dried out. In hot weather use cold water, soft water preferably. In cold weather, warm water; though many people advocate hot water we find that this has a tendency to start temporary moults, the very thing one wants to avoid during show season.

The quantity of water put on the birds depends upon the weather at the time. A mild day, and we soak them; a cold day, and we spray lightly. On those damp raw days of fog and drizzle we never spray, for nothing ever seems to dry at such times. On very cold freezing days, if we must spray we take the birds inside the house to do it, keep them in a warm room until dry, and then transfer to a cold room for the night, putting them back into the aviary the following morning.

A bird that is fit has a gloss upon his feathers; the water will abstract some of this oily matter, leaving the feathers dull, but they will recover the sheen in two or three days. So don't spray your birds the day before a show.

FOOD.

The correct diet for your show birds is half good-quality Spanish and half best white millet; a little Indian millet may be added occasionally as a change. A tonic once per week is a good thing for them. Soak millet sprays in water to which chemical food has been added, one teaspoon to the pint. Allow to soak for twelve to twenty-four hours, shake off the superfluous water and give wet. The birds will enjoy this and eat it readily. This is the best way to give budgerigars medicine, for they drink so little from the pots out of breeding season.

Forty-eight hours before a show, a millet soaked in water and citrate of iron with ammonia will tighten them up and make them fit. Use enough of the iron to colour the water a deep red.

A good tonic at any time, but especially for birds that are inclined to fatten, is a millet spray soaked in Glauber salts, one teaspoon to the pint. Always give wet.

Green food should not be given to exhibition birds ; only as a titbit very occasionally.

If one wishes to compete for points or trophies extending over the season, one should aim at having more than one bird of each colour, so that should one fail just before a show another may be substituted.

PICKING THE WINNERS.

Birds which have been tried out and won, of course don't need any picking, neither does that ' stormer ' —he always stands out a mile ahead of the other birds ; but unfortunately there are not many of these super birds, and the beginner is always puzzled which birds to try. In this case he is rather inclined to lean too much to individual features, such as colour or spots. But here is a tip which will enable you to puzzle the judges somewhat.

Pick out your birds which are best balanced in all the features, i.e. good all round. The judge will usually see the head the first thing, so choose birds with good heads. In a big class the judge will want to thin them down as quickly as possible to allow himself time to spend on the last seven birds which will take the cards. The first thing he does is to pick out all the bad-headed birds, for they are obvious to everyone who sees the class, and he has his reputation as a judge to consider. So aim at surviving that first elimination process. The longer your bird can stop on the bench the better his chance for his finer points to be considered.

Also, as we have said, have your birds steady, for after he has thrown out the bad-headed birds the judge will still want to get rid of some more if the class is a big one, and he will probably get the unsteady birds out of the way. Survive that.

The next thing the judge will do is to clear out the small birds, so endeavour to have size in your birds ; get this and you will still have a chance. The birds will be getting thinned out by this time, but there may still be ten or twelve birds left, and the judge only wants seven or eight for his final sorting out, according to the plan by which he works. He will probably take colour into his calculations now, so see that your bird is of a good colour and you will probably survive the final elimination process ; if you do, your chances with a well-balanced bird are decidedly good.

The judge during these elimination tests will probably have got his eye upon the really top-hole birds in the class, and will have gradually got them placed 1-2-3-4. You still have a chance with your well-balanced bird, even though he may not be a ' stormer ' ; a good all-rounder that is fit, perfectly put down, and steady will puzzle the judge. Then there is always the chance that the judge will spot a minor fault in one of the birds which at the moment is standing higher than your bird ; down it goes, and UP goes yours. Sometimes a better bird whose training is not of the best suddenly loses its patience and goes wild before the judge has finished ; then up you go again.

A good judge who knows his bird will never throw

out a good, well-balanced bird, even though he knows it is not a ' Palace ' winner, until he has found something to beat it. But do remember that condition and training will pull your bird through most of the first stages of elimination. Remember that a judge does not commence his work by comparing the finer points of one bird against the one in the next cage, but by getting rid of his bad birds ; so aim at surviving these trying times, and then every good feature your bird has got will be counted against the others.

There is still one point which helps a bird considerably—

CLEAN CAGES.

Put your birds down in the cleanest cage that you possibly can. We often hear remarks about : " The judge should judge the bird and not the cage." These remarks usually come from lazy, disgruntled people ; they are too idle to clean their cages, and think that the man who is not should be penalized to their level. This is rot !

Any sensible man who stops to think knows full well that the judge looks at the bird, and not the cage ; but only the born fool cannot see that a good bird in a spotlessly clean cage looks smarter. The clean cage with its spotless white enamel enhances the bird, the old, dirty cage detracts from it.

If you were called upon to judge a beauty contest you would never dream of putting the fair ladies up against a dirty backyard wall or judge them in a coal mine. We have heard all the arguments about a contrast showing up the goodness . . . don't be had, it's a fallacy !

We were one of the first in this district to realize the value of the white-enamelled wire fronts when other people were painting theirs black, to get that contrast. When we took home the prizes consistently, the others began to follow our lead; now the white front is standard.

Whilst on with show cages, don't be niggardly with the seed in the bottom; it is your bird's funeral if it should be spilt out in transit and the bird starves. We have even seen birds sent to shows, not on odd occasions, without even a single seed in the cage. Surely your conscience should see that there is more in the cage than is necessary for the trip; the remainder can be riddled after the show, and fed to the birds in the flights.

The seed on the bottom of the cage is half white millet and half canary; any other mixture may lead to disqualification.

SCHEDULE AND ENTRY FORM.

The beginner should study his schedule and the rules before making out his entry form. It is surprising how many silly mistakes are made at each show, all for the want of a little thought and common sense. If there is any point upon which you are doubtful, write a note and pin it to your entry form and send them together to the secretary of the show. He will be pleased to put you right. But don't send your note by itself two or three days afterwards; this causes the secretary double work, and the catalogue may be in print. He is not bound to comply with your request at that time if he is rushed with work.

One should not forget that the exhibitor is only concerned about his own birds, but the secretary is concerned about *all* the birds, which is a vastly different matter.

Remember, a fancy or exorbitant price may be put on your bird, but do see that it is beyond dispute. Don't put 25/- if you mean £25 os. od.

191

Send your birds off in good time to reach the show and to have time to settle down and perhaps feed before they are again moved about for judging.

RETURN.

Immediately your birds arrive back from a show, check them to see that you have received your own rightful birds back. Then look your birds over to see if they are all fit, not showing signs of chill or looseness in the droppings; if they are, put them where they have heat to bring them round. Examine for dirt; some shows are very dusty. If your birds are all fit, spray them as soon as possible after a show to get the dust out and as a prevention against moulting.

Sprinkle a little Bismuth carbonate on seed.

COMMON AILMENTS AND DISORDERS.

The chief troubles which the budgerigar breeder experiences are as follows—

Chills, which usually develop into pneumonia or enteritis.
Egg-binding.
Feather-plucking.
French moult and runners.
Undershot or overgrown beaks.

There is not the slightest reason why anyone should be unduly perturbed by this list; for, having bought sound healthy stock at the beginning, then by keeping them in sanitary aviaries and feeding with good sustaining food, very few cases of serious disease will be experienced. The budgerigar, because of his continual activity, is a very healthy fellow, and his extraordinary freedom from disease makes him a very fascinating one.

CHILLS AND ENTERITIS.

The budgerigar does not get cold upon his chest as humans do ; he gets cold in his back. Because of his anatomical construction his ribs are at the back, and this is where you should take care no draught strikes on to him. When a budgerigar goes to sleep, he ruffles up the feathers on his back to keep these cold draughts from striking him there. The feathers then act as a down quilt and keep him snug and warm. When a bird is fluffed out, that is not a sign of illness provided he draws his feathers in when wakened ; of course he is ill if he stands huddled the whole time, with his feathers all on end. But when he gets to that state he is *really* ill, and there is not always a good chance of curing him.

The thing to do in bird keeping is to aim at prevention rather than cure. People will say : " That's all very well, but how can we tell when a bird is sickening ? " Well, there is one infallible sign which one should never ignore, though the bird does not seem to be ill in itself. When one has anything from one hundred to five hundred birds there are bound to be odd cases of birds being taken ill. Mostly these can be cured quite simply if caught in time. But it is hard to spot the bird slightly off colour with a flock of any extent unless one goes about the business systematically. Yet if observation is kept on the birds in this way it is surprising how the faculty of spotting the weakling grows on you. You can spot the ' off colour ' bird at a glance.

This is the way that we go about it. Every time we enter the aviaries, no matter what for, we have trained ourselves unconsciously to get the habit of looking at that last bird which does not move, when the others fly across the cage or flight. Usually, when one enters the aviary, the birds which are well immediately fly across to the opposite perch, but there are odd occasions when some bird will remain where it is, or hesitate; these sluggish birds are the ones to observe.

The bird may seem well enough, and not even ruffled in his feathers, but look at his head; here is the infallible sign which we mentioned. If the feathers about his head and back of the skull seem as though they have all been dipped in water or gum, and have the extreme points stuck in tiny needles, then catch the bird at once and examine him closely. These tiny needle-points will be more conspicuous when you hold him in your hand; they will appear just like the tips of a waxed moustache. That is the bird which is sickening!

Turn him over and look at the vent. If it is clean you can congratulate yourself that you have caught him in the first stages, and there is every chance that you will cure him or prevent him from being really ill. If the vent is soiled with greenish excreta, then the illness has advanced further than desirable, and you will have to take steps to doctor him at once unless you desire to lose him. These little symptoms are those of colds or enteritis.

The bird whose vent is clean will most likely be perfectly well again when he has had a couple of days in the hospital cage in a heated temperature. Mr. Andrew Wilson, of The New Zoo, Argyle Street, Glasgow, has invented such a cage, heated by electricity, and which is worth its weight in gold; every keeper of a large flock cannot afford to be without this wonderful gadget. Get the temperature up to about eighty to ninety degrees and put the bird in; he will soon begin to pick up and one can observe his excreta. A millet may be put to soak in chemical food, and be given to him when ready; this will be probably the only treatment that he will need. Heat is the best cure for bird illnesses.

The bird whose vent is soiled with excreta should be treated slightly differently. The hospital cage should be heated to about one hundred degrees for him, and he should be given a dose of 'Dwek' and water by means of a fountain-pen filler. As soon as a millet spray can be soaked in 'Exonia' the better for him, for you must endeavour to keep the bird eating; they soon lose their appetites when unwell. Before you place the bird in the hospital cage, you should clip the matted feathers from the vent, taking care not to clip the skin. If you don't do this the odds are that he will soon die from stoppage of the bowels, for the matted feathers will dry in the heat of the hospital cage and seal his vent. Keep your eye on this bird; you will soon see him drop watery green excreta on to the blotting paper in the cage now that you have cleaned his vent; if he does so, he has got enteritis. Try to tempt him to eat and dope him with 'Dwek'; sprinkle some of the powder on his seed.

A good plan is to go to the flight where you got him from and sprinkle some powdered 'Dwek' over all the seed-pots; the other birds will get it when they eat, and it will do them good, and help to prevent more from sickening. All the droppings in that flight should be at once cleaned up and the other birds examined for soiled vents.

As the droppings of the birds in the hospital cage become normal the heat may be cut down gradually, for they will soon be tight in feather; then cut the heat out altogether during the day, putting a little on for that first night; the following morning, if the birds look well, cut it out altogether and leave the heat off that night. Should the birds still look well and have not had a relapse, then take them out of the cage and keep in a warm room; but don't take back to the aviary until you feel sure that the cure has been successful.

EGG-BINDING.

If by any chance you should have a sitting hen become egg-bound, you will soon know, as she will be huddled on the floor of the pen looking very sick. Take her into the house and drop a few drops of warm olive oil on to the vent and put her in the hospital cage at a temperature of about ninety to a hundred degrees. The heat will soon take effect and she should soon pass the egg. Plenty of heat without roasting the bird is usually successful. After she has rid herself of the troublesome egg she should be put into a flight to recover and to exercise before allowing her to go back to the breeding pen. Her other eggs should be scrapped, as they will have gone cold and be spoilt; they would be addled.

Should a hen be egg-bound and not part with her egg, it soon becomes a matter of life or death with her, and then other means have to be taken to get the egg away; unless you do, the hen will certainly die. A beginner should never try to take an egg away from a hen unless he has seen the operation performed by someone who knows how to do the job; a hen can easily be ruptured and ruined if the job is not done correctly, to say nothing of the pain which the hen will be subjected to by unskilled amateurs. It would be most advisable to go to a more experienced breeder and ask him to do the job for you.

The Author has successfully taken eggs away from hens in most stubborn cases, and where it seemed impossible for the hen to live. Here is a description of the operation; in these extreme cases the use of a hospital cage is imperative, and it should be heated to about one hundred degrees.

The job should not be hurried; you must not get flurried or excited because the hen looks like dying at any moment; only patience will do it satisfactorily. First drop some warm olive oil on to the vent, pressing the egg gently forward as you do so, to open the vent and allow the oil to work its way in. When the oil has trickled into the vent let it close, put the bird into the hospital cage for a while and observe her. She will probably endeavour to expel the egg, and first of all black droppings will exude from the vent; if these do appear she will probably pass the egg herself. If, however, she simply lies gasping for breath, making no effort to part with the egg take her out again and repeat the performance, squeezing the egg a little more towards the vent this time.

The egg should appear in the wide-open vent as though covered with a thin red skin; this is the oviduct, and care should be taken not to touch or split this. As the pressure is increased, a tiny white speck should appear in the red skin; this is the end of the oviduct from which the egg exudes. Drop a little warm oil on this speck of white, and let the egg go back gently; the oil will go with it and lubricate the muscles of the oviduct.

Place the bird back in the hospital cage and let her rest for a few minutes; if she does not make any attempt to expel the egg then it will be a matter of minutes only, or she may die. Take her out again, handling her very carefully each time, and gently press the egg forward again. Drop some more warm oil on to the vent as it opens; this time as the oviduct is pressed forward the white egg should be showing more distinctly in the aperture, the oil should have done its work and be releasing the contracted muscles. Press the egg gently forward and suddenly it will roll into the hand. Have some more oil ready to drop on to the oviduct as it slides back into the vent, and then put the bird back into the hospital cage; she will probably lie on her side gasping as though dying.

A fellow fancier who saw this operation performed at our aviaries looked at the hen and said, " She'll be dead in a few minutes," and was greatly surprised to hear the reply, " She'll be on the perch in half an hour, and chirping." Much to his amazement she was, and eating seed, too. Within ten days she had perfectly recovered and was starting to lay again ; the eggs were all fertile and hatched, the chicks no different from those of a normal case. But don't do this operation unless you have seen it done.

The only experience of egg-binding at ' Duchy Aviaries ' has been with hens which have been shown for a long period—*verb. sap.*

Please do go the rounds of the breeding pens each morning and see that the hens are all right. Don't leave a hen in pain until lunch-time ; probably if you do she will be dead by that time.

FEATHER PLUCKING.

Occasionally a hen will develop the annoying habit of plucking her chicks. Why they do this no one can give a satisfactory reply. It seems that they do it for sheer devilment, or to pass the time away between meals. One theory, however ridiculous, is as good as the next.

Some hens take the tiny quills from the heads of the chicks as they form ; some take the down only, which is not so important ; some take the whole lot with the exception of the flights, which they cannot pull out. You might have a hen of this description which appears to be the ideal mother ; the chicks are almost ready to leave the nest, and then you go in to examine the nests and find that she has stripped the youngsters in a day. Fortunately these cases are very few and far between ; the budgerigar is almost a model bird.

If the hen strips the lot after they are fully feathered,

she should be destroyed unless she is a very valuable exhibition hen, in which case her eggs should be fostered out. Where the hen just takes the tiny quills off the heads of her babies, a shiny appearance will be seen on the back of the skull; once this is seen transfer the chicks to other nests where the hen can be relied upon. The chicks will be no worse for this experience, and the feathers will soon grow again.

When breeding with young hens which are untried this should be guarded against, and you should be ever on the watch for this annoying little trick, or you might have a valuable specimen ruined.

All kinds of experiments have been tried with these birds, but without success. Why they do it one cannot tell, but fortunately the percentage of pluckers is very small; you may go years and never have a hen who does it.

FRENCH MOULT AND RUNNERS.

One usually approaches this subject with feelings of trepidity. There have been so many theories put forward by men of great experience on this subject, men who are in a position to expound their theories backed with knowledge, that one hesitates to add to the list. Yet though 'Runners' have been termed French moult birds, we at 'Duchy Aviaries' are by no means convinced that this is so. In fact, in face of the experiments which we have performed in search of knowledge on this subject, we might go so far as to state that we fully believe that the two have no connection; that is our opinion, but we do not state it as a proved and accepted fact.

French moult makes its appearance in the form of chicks which fully feather for a time, and which suddenly shed all their feathers whilst still in the nest. Examination of the feathers show that they are curled, and any subsequent feathers which form drop out later.

In our aviaries we have had only one experience of this, which rather refutes the evidence given in a treatise on this subject which we think was prematurely published by The Budgerigar Society.

Four years ago we had a hen which was egg-bound; as she did not expel the egg herself we took it from her. For two years she had bred perfectly feathered youngsters. As it was getting near the end of our breeding season when the hen became egg-bound, we decided not to allow her try that second round over again, but put her out into the flights. Now, we never use three-year old hens for breeding unless we have done exceptionally well with them; in the case of this hen we had done well with her and desired to use her for one more season.

She was mated up, and her eggs were fertile; they hatched and the chicks thrived. Then came disaster. About a week before the first was due to leave the nest it shed all its feathers; they were curled. We tried a second round with the same results, so the hen and all her chicks were destroyed. The cock, which was a young one, we tried with other hens, and had perfect youngsters, so we kept him. That was before the treatise on French moult was published, or we should have carried our experiments further with the hen. That was the only case we had of French moult to date. We are bound to believe that the cause of the trouble was some derangement of the bird through being egg-bound, or some damage we might have done to her in taking the egg away.

Further remarks about French moult we cannot give, but we should not advise anyone experiencing the disease to keep the parents, but destroy them. But in spite of all that has been said we prefer still to keep an open mind, and until such times as we can be convinced that the statements made in that pamphlet are true, with all due respect to the author, we shall continue to do so.

RUNNERS

Unfortunately, these cases are rather more frequent than those above. The 'runner' is the budgerigar which leaves the nest fully feathered, and then, a few days later, the flight feathers drop out and the bird is unable to fly ; so, as its name implies, it runs about the cage floor and climbs about the wires. After about a month to six weeks new flights grow, the bird flies like any other, and it would seem impossible to tell it from a bird which had never dropped a flight.

In spite of all the evidence which has been put forward in the treatise on French moult, we can never accept the theory that this is hereditary, but firmly believe that this bird has no connection with the genuine French Moulter.

Probably, much more evidence than that given in favour of the theory of inheritance is to be had showing that birds which have—shall we say, by accident or some outside influence—bred such 'runners' at one period, which have in turn bred many other birds none of which have ever dropped a single flight except at moulting times. Is this phenomenon but a 'childish' ailment such as fever or some similar disorder ? The Author urges all experimental breeders to continue their efforts but with an open mind as he cannot accept the theory of a recessive factor without more proof.

Neither could we accept the theory that the 'feather plucker' is related to the 'French Moulter' genetically.

Let us examine our own experience of 'runners'. We quote the number of young bred in the last five years at our aviaries; and the number of runners is interesting.

Year	Bred	Runners
1933 ...	126 ...	... Nil
1934 ...	186 ...	... Nil
1935 ...	230 ...	... 30, plus four from split cin. mating
1936 ...	252 ...	... Nil
1937 ...	313 ...	... Nil

It seems very strange that we should only experience this phenomena in the year 1935 and never since. Yet we have bred again and again with the same stock which produced the ' infected ' birds, with no recurrence.

The original stock which we had bought had been all good, strong, healthy specimens (bought from a reliable breeder who had no experience of F.M.); we had not *inbred* with them; they produced many well-known winners; and then in 1935, suddenly, without a sign of warning, we bred about 30 runners. These birds were big, strong, healthy birds which, when they came out of the nest, gladdened our hearts. Why? Because they were of a colour of which it was very hard to get size in the best coloured birds. We had that good colour, and thought we could get the size by artificial means, by feeding and not by breeding for it; and that was where we had erred.

It was a very bitter lesson to us, for we destroyed all those youngsters, some of which, if we had kept them, would have recovered their flights and made extraordinary good show birds. But we had been so frightened by the tales of these monsters that we executed the lot *en bloc*.

Surprising to say, these birds had appeared in the first rounds in the nests of our best birds, so we sat down and studied the problem to find where we had gone wrong. Naturally we compared our procedure with that of previous years; the only difference had been in the feeding. So keen had we been to get that *size*, we had thought that by packing the birds with all kinds of rich food we could get it.

Our food that year was composed of the following dishes—

Cod liver oil seed, the oil generously used.
, A brand of soft food containing cod liver oil.
Giant Spanish, White Italian Millet, French Indian Millet.
Groats.

Not content with this, we had made a cake from pea-meal, eggs and lard; baked this in the oven, cut it into squares and strung these on wires in the breeding pens. (This is a food we made at home for young nest birds, i.e. wild birds taken from the nests to be hand-reared. We used to soften the cake with water and feed with a stick.) The birds ate this freely; the hens were laying their second rounds long before the first chick was ready to leave the nest. Amazing clutches of eggs were being laid. It was common to get tens and nines, in some we had twelve, and in one fourteen eggs. We soon realized what we had done, at once cut out all the heating foods and went back to our feed of hard tack: half canary and half white millet and Indian millet in separate pots.

We scrapped a lot of eggs in the second rounds, and to our relief did not have another runner. That experience does not tally with the information given in the pamphlet on French moult, except " C.L.O. treated seed was supplied; the best of canary and Italian white millet provided; green food given constantly and renewed regularly; cuttle-bone, mortar, sand, clean water, everything one could think of. In fact, this lot of birds enjoyed greater attention and were better fed than the ordinary stock birds." (Page 8, Supplement to *The Budgerigar Bulletin*, March, 1936.)

But we noticed something else which perturbed us far more than anything else. The heating foods not only overheated the blood of the babies, which were very hot to the touch when handled, but it heated the blood of the hens, and for the first time in our breeding we experienced lice in the nests.

That fact, and the fact that some of the feathers which had dropped from the chicks showed that they seemed to have rotted off near the base of the quill, set us thinking. We determined to make an experiment. We had that wonderful light green which won for us in the first closed ring class which had ever been put on, and third best budgie in the whole show, at The First National All Budgerigar Show, promoted by the Budgerigar Society in conjunction with Shipley Society in November, 1934.

He was a wonderful bird, and had been run over; his sister, a marvellous hen, had also been run over, so we mated them together. Then we took a pair of unrelated greywings and mated them, too.

The two pairs were isolated from all the other birds and allowed to breed. They were fed on the rich foods previously used, and the nests were never touched from mating to the last youngster leaving the nests. All eggs were fertile, and all hatched, and all the chicks left their nests fully feathered. Within a week every one dropped the whole of their flights. The nests were examined and were found to be full of lice. About seven different kinds were collected, put into a test-tube and sent to Mr. W. Watmough, who sent them to Dr. Tom Hare, of the Poultry and Game Research Laboratories, London, with my request to see if these were, as I supposed, blood-sucking lice. I had recognized one or two of the parasites as a kind of flea.

Dr. Hare replied : " The parasites received from Mr. Frudd are lice belonging to the family of biting lice, or Mallophaga. . . . A heavy infestation of these parasites leads to loss of condition and depression, owing to the irritation of the bird's nervous system."

Then followed a request to send some of the infected birds to Dr. Hare for inspection, but unfortunately the whole of the chicks had been destroyed—they had in this case been very weak things. It was a great error having destroyed these birds, or we might have carried the experiment further.

Later that year we had still a further case of ' runners '. In 1934, when cinnamonwings were rather scarce, we purchased a young split cock. He was of a poor type, weakly, and had been inbred. We got four normals in the first round which were all runners, and during the feeding of them he died. We had paid a good price for this bird, who was barred when we had bought him. That was our first exploit in breeding with that new colour, which gave us nett result—nil ; for we destroyed the four normals, being of no use to us.

From our experience we have had to come to the conclusions that runners are perhaps the result of either inbreeding, wrong feeding, or insanitary conditions. In any case we think that further research is necessary before one can state with confidence what the real cause is.

The beginner need have no fears about this annoying trouble, for he may never experience it if he keeps to the instructions given in this book.

Although the Author cannot at present accept the findings published in the pamphlet on French moult as issued by The Budgerigar Society, he urges all breeders of these so-called ' runners ' to destroy them, unless they are kept solely for experimental breeding, as until the cause of this phenomenon is established no useful purpose can be attained by their retention or sale.

The Budgerigar Society is again enquiring into this matter.

UNDERSHOT OR OVERGROWN BEAKS.

This is an irritating trouble, for it usually is bad luck enough to come where you don't want it, on a good bird.

The undershot beak is where the lower mandible grows upwards, covering or overlapping the top one; it is caused by dirty feeding by the mother. Sometimes one gets a hen who allows food to collect on her beak and who does not rub it off after feeding; this gets stuck to the top beak of the chick, causing pressure and forcing the mandible inside the bottom one, and the top one to grow malformed. Sometimes a little food gets under the tongue of the chick, goes hard and forces the bottom mandible out, having the same effect.

These birds should be killed; trimming the beak acts like pruning, making it grow faster. A dirty feeder can be spotted by the food stuck to her beak; she should be caught up and her beak cleaned.

Overgrown beaks take the form of a beak which looks like a miniature elephant's trunk. The trouble usually occurs in old birds, who seem to be too old to manicure their beaks on the builders' lime put in the flights for that purpose. Trimming does no good with them, either. It is better to dispose of them painlessly.

People have often asked, " How can you destroy a bird painlessly ? " It is quite simple. Take the bird in the hand, the four fingers under the back of the bird, the thumb on the breast-bone, and apply pressure gently. This pressure acts upon the heart and the bird does not cry out or struggle, for it immediately goes into a state of coma. Hold the pressure for a minute, and the heart stops beating.

PSITTACOSIS.

You will wonder why this is included, but not under the headings of budgerigar ailments. Psittacosis is a parrot disease which is communicable to man, of which the authorities say that the origin and causative bacteria is a mystery. Budgerigars certainly belong to the parrot family, being parrakeets, but we have yet to hear of any single case of this disease being given to anyone by a budgie, or even of a budgie ever having the disease.

One need have no fears with our little pets. Thousands of pet budgies have been fondled by their owners, have been ' kissed ' etc., and yet not one case. Therefore it is not included in the ailments until such times as we have proof that it can be communicated to man by our pets.

Anyone taking up this fascinating cult and keeping his birds properly should have very little illness amongst his stock ; as a matter of fact there are no other species of livestock which are so immune from troublesome diseases as budgerigars.

We should like to impress upon the mind of the reader one point—don't keep 500 where you have only the convenience or the time to keep 50. Apart from the poorer results the labour entailed makes the hobby become a toil of a pleasure.

Buy a young budgerigar and tame him and you will find him a very fascinating little fellow. Start a small aviary and keep and breed and few and you will find it a fascinating hobby.

.   .   .   .   .

Every keeper of budgerigars is recommended to purchase Dr. H. Duncker's lists of *Budgerigar Matings*, published by The Budgerigar Society.

This wonderful book gives the expectations of nearly 2,000 different matings, as well as information on the difference between Type I and Type II birds.

Every breeder of budgerigars should join The Budgerigar Society or some local society; by doing so you will soon have access to all the information and benefits which we older breeders enjoy.

The address of The Secretary of The Budgerigar Society is—

      Mr. C. H. ROGERS,
      Lawn Cottage, Abington, Cambridge.

QUESTIONS—ANSWERED.

During the course of the many lectures which the Author has given the following questions have been asked him many times. They are reproduced here because they are points which often puzzle the man who is only just beginning to build up a strain.

Why do YOUNG birds often win as youngsters but fail as adults?

In judging young bird classes *colour* counts more than type, which has probably not begun to show itself. Therefore judges incline to the deepest coloured bird; yet often this colour is too deep or patchy on the adult specimen. A notable example is with greywings. The judge wants to see youngsters showing a distinct greyness about the wing markings and flights; these often moult out in the adult plumage into very dark, almost black, markings which are not desirable in the adult. The adult plumage of all budgerigars is deeper than that of the nest feather.

What good is a pedigree?

It tells you what the eye cannot see. If the breeder is truthful in his pedigree one sees *behind* the appearance of the bird. Much time is saved by not having to prove every bird when one knows the pedigree.

Why do you advocate NOT showing the breeders? Surely the best birds, the winners, are those which one should breed from?

Surely the second part of the question answers the first. A breeder in a big way usually keeps two or even three sets of birds ; one he exhibits to keep his name to the front, the others he keeps at home to breed with. Showing birds tires them out and does not tend to induce breeding condition.

Why take only two rounds?

Because breeding is naturally a strain upon all beings and should never be abused. Two rounds per season is ample for any pair of birds. In some cases, with very valuable birds, the expert breeder may take only one round, or even foster out all the eggs and so place no strain whatever upon his show birds. Third and fourth rounds have been known to produce " runners " when there has never been this phenomenon in the strain before.

Why advocate the killing of " runners " if you don't believe that this is hereditary?

For the simple reason of ' safety first '. Until the real proof of this phenomenon and the actual cause is established beyond dispute, there is no sensible reason for the keeping of them except for experimental breeding.

Do you desire a variation in the heads of male and female?

Most decidedly ! The silky feather of the female is a feminine property or attribute ; and, obtaining this,

209

one is bound to get a difference in the shape of the head.

If you desire a distinct type for the male and one for the female, how can you expect to breed males at all?

This was the silliest question ever asked the Author at the end of one of his lectures, and it came from an old breeder. The question of type has nothing whatever to do with the actual distribution of the sexes, though it may have very important consequences upon the progeny produced.

The distribution of the sexes is controlled by the action of the different chromosomes. Both male and female sperm is made up of two chromosomes; the female—X and Y; the male—X and X. If an X chromosome of the cock meets the X chromosome of the hen this produces a youngster—XX, the male; likewise, if the X chromosome of the cock meets the Y chromosome of the hen the youngster produced —XY, the female. The type of the parents only acts upon the youngsters under the laws of heredity, colour under the Mendelian law. There are birds which have a tendency to produce good specimens in one sex only, the other being very mediocre stock; this should be noted and made use of.

Why don't you like a masculine female?

Because it is not natural. The masculine female usually makes a very bad mother, if a breeder at all. These Amazons are too fond of aping the male. The masculine hen is not a good sitter. Remember the superstition of the ages against the crowing hen; these superstitions are not built upon fanciful conjectures in all cases, but have always been the omens of —ill-luck.

SHOW PREPARATION CHART

8 weeks before show	4 weeks before show	one week before show	48 hours before show
Catch up 'probables.'	sort out the best 'balanced.'		
examine for broken feathers remove stumps.	new tails will grow in eight weeks. ,, Flights ,, ,, ,, ,, ,, ,, Spots ,, ,, ,, four ,,	cut out all greenfoods. feed with hard seed.	give spray soaked in citrate of iron with ammonia.
Note cleanliness.	very dirty —hand wash remove all soapy lather. only flights soiled. —hand wash flights only. spray regularly twice a week	spray lightly. pick out birds to enter. pick out any likely substitutes.	
note condition.	too fat —give glauber salts twice per week. too lean. —give cod liver oil seed. condition seed, or a few groats occasionally.		
put into large indoor flights.	gradually reduce flight. remove to training cage proper. teach to get accustomed to show cage. teach to be unafraid when moved about get used to stick or pencil.		

What are the most common causes of failure?

Greed and the tendency to take ' short cuts '. Some men get satiated with success, others become ' financiers ' not ' fanciers '. Others want to produce in every youngster a winner. They will not take advantage of the matings which may only produce a proportion of good colours. They don't like to make sacrifices, yet some of these matings produce some of the best birds.

What is the difference between TYPE I and TYPE II birds?

The beginner is usually puzzled with this definition of a bird on a pedigree. It has nothing to do with Type as shape, but is the guarantee of a hidden factor that is not visible to the eye.

Owing to a " linkage " between the factors F (the yellow factor) and B the brown factor) Type I and Type II birds do not follow the same rules as birds with other factors. (From the B.S. matings list by Dr. Duncker.)

Simplified, this means that all the beginner has to remember is that when mating Dark Green/blue to Skyblue—

Type I birds will produce more of the lighter blue —Skyblue.

Type II birds produce more of the deeper shade of blue—Cobalt.

Similarly when using Type I and II birds in matings producing Olives and Mauves, the Type I bird produces more Olives and the Type II bird more Mauves.

Type—FAULTS CHART

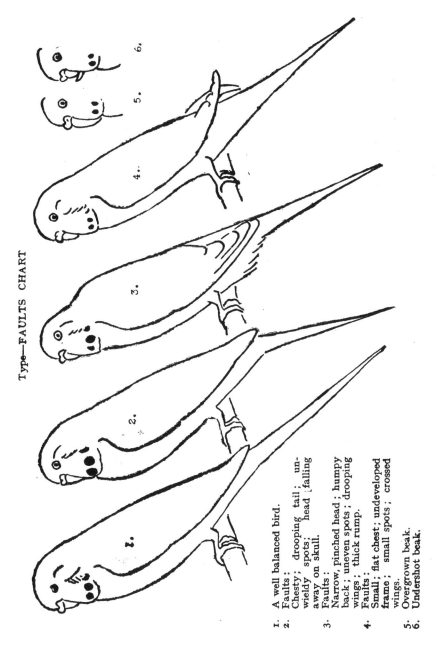

1. A well balanced bird.
2. Faults:
   Chesty; drooping tail; un-wieldy spots; head falling away on skull.
3. Faults:
   Narrow, pinched head; humpy back; uneven spots; drooping wings; thick rump.
4. Faults:
   Small; flat chest; undeveloped frame; small spots; crossed wings.
5. Overgrown beak.
6. Undershot beak.

AILMENTS CHART

Bird "Off colour"	Symptom	Treatment	Outcome	Action
	Merely sluggish	Keep under observation give one dose of powder Dwek and repeat in 8 hours. Wash down Dwek with 2 drops of distilled water	Bird recovers	Keep under observation until perfectly satisfied cure complete. Put Exonia in water. Give Millet spray soaked in Exonia solution.
			Bird gets worse	Remove to hospital cage and give heat 80°. Give Dwek every 3 hours.
	Bird Huddled. Vent clean.	Remove to hospital cage. Temp: 80° Administer Dwek—also millet spray soaked in Exonia solution.	Bird improves	Gradually cool off before returning to flight. Keep a tray of 'Calci' in flight.
			Bird gets worse	Give Dwek and gradually increase heat to 90-100°.
	Bird huddled. Vent soiled with green excreta	Remove to hospital cage administer Dwek and water by means of filler. Give heat—90-100°	Bird improves	Gradually cool off. Give powder Dwek on seed and return to flight when droppings normal (black).
			Bird gets worse	Will probably die. Give powder Dwek every 2 hours. If this does not effect a cure, bird has probably an internal laceration.

Bird "Off Colour"	Bird Egg-Bound	Remove to hospital cage. Temp.: 90-100° Administer warm olive oil to vent, also Exonia to beak by filler. I part Exonia to 6 parts water; give 2-3 drops only	Bird expels egg	Gradually cool off; when bird has recovered put into exercise flight to recuperate. Never put straight back to breeding pen. Give Exonia and sprinkle Calci on seed.
			Bird gets worse—'Life or death'	Remove egg according to instructions. If inexperienced, get someone who is to do the job for you. Give Exonia, keep warm and quiet until perfectly recovered.
	Bird Wheezing	Remove to hospital cage. Temp. 80°. Put Valpine in diffuser, also Exonia into water. We find a weak solution of Iglodene a good throat antiseptic.		
Bird Moulting	General dropping of feathers	Keep warm in an even temperature free from draughts. Give Exonia, Calci in dish also old brick mortar. Birds require lime, in moulting period especially so.		
	Chicks drop feathers in nest	If curled—FRENCH MOULT—Destroy! If plucked, remove to foster.		
	Flights dropped after leaving nest	"Runner:" Destroy until further information is available regarding this phenomena. Examine food-pots for over heating food; examine nests for lice.		

In giving the reader the " Ailments chart " printed on pages 214, 215 the Author does so in the hope that it will assist the worried fancier to find ' at a glance ' what to do in moments of emergency and anxiety.

There are many tonics which may be had which will probably prove successful in the saving of your pets. Those mentioned in the chart can be fully recommended by the Author, with every confidence.

As most troubles which beset the budgerigar are largely caused through unsuitable grit, the fancier would be advised to not use those containing sharp particles of oyster shell. Sea-sand no larger than granulated sugar is best. Perfecto grit specially prepared by Mr. Percy Glover of Fareham, Hants, may be safely used.

One of the troubles which worry the exhibitor at show times is the abundance of fat which the old bird puts on after breeding is over. This is really one of nature's aforethoughts in providing the bird with extra flesh to keep his vitals warm during the moulting period ahead. One should never be too keen to reduce these birds. Glauber salts dissolved in water may be used as a reducer—the best way to administer is to soak a millet spray in this, and shake off the superfluous water and give wet.

The fancier's motto should be ' prevention is better than cure ', therefore aim at keeping your bird fit by coupling to that slogan—' cleanliness is next to Godliness '.

CHAPTER XXIII

THE MARCH OF TIME

A Fantasy

A SHORT time ago, one heard the exhibitor say, " How can we hope to win by showing YOUNG birds against old ones, in the same classes ? "

So to please the exhibitors, the promoters of shows placed on the schedules, classes for *young* birds bearing the current year closed ring.

.   .   .   .   .   .

A steward, at a show in 1936 watched the Author judge a *young* bird class ; the exhibits were all wearing the current year's closed ring. Some time afterwards, the same steward said to the Author, " I was amused to see you give ' first ' to such and such a bird, it is an old bird ; last year, it had another ring upon its leg and won at certain shows ; I know the bird."

.   .   .   .   .

At a show this year, where the Author was judging ; a fellow judge who had finished his section first, and who had idled his time, until ' specials ' were to be awarded, looking at some of the classes yet to be judged, came up to the Author and said, " When you judge the *young* bird class, come and tell me how many old birds there are in the class." All the birds in the class were wearing the current closed ring.

.   .   .   .   .

At another show, where the Author was judging the budgerigars; the canaries were being brought out for the special for the ' best *unflighted* bird ' which is paramount to the closed ringed young budgie.

One of the stewards whispered something to the judge; a look of horror spread across the features of the man making the awards. The Author asked him what was the matter.

" It is an old bird," said the judge.

" But it has the greenish uncoloured feathers in its flights," returned the Author, looking carefully at the bird. in question.

" Quite ! " said the canary judge, " But people wishing to pass off an old bird as a young one have found out a way to do so. They pull out all the flights of the bird after they have finished colour-feeding ; and the bird then grows another lot of feathers which are not coloured ; it is a cruel and a most horrible thing to do."

.   .   .   .   .

Lest anyone should think that it is impossible to put the B.S. closed ring upon an old bird, the Author wishes to say that he can put the present ring upon almost any old bird.

Here is something which requires looking into quickly ; should the closed ring be made smaller ? or should our experts endeavour to find the difference between a first-year bird and an old one—there must be some subtle difference by which the two may be distinguished. Or, must the young bird classes be won by birds which are not quite good enough for the old bird classes. How soon will it be before the exhibitor murmurs, " We cannot win the *Young Bird* classes with a young bird."

The Author points out that there are certain features in the bird which would bear close investigation—

The March of Time

The Beak   (Scaling at the point)
The Cere   (The old soiled look, lack of freshness)
The Feather (Stronger and deeper colour)
The Feet   (Scales and lack of freshness)
The Structure (Substance, the budgie does not
      fully develop in the first year)

.   .   .   .   .

Just as we are going to print we learn with pleasure that the Budgerigar Society is to consider the question of the size of the closed ring in the near future.

ADDENDA

We are able at the last moment to include further information in regard to our experiments on the ' Runner ' question. As previously stated we regard this phenomenon greatly attributable to lice and wrong methods of feeding. Bearing this in mind we are not endeavouring to *produce* them, but to prevent a recurrence of our 1935 troubles.

Last year we made two experiments which we have again repeated this season, and fortunately we are able to state with satisfaction that out of our first round of youngsters we have not had that recurrence. We should have included this information earlier in the book, but we desired to still further test our methods.

First, we have again used clipped oats in preference to groats for feeding breeders. Oats keep their freshness, and if given dry are relished by the birds and there is no danger of stale or sour food. Note we never give soaked seeds or soft food of any description to our feeders—nothing but plain hard tack. All youngsters out of nests at the present moment are doing well and are perfectly feathered.

Secondly, and this we consider to be one of the most important of our experiments—that of combating lice. Following up our theory of lice as a causative factor in the production of 'runners', we resolved on a very daring experiment last year, and one that we have again repeated with great success.

Instead of creosoting the whole of the insides of our nest boxes and allowing to thoroughly *dry* before hanging, we now wash out our boxes at the end of a season with strong disinfectant before putting away for the show season. At the beginning of a new season we get them out, brush the woodwork with a stiff brush and then creosote the inside of the bottom of the box (under the concave) and for about 1 in. up the sides ; putting plenty of the liquid into the corners. Then, we put in the copper sheet, replace the concave, rub a little sawdust into the crevices and hang the box at the time of mating with the *creosote still wet*.

The sawdust absorbs the liquid which soaks up the sides and does not soil the hen. The hens do not seem to mind the smell, and they use the boxes just as freely. It seems to have no ill effects on the incubation of the eggs or on the newly hatched chicks. It does not interfere with the action of the copper sheet, we still get condensation on the upper surface under the thin part of the concave, and which soaks into the wood beneath the eggs.

No lice are being bred during sitting, and no runners are appearing. To the sceptic who says that he does not breed lice in his nests during breeding we would advise him to look with a microscope—they are so minute. Creosote which has dried soon loses its power to kill these little pests In aviaries which have been built of T & G boards and which have been in use for a number of years, it is remarkable what does come out of those crevices just when you don't want it.

We were certain that our birds did not breed lice when sitting, so faddy were we about cleanliness, until we looked among the droppings in the boxes with a very strong magnifying glass.

INDEX

14429017R00155

Printed in Great Britain
by Amazon

HORSES TO FOLLOW
2010/11 JUMPS SEASON

TIMEFORM
THE HOME OF WINNERS SINCE 1948

TIMEFORM

© PORTWAY PRESS LIMITED 2010

COPYRIGHT AND LIABILITY

ISBN 978 1 901570 79 3   Price £7.95

Printed and bound by the
Charlesworth Group,
Wakefield, UK 01924 204830

TIMEF◖RM
HORSES TO FOLLOW
2010/11 JUMPS SEASON

CONTENTS

Timeform's Fifty To Follow

Timeform's Fifty To Follow, carefully chosen by members of Timeform's editorial staff, are listed below with their respective page numbers. A selection of ten (**marked in bold with a pink ★**) is made for those who prefer a smaller list.

in an above-average bumper at Kempton in February. As expected, he came on plenty for that experience and was unbeaten in three novice hurdles during the final months of the campaign. The first two of these were wide-margin wins in ordinary contests at Kempton, but the competition was much stiffer for his final start at Cheltenham's April meeting and Captain Chris passed the test in extraordinary circumstances. Racing away from Kempton for the first time, he hung markedly to the right and gave Richard Johnson a torrid time in the final third of the race, yet still travelled with menace and was able to overcome the ground lost to beat Salden Licht by three and three-quarter lengths. At this stage it's almost certainly best to put that errancy down to greenness, and he'll surely prove himself more professional with another summer under his belt. A year older than Menorah, it is understandable why connections are leaning towards a novice chase campaign in 2010/11, particularly given he's a strong sort who'll take well to the fences, and he could go to the very top in that sphere. **P J Hobbs**

Philip Hobbs (trainer): I imagine, all being alright, he'll run in a listed novice hurdle at Kempton on October 17th as he's still a novice until November 1st, and then I'd have thought he'll be going novice chasing, but if he were to impress at Kempton we'd have to look at the Greatwood Hurdle at Cheltenham.

Castlerock   h111p
6 gr.g Kayf Tara – Jessolle (Scallywag)
2009/10 F16g³ 16v 17s² Mar 27

In light of some decidedly iffy jumping, Bakbenscher's record of two wins from five starts for last season's 'Fifty' wasn't a bad return. His half-brother Castlerock is expected to do even better, though. Castlerock first gave notice of his ability in a bumper won by Cavingdon at Chepstow in the autumn, impressing in the paddock (well-made sort) and also the race as he travelled well and ran on into third, despite a ride mindful of his obvious inexperience. Hurdling was the next step for Castlerock, and it was his second start in that sphere that really marked him down as one to follow, showing an above-average level of form as he pushed Mister Stickler to a length in a Bangor novice under yet more considerate handling; it's likely Castlerock wasn't expected to show so much that day, sent off at 18/1, so it says plenty about just how high he could go this season with the aid of further experience and more vigour in the saddle. Handicaps look the likely route with Castlerock, and he's with a master when it comes to the placement of such types, but he shouldn't be ruled out when lining up for a maiden or novice on his reappearance, especially one at two and a half miles plus. And there's always the option of chasing, too; he surely can't be as clumsy as his sibling proved! *Jonjo O'Neill*

Jonjo O'Neill (trainer): We thought he was going to make a nice horse but he's had niggling problems and had been a bit disappointing before running a cracker at Bangor. Hopefully he's just maturing now and we may go chasing with him.

Cavite Beta (Ire) F106

4 ch.g Old Vic – Kinnegads Pride (Ire) (Be My Native (USA))
2009/10 F16v* F16g Apr 22

Three runs, consisting of two no shows in bumpers and a remote seventh in a novice hurdle at Thurles, were all Kinnegads Pride could muster in her brief racing career. It's doubtless a relief for those connected with her, therefore, that she's made a much bigger impression at the paddocks. Her second offspring, Bangkok Pete, was a useful bumper winner for Brendan Powell prior to winning twice in novice hurdle company last season, and third foal Cavite Beta seems set to scale even greater heights after a most encouraging start to his career in 2009/10. A wide-margin win in a maiden point was followed by a similarly impressive success in a Towcester National Hunt Flat race, and the chances are he'd have been fighting it out with the likes of Bishopsfurze in a winners-of-one bumper at Punchestown on his final start but for a slipped saddle, a race won in previous seasons by Go Native and Quel Esprit no less. Cavite Beta could hardly be in better hands with an eye on taking to jumping, either, hands that guided his dam's half-brother Trabolgan to success in the RSA Chase and Hennessy during his light career. *N J Henderson*

Nicky Henderson (trainer): We didn't get to find out how good he was at Punchestown as his saddle slipped. He'll go novice hurdling, and he'll win races in his grade.

Coup Royale (Fr) h115p

6 b.g Balleroy (USA) – Coup de Rouge (Fr) (Quart de Vin (Fr))
2009/10 16s^5 17v^4 17s^3 16s* Mar 22

It is a notably impressive strike rate for little known French-based sire Balleroy—just three of his offspring competed on British soil in 2009/10 and two of that trio have made it into these pages! Along with exciting bumper performer Quousko de L'Isop, Coup Royale promises to provide the virtually white stallion with further success on the racecourse in 2010/11.

Coup Royale showed ability without being able to make any meaningful impact at the business end of a couple of bumpers in late-2008/9, but there was soon plenty more encouragement when he embarked on his hurdling career last winter. Soon spared a hard time on his first two attempts three months apart, he stepped up his form when third to You're So Vain in a maiden at Folkestone in March, even though a few mistakes crept into his game. He didn't need to progress much further to get off the mark at the fourth attempt when beating Wizard of Odds a length and a quarter in a Plumpton maiden later that month. Although Balleroy only showed his Flat form at up to a mile and a quarter, he's imparted plenty of stamina into those other performers of his who've made it across the English Channel so far and there's reason to imagine there will be further improvement from Coup Royale as his stamina is drawn out. Though, that said, he looks well handicapped as it is from an official mark of 112 even if kept around two miles! *C L Tizzard*

Colin Tizzard (trainer): He was big and babyish at three and four and we had a setback in November of last year. We ran him three times after that and won with him on the final one. I think he's a dark horse. We'll go over fences, starting off at two and a half miles in all likelihood.

Court In Motion (Ire) ★   h132p F101+

5 br.g Fruits of Love (USA) – Peace Time Girl (Ire) (Buckskin (Fr))
2009/10 F16s³ 19v^F 19v² Feb 26

Big, athletic-looking hurdlers emerging from Emma Lavelle's burgeoning yard are nothing new, certainly with regards recent seasons: Crack Away Jack has of course been the flag-bearer for the stable during its rise up the ranks, his Fred Winter win in 2008 followed by a fourth-place finish in Punjabi's Champion Hurdle a year later, while Kangaroo Court, although yet to hit the heights he so richly promised, was soon deservedly mixing it with the best in his novice days. Racing in the same colours as Kangaroo Court, we see Court In Motion as another Lavelle charge sure to take his place among the top novice hurdlers in 2010/11.

Like Kangaroo Court, Court In Motion was given just a single outing in bumpers, though his form reads much better than that of his year-older stablemate, finishing third in a hot Newbury contest behind Oscar Whisky and Midnight Prayer, with Rock On Ruby in fourth. Subsequently given plenty of time before his next run, Court In Motion was set to make a winning start to his hurdling career at Exeter, eleven lengths clear of Diamond Brook when stumbling and falling after the last. Although meeting with defeat in trying to make amends at Warwick just over three weeks later, Court In Motion enhanced his reputation in going down by half a length to Peveril, another of our 'fifty', that ones greater experience as well as the talented David Bass' 7 lb claim proving the difference on the day as the odds-on Court In Motion had travelled the stronger, the pair pulling well clear despite a steady early pace. What makes his apparent speed all the more impressive is that Court In Motion comes from a family of stayers, most notable among his half-siblings last season's World Series Hurdle runner-up Bensalem. With everything seemingly going his way, we see Court In Motion as one of the brightest prospects over hurdles this season and will be surprised if he doesn't feature in some of the spring's premier novice events. **Miss E C Lavelle**

Emma Lavelle: He's a lovely, lovely horse. He was still a bit green last season and accordingly, so I thought what's the point? We'll keep him as a novice and give him a proper season. We'll keep him to hurdles and I think he should be very good. He's beautiful, he's got loads of scope and he's that bit bigger and stronger than he was last year.

Cue Card ★   F132

4 b.g King's Theatre (Ire) – Wicked Crack (Ire) (King's Ride)
2009/10 F14s* F16g* Mar 17

The Champion Bumper at Cheltenham is an obvious starting point when it comes to pinpointing those likely to take high rank among the next season's novice hurdlers, and from the 2010 renewal we have not only included the winner Cue Card in the `Fifty' but also Megastar and Dare Me, who finished fifth and sixth respectively. In eighteen renewals of the Champion Bumper Cue Card is only the fourth winner to come from a British stable, and he put up a performance on a par with the best in the race's history. All the more commendable was that his success was achieved as a four-year-old, only the third in all from that age group to come out on top.

Cue Card had won in very good style at Fontwell in January on his sole start prior to Cheltenham, but the form he showed there was some way removed from what was required to get in the shake-up in the Champion Bumper, for which he started at 40/1 in a maximum field of twenty-four. In a race where the pace set by Al Ferof ensured a proper test of stamina, Cue Card, turned out in magnificent condition, belied those odds with another impressive display, joining issue on the bridle entering the straight before quickening away once asked, despite showing signs of inexperience by edging left. Al Ferof kept on well to finish a clear second, but he was still eight lengths adrift of Cue Card at the line.

Two of the previous British winners of the race, namely Dato Star and Monsignor, went on to do well over hurdles, the latter showing himself a brilliant novice

40/1-shot Cue Card storms clear to put up one of the best bumper performances in Timeform's history

hurdler the following season, which ended with a victory in the Royal and SunAlliance Novices' Hurdle. Not surprisingly, Cue Card was priced up after Cheltenham as a leading contender for the 2011 Supreme Novices'. However, given his pedigree—his dam was a useful hurdler/chaser who stayed three miles, while there are plenty of other useful staying chasers in the immediate family—there could well be a bigger chance that Cue Card could try to emulate Monsignor in what is now the Baring Bingham. Either way, Cue Card, a useful-looking individual with scope, looks a very strong candidate for top novice honours this season. **C L Tizzard**

Colin Tizzard (trainer): He's schooled beautifully. His dam had a run round in the Grand National, so it was a bit of a surprise he ran like he did in a Champion Bumper, he really should be more at home over hurdles and fences. He's definitely bigger than he was last year; he looks superb now. We'll start off in a National Hunt novice hurdle somewhere.

Dare Me (Ire)   F120

6 b.g Bob Back (USA) – Gaye Chatelaine (Ire) (Castle Keep)
2009/10 F16s* F16g^6 F17g^2 Apr 10

While the appearance of the word `Cherry' in a jumper's pedigree might point to a connection to the family of Arkle, so the word `Gaye' suggests the likelihood of a link to some of best-known National Hunt performers of the 1980s. That's certainly the case with Gaye Chatelaine, the dam of Dare Me, as she is out of a half-sister to, among others, the 1983 Champion Hurdler Gaye Brief and the Sun Alliance Novices' Hurdle and Stayers' Hurdle winner Gaye Chance. Dare Me himself could well be destined for Cheltenham Festival glory one day, perhaps as early as 2011. One of the leading bumper horses of last season, Dare Me is a lengthy still somewhat unfurnished individual with the size and scope to make his mark at the highest level in novice hurdles, and come March it would be no surprise to see him as a leading contender for the Baring Bingham.

It didn't take long for Dare Me to show that he was fully over the problems which kept him off the course for fifteen months after he'd make a successful debut in November 2008, impressing again when successful at Ffos Las on his return. Subsequently stepped up in class, Dare Me showed further improvement when sixth of twenty-four to Cue Card in the Champion Bumper at Cheltenham and when one and a half lengths second to Megastar in a twenty-runner Grade 2 event at Aintree. In the latter, Dare Me started his effort from further back than the winner, was forced to switch before quickening and then was bumped as he drew alongside.

Dare Me's half-brother, the fairly useful hurdler Wild Ocean (by Old Vic), stayed two and a half miles and the step up to that sort of trip will suit Dare Me well, though there is no doubt that he's capable of winning novice events at two miles.
P J Hobbs

Philip Hobbs (trainer): The plan with him would be to go novice hurdling and I think he'll be ready for the maiden hurdle at that October meeting at Cheltenham and we'll see where we go from there. He's got enough pace at the moment but he'll probably want further in time.

Evella (Ire)   h119

6 ch.m Beneficial – Drimadrian (Gildoran)
2009/10 F16s^2 F16v^4 21v^6 21v* 21s^4 20s^F 21g* 21s Mar 27

It will be no great surprise if Evella, who finished seventh in the latest running of the European Breeders' Fund Mares' NH Novices' Final, turns up at Newbury next

March for the chase equivalent of that contest. Fairly useful though she is over hurdles, it's when she goes fences that Evella will really come into her own, and she should prove well worth following in mares novice events this season.

Evella, a big mare who won a maiden point in Ireland in May 2009, had a couple of victories to her name in mares novice hurdles prior to Newbury. On both occasions she made the running and scored by a wide margin, by twenty-seven lengths at Plumpton in January and twelve lengths at Towcester in March. She was also running well when falling at the last at Southwell, a clear second behind smart novice Banjaxed Girl at the time. That mishap clearly had no lasting effect, as Evella was most fluent at Towcester next time out. Evella, who will stay three miles, has raced only on good ground or softer to date, and her Plumpton win was gained on heavy. ***N B King***

Neil King (trainer): She was very pleasing last year and didn't do a whole lot wrong. The plan with her is probably to have her first run over hurdles then go novice chasing. She's a big, scopey mare and I've always though of her as a three-mile chaser rather than a hurdler.

Finian's Rainbow (Ire) h141p

7 b.g Tiraaz (USA) – Trinity Gale (Ire) (Strong Gale)
2009/10 16d* 21v³ 19s* 21g⁵ Mar 17

The playing career of Iain Dowie spanned almost two decades and featured sixty-nine goals at club level and another twelve for Northern Ireland. Hardly a bad return for a striker, yet in recent times he's arguably best remembered for his coining of the word 'bouncebackability' in a post-match interview, a term that made it into the Collins English Dictionary in 2005. 'Bouncebackability' was defined as the 'ability to recover after a setback, particularly in sport', and could have been tailor-made for Finian's Rainbow, as much as it was for Dowie's Crystal Palace team at the time.

Finian's Rainbow's setback came in the shape of a last-fence fall in an Irish maiden point with the race at his mercy, and he hasn't looked back since. An impressive bumper win at Kempton followed in March 2009, and connections can't have asked for much more in his novice hurdle season, with easy wins at Newbury and Ascot split by a strong-travelling third on heavy ground in the Challow. His season ended on the up, too, Finian's Rainbow showing a very useful level of form in finishing fifth in a well-contested renewal of the Baring Bingham at Cheltenham, despite again leaving the impression twenty-one furlongs stretched his stamina.

Finian's Rainbow looks a smart novice chase prospect for 2010/11

There's much to look forward to with the rangy Finian's Rainbow over fences this season; let's just hope he doesn't have to display his bouncebackability again.
N J Henderson

Nicky Henderson (trainer): He's a smart horse. He jumps well, and will go novice chasing. I don't think he'll necessarily need three miles.

Fleur de Vassy   h97p
6 ch.m Alflora (Ire) – Royale de Vassy (Fr) (Royal Charter (Fr))
2009/10 20s 21v^6 16d 20s^3 22s* 22v^F Mar 30

A lightly-raced, useful-looking individual who starts off her career at the right end of the handicap. What's more, she's trained by Venetia Williams. Some of the entries in this publication really do pick themselves! Fleur de Vassy began reasonably brightly when runner-up in a bumper on debut in 2008/9 but initially struggled to find her feet when sent over hurdles. Three nondescript runs, however, resulted in a very lowly mark of 83, and she duly took a step back in the right direction on her handicap debut when a free-going third at Huntingdon in February. That was just a hint of what was to come, clearly learning fast by this point, and she ran out a comprehensive winner of a two-and-three-quarter mile conditional jockeys' event at Fontwell the following month, having most of the fifteen-strong field in trouble fully a circuit out and still in control when her nearest challenger fell at the last. Unpenalised for that success back at the same track nine days later, Fleur de Vassy was understandably sent off a very short-priced favourite. Unfortunately, it all went awry for her supporters at the first when she was rather crowded out and came down. Never mind, that is likely to prove no more than a blip in her overall progression, and there's little question she remains some way ahead of the handicapper from a mark just 7 lb higher than her initial success—she can stay that way for some time to come, including over fences. ***Miss Venetia Williams***

Venetia Williams (trainer): She'll probably go over fences. She's a big, strong mare who looks like a chaser and hopefully she'll be better than over hurdles.

Galant Nuit (Fr)   c137

6 b.g Comte du Bourg (Fr) – Little Blue (Fr) (Reve Bleu (Fr))
2009/10 c25s² c24m⁶ c27s* c25g³ Mar 18

He might not have won the big one yet and the Welsh version has also eluded him, but Ferdy Murphy has enjoyed much success in other Nationals over the years, winning the Scottish with Paris Pike, Joes Edge and Hot Weld, the Irish with Granit d'Estruval and the Midlands with Ackzo. Murphy's lack of success in the Welsh National is hardly surprising given that he's had so few runners in it—Granit d'Estruval was the most recent, finishing sixth in 2005—but he's set to be represented in the next renewal by Galant Nuit, who looks an ideal type for the race.

Galant Nuit, who has been brought along steadily, won a maiden in his first season over fences and a handicap at Cheltenham in his second, the latter the Servo Trophy run over a distance of almost three and a half miles on soft ground in November. A good gallop helped place even more of an emphasis on stamina that day, which suited Galant Nuit ideally. Patiently ridden, he made up his ground smoothly and found plenty to edge ahead of subsequent Grand National winner Don't Push It near the finish. Back at Cheltenham for the Fulke Walwyn Kim Muir, Galant Nuit faced a shorter trip and much less testing ground but improved again despite that, making relentless progress from three out to finish one and a quarter

Galant Nuit (centre) gets the better of Grand National principals Don't Push It (left) and Hello Bud (spots)

lengths third to Ballabriggs. A return to further will see Galant Nuit do better still, with the distance of the Welsh National (almost three and three quarter miles) sure to be right up his street. Galant Nuit, an angular gelding, acts on soft going and probably on good to firm. **Ferdy Murphy**

Ferdy Murphy (trainer): He'll have one run, probably at the Paddy Power meeting, before going for the Welsh National. We've always thought he's the ideal type for that. He's a big-framed horse and he's a lot stronger now. I'm very happy with him.

George Nympton (Ire) ★   h119

4 br.g Alderbrook – Countess Camilla (Bob's Return (Ire))
2009/10 17g 17s² 17s² 17s⁴ 16g Mar 17

Nick Williams has held a licence for around ten years now and, along with his wife, Jane, he's established—on a relatively small scale—one of the most effective training set-ups in Britain. The likes of Dom d'Orgeval, Philson Run, L'Aventure, Beshabar, Reve de Sivola, Diamond Harry and Me Voici have all been sent out from a small, sleepy village in Devon called George Nympton to big-race success. Indeed, the last-named trio captured a pretty astonishing four Grade One wins between them in 2009/10 alone. This season the Williams' get the opportunity to put their base on the map more figuratively with the four-year-old who shares the same name. George Nympton, the horse, did particularly well to reach the level as he did as a juvenile hurdler in 2009/10 given he lacked the prior Flat experience of the vast majority of his contemporaries. Admittedly, he failed to win in five starts, but his debut season resembled that of Reve de Sivola's in many respects and, even if the latter had achieved a good bit more in form terms, the fact he was able to go on to all the success he did as a second-season novice can only augur very well for George Nympton as he goes down the same road. His hurdling debut in September was all about gaining experience, and he showed the benefit on his next two starts when runner-up in juveniles at Bangor and Cheltenham, beaten two and three-quarter lengths by Olofi on the second occasion. He was sent off at just 3/1 for the seven-runner Grade 2 Finesse at the latter track on his fourth start and was still going strongly when making a bad mistake two out. At the Festival there nearly two months later he was anything but discredited when eighth in the Fred Winter, simply lacking the sharpness of most of those around him, and it will surely be over further than two miles that he comes into his own this season. Longer term, however, fences promise to suit this rangy gelding even more, and we've got little doubt he's going to be adding further to the long line of success that has emanated from North Devon over the past decade or so. **Nick Williams**

Nick Williams (trainer): The plan is to run in the four-year-old hurdle at Chepstow in October.

Get Me Out of Here (Ire) h147p

6 b.g Accordion – Home At Last (Ire) (Mandalus)
2009/10 F16g* 16g* 16g* 16s* 16g* 16g² Mar 16

Given the progress made by Get Me Out of Here in his first season, it would be no great surprise to see him develop into a high-class hurdler in his second; while he also has plenty going for him as a prospective chaser, and would almost certainly win good races in novice company should connections decide to go down that route with him.

Get Me Out of Here made a successful first appearance in a bumper at Uttoxeter, and that was followed by four straight wins over hurdles, the last of those coming in the totesport Trophy at Newbury in February. It was a fiercely-competitve renewal of the season's most valuable handicap hurdle and, in view of his relative inexperience, it said much for Get Me Out of Here that he was able to account for twenty-two mainly battle-hardened rivals so decisively. Travelling strongly, and holding his position with some very accurate jumping, Get Me Out of Here was

Get Me Out of Here and Tony McCoy

poised to challenge when making his first mistake at the last, from which he recovered well to beat Ronaldo des Mottes by a length and three quarters. The totesport Trophy, in all its guises, has never been won by a subsequent winner of the Supreme Novices', but Get Me Out of Here can be counted as unlucky not to complete that particular double. A much more sedate gallop compared to the one at Newbury told against Get Me Out of Here, and he just failed to peg back Menorah, who had got first run on him into the straight. The well-made Get Me Out of Here has raced only at two miles so far, but he is bred to stay a fair bit further than that, by Accordion out of an unraced half-sister to the top-class staying chaser Harbour Pilot. The ground has been good for all of his starts apart from when successful in a conditional handicap at Newbury on soft. ***Jonjo O'Neill***

Jonjo O'Neill (trainer): He's in great nick and will definitely go chasing bar an accident. He needs to go this year if he's going to go at all. We'll stick to two miles for now. He has to be the best I've got at the moment.

Glenwood Knight (Ire) ★   h122

7 ch.g Presenting – Glens Lady (Ire) (Mister Lord (USA))
2009/10 20s³ 23s* 20v² Apr 3

Emile Heskey's participation in the 2010 England World Cup team. Alex Bogdanovic's succession of wildcard appearances at Wimbledon; just two of the many sporting examples where the unflinching faith of selectors has backfired on the big stage, though it doesn't always go badly wrong, as anybody who followed Sebastian Coe's path to Olympic gold medal glory in 1984 might testify. With just one remaining spot on the team, Coe had come off second best to Peter Elliott at the AAA Championships only to get the nod ahead of that rival when the squad was announced, much to the wrath of the British media at the time.

It remains to be seen whether our old face Glenwood Knight proves to be a Bogdanovic or a Coe, and it's certainly asking a lot to think he'll be chosen in his trainer's team for racing's Olympics at Cheltenham in March, but there are certainly valid reasons for thinking he's worth another chance to make up for lost time this time around after a 2009/10 that yielded one 5/1-on tap-in from only three appearances.

For one, chasing is reportedly on Glenwood Knight's agenda this time around, a job for which he laid sound foundations by finishing second in Haydock's Fixed-Brush Final in the spring and for which he's very much built and bred; he's a big, imposing gelding and is out of a half-sister to none other than Grand National winner Papillon, who landed the Aintree showpiece in 2000, four years before Donald McCain Snr tasted success in the big race for the fourth time courtesy of Amberleigh House.

McCain's work last season with Ballabriggs shouldn't be forgotten, either. A similarly lightly-raced sort, Ballabriggs improved out of all recognition on getting a belatedly clear run at his racing, culminating, strangely enough, with the Festival success that our harshest critics may feel Glenwood Knight needs to produce to justify our unflinching faith in him. ***D McCain Jnr***

See trainer interview, page 68

Humbie (Ire)   h113p

6 b.g Karinga Bay – South Queen Lady (Ire) (King's Ride)
2009/10 22m² 22v³ 22d* :: 2010/11 22m⁶ May 19

For the sake of interest, Humbie is a very small Scottish village around fifteen miles south-east of Edinburgh. Now we can move on to the business at hand, namely Pauline Robson's lightly-raced handicapper from the family of Denman who remains with loads of potential despite a disappointing run when last seen in May, that an effort, which as we will see, is certainly best disregarded. Having raced exclusively over two and three-quarter miles at Kelso in four outings to date, Humbie started off finishing placed in maidens the first twice, that sufficient to qualify for him for an official mark nowadays. Returning from a four-month absence in March, Humbie improved no end to make a taking winning start in handicaps. Given a no-nonsense ride by Richie McGrath, Hunbie clearly had the twelve-runner race in the bag a long way out before showing residual greenness as he idled, finishing with three lengths to spare over the in-form Young Buddy. That impressive display came on good to soft ground and it's presumably the case that less testing conditions were against him two months later when only sixth in similar company at the same track, but he still shaped a good bit better than the result, swallowed up only on the run-in and appearing to lose his action. Either way, his win there is very much the one on which to judge him and, in excellent hands, it's almost inconceivable he won't win further handicaps before switching to fences, something his pedigree and demeanour suggest are sure to suit down to the ground. **Miss P Robson**

Raymond Anderson Green (Owner): He was disappointing on his last run, but he wasn't quite right and we've got high hopes for him; with a bit of luck, he'll turn into a really decent long-distance chaser. We'll let him find his level, and the dream is to have him in the four-miler at Cheltenham next spring.

Locked Inthepocket (Ire)   h104 c96p
6 b.g Beneficial – Ruby Rubenstein (Ire) (Camden Town)
2009/10 16g³ 17d³ 22v² 20d⁶ 20v² c20d⁶ Mar 21

That he is the most represented of all the owners in this year's publication says much about the type of horse in which Raymond Anderson Green specialises. Anderson Green has four inclusions, all late-maturing chasing types from National Hunt families, and Locked Inthepocket arguably has the most room to manoeuvre amongst the quartet from a current BHA mark in the low 100s.

Granted, Locked Inthepocket has yet to win a race, but he's still unexposed after only five starts over hurdles and just one over fences and there's surely improvement in him, especially in the latter sphere. In addition, he's well treated on his form as it stands. His clear second to then-thriving Mister Pete in a handicap hurdle at Newcastle represents strong form; and he'd have been bang there with some fairly useful chasers at Carlisle on his sole try over fences had he been ridden with more enterprise, jumping soundly and staying on encouragingly under tender handling as he took sixth behind Award Winner. There are still untapped reserves of stamina where Locked Inthepocket is concerned, as he's yet to race beyond two and three quarter miles; while, as a six-year-old, he also has age on his side as he embarks on only his second full season. **Miss P Robson**

Raymond Anderson Green (Owner): He's been unfortunate not to have won a race, yet has shot up in the handicap. Having said that, I think we can have a good campaign with him in novice handicap chases; he's not devoid of pace, but I think he will stay three miles.

Me Voici (Fr)   h133
4 b.g Saint des Saints (Fr) – Battani (Fr) (Top Ville)
2009/10 17m 16s² 16v* 16s* 16d⁶ Apr 8

'Whatever he's achieved so far is a bonus' is a well-worn phrase usually applied to a prospective chaser who has done well over hurdles, and in the case of Me Voici it's a most appropriate one. The big, useful-looking Me Voici, who is very much a chaser on looks, apparently had been bought as a potential Gold Cup horse as a yearling, and it speaks volumes for him that he was able to show useful useful form and win two races, including a Grade 1 contest, in his juvenile hurdle season.

Me Voici showed some promise on good to firm ground on his debut, but subsequently he appeared very much at home when the mud was flying and it was on heavy that he opened his account, in the Coral Future Champions Finale Juvenile Hurdle no less at Chepstow in December. A 10/1 shot in an eight-runner field, Me Voici travelled strongly and gave a faultless display of jumping, unlike even-money favourite Sang Bleu, who made a mistake two out when holding a three-length lead. Me Voici was quick to take advantage and asserted under hands and heels approaching the last before going on to beat that one by ten lengths. An easy win at Haydock followed and, while he failed to make much of an impact in another Grade 1, at Aintree, on his final start, Me Voici impressed beforehand as the best type physically and remains a fine prospect for novice chases.

And don't forget, there's still plenty of mileage left in Me Voici as a hurdler, too, including over longer trips, so it'll pay to follow him whichever path his much-respected trainer chooses to take. **Nick Williams**

Nick Williams (trainer): The plan is to go to Auteuil from mid-October to mid-November due to the lack of four-year-old hurdle races in Britain. If the first race in France is a disaster, then he could end up running back here at that time instead.

Megastar   F121

5 b.g Kayf Tara – Megalex (Karinga Bay)
2009/10 F16d* F16s² F16g⁵ F17g* Apr 10

Having put forward Dare Me as one who could take high rank among this season's novice hurdlers, it would be foolhardy to overlook another smart bumper performer who finished one place ahead of him on the two occasions that they met. Megastar looks to have just as much potential as the year-older Dare Me, and he too will be making his mark in the top novice races at up to at least two and a half miles.

Apparently Megastar's trainer Gary Moore took a shine to him on the day he did his first piece of work with his then stable-companion Mourilyan, a pattern-race performer on the Flat, and there was plenty of confidence behind Megastar when he made his debut at Sandown in November. That confidence proved not to be misplaced, Megastar showing his inexperience after quickening to the front two furlongs out but still keeping on too well for runner-up Wayward Prince. It says

The whips are up as Megastar (white face) gets the better of fellow Fifty member Dare Me

much for Megastar's prospects over hurdles that Wayward Prince, who also features in this publication, then went on to show himself one of the season's best novice hurdlers, winning the Sefton at Aintree on his final start. Megastar was also successful at Aintree's Grand National meeting, which followed his good effort when finishing fifth of twenty-four to Cue Card in the Champion Bumper at Cheltenham. Megastar beat Dare Me one and a half lengths in a twenty-runner Grade 2 contest at Aintree, still looking green after taking over two furlongs out but battling on well once joined by the runner-up. A tall, good sort, who certainly looks the part for jumping, Megastar is the second foal of a two-and-a-half hurdle winner who has already produced one winning hurdler in the shape of Megastar's sister Megasue. It won't be long before Megastar is another. **G L Moore**

Gary Moore (trainer): We'll look to start off somewhere pretty low key where the ground's decent, just an ordinary novice hurdle before something similar again, and if he's done that all right we'll probably look towards the Tolworth. He's completely different to his sister Megasue; he's a good hand and a half higher and a big, strong horse.

Midnight Tuesday (Fr) h116

5 b.g Kapgarde (Fr) – Deat Heat (Fr) (Volochine (Ire))
2009/10 F17g^2 F16s 16s^3 24g Apr 9

Even members of editorial at Timeform House were seen raising eyebrows and hurriedly referring to old editions of Chasers & Hurdlers when Mr Thriller strode clear in a handicap hurdle at Chepstow on his reappearance last season. Just who was this sire, Kapgarde? Research showed Kapgarde was a half-brother to very smart hurdler/chaser Geos and made his name as a useful jumper in France for Guillaume Macaire, but through the likes of Mr Thriller, dual bumper winner Problema Tic and hopefully this season Midnight Tuesday, his influence as a sire could be far more profound. Midnight Tuesday certainly caught the eye in his debut season, from the first time he stepped into the paddock prior to a bumper at Aintree in fact, Timeform's racecourse reporter noting he 'really looked the part' and was 'gleaming in condition'. The favourable impression extended to his performance, too, Midnight Tuesday travelling like the best horse at the weights only for his lack of wherewithal to tell against the now-useful hurdler Solway Sam. Softer ground and a quick turnaround easily explain away his flop at Cheltenham the time after, and he was back to promising plenty in a hot novice at Newbury on his hurdling debut, when finishing third behind useful hurdlers Master of The Hall and Nice One Eric. Midnight Tuesday, understandably, then found the Sefton Novices' Hurdle at Aintree a bridge too far at such an early stage in his development, but we fully expect him to fulfil his potential this season. Given his sire's strike-rate in Britain, he can't fail to win races over jumps, can he?

N A Twiston-Davies

Nigel Twiston-Davies (Trainer): He's a nice, young horse. He isn't even back here yet. He showed a lot of promise last season, so we'll probably carry on in the same way, novice hurdles starting off, but he's big enough to go over fences.

Mister Stickler (Ire) h109

6 b.g Alflora (Ire) – Almost Trumps (Nearly A Hand)
2009/10 16d 17s^2 17s* 16g^3 Apr 21

Whoever first uttered the phrase 'form is temporary, class is permanent' could conceivably have been referring to Alan King. Long since in the upper reaches of the trainers' table, and with a host of big-race successes on his record, including the Champion Hurdle (Katchit), World Hurdle (My Way de Solzen) and Champion Chase (Voy Por Ustedes), King suffered something of a downturn during the latest season. That was largely due to a much-mentioned muscle enzyme problem that afflicted his yard seemingly from the word go. Numbers in all categories understandably declined, winners from a career-high 136 down to 76, but it's not all bad news for the trainer now the problems seem to be in the past, as several of his runners who were in action during the lean spell are now potentially very well treated.

It would be unfair to say Mister Stickler struggled in 2009/10, but there was definitely a whiff of untapped potential about him, while his powerful physique points to chasing proving the making of him. Mister Stickler has always shown promise, starting with his fourth to Our Bomber Harris in a warm Uttoxeter bumper on his debut, and his four starts over hurdles were perfectly creditable considering both stable form and the fact hurdling was never going to be his game. For instance, at Southwell on his final outing, Mr Stickler did well to fill third behind a couple of natural two-milers when longer trips are almost certainly going to suit him—he's out of an unraced half-sister to fair hurdler Teletrader, who needed a real test to show her form around the minimum trip and boasted a pedigree that screamed stamina. Fingers crossed, for the stable's sake as much as ours, that King enjoys the sort of season we've become accustomed to this time around, as Mister Stickler has all the hallmarks of a useful chaser in the making.
A King

Alan King (trainer): I haven't schooled him over fences yet, but we think he'll be alright and he's one that can certainly improve. He's a big, strapping horse and his mark looks fair enough.

Morgan's Bay   F103p

5 b.g Karinga Bay – Dubai Dolly (Ire) (Law Society (USA))
2010/11 F17g^2 May 14

It was a well-timed racecourse bow from Morgan's Bay at Aintree in May, one that helped see him fetch £100,000 at the Doncaster Horses in Training Sales just four days later. That figure was clearly a lot more than original owners Joss and Nicky Hanbury, in whose well-known Mighty Man colours he was seen at Aintree, might have expected to recoup had he not shaped with such promise. Whilst unable to cope with a previous winner in the closing stages, going down by three quarters of a length to front-running Problema Tic in the nineteen-runner event, Morgan's Bay still finished clear of the third and had done more than enough up until that point to suggest he possesses the ability to win plenty of races, in a similar bumper before making the transition to obstacles. After travelling smoothly into contention from mid-field Morgan's Bay knuckled down well to make the winner pull out all the stops despite understandably showing signs of greenness. To some degree his sales price also reflects an impressive physique, well made and looking just the sort who'll thrive over hurdles, with two and a half miles sure to suit him well in that sphere. Following his sale Morgan's Bay left Henry Daly's yard and is now in the care of the very capable Tom George. **T R George**

Tom George (trainer): We'll probably go straight over hurdles rather than running in another bumper. He looks the part and we've been very impressed with him.

Notus de La Tour (Fr)   h138
4 b.g Kutub (Ire) – Ridiyla (Ire) (Akarad (Fr))
2009/10 18s⁴ 18d³ 18s⁶ 18v* 16s* 16g² 16d Apr 8

When it comes to improving horses acquired from claimers the Pipe yard is second to none. The likes of Her Honour, Pomme Secret, Out Ranking and Quick were all prolific winners for fifteen-time champion trainer Martin, while Corum started on a similar trajectory for David last summer before falling by the wayside. King among the claims, however, is surely Make A Stand, who won ten times in all for the yard, culminating in the 1997 Champion Hurdle when still a novice. Similar

Fred Winter runner-up Notus de La Tour (noseband) could benefit from an early switch to the larger obstacles

expectations may prove too ambitious with regard to Notus de La Tour, claimed from a three-year-old hurdle at Auteuil last December, but we still see him as one who could well have an excellent 2010/11.

Seemingly useful in France, Notus de La Tour didn't have to come up to that level when making a winning British debut at Plumpton in January, though the subsequent exploits of runner-up Ranjobaie (winner of a novice at Market Rasen before finishing third in Sandown's EBF Final) advertised the form as strong even before his next run the Fred Winter at the Cheltenham Festival. Sent off second-favourite in that race, Notus de La Tour proved himself well handicapped in finishing runner-up behind Sanctuaire, facing a near-impossible task in conceding 7 lb to a clearly smart juvenile, paying for trying to take on that rival and shaping even better than the result. The effects of a hard race there likely told on the son of Kutub on his only outing thereafter, when a laboured seventh in a Grade 1 at Aintree. Clearly unexposed in Britain as it is, Notus de La Tour has plenty of options for the coming season, including the tempting prospect of taking advantage of a generous four-year-old allowance over fences. **D E Pipe**

David Pipe (trainer): He did very well last season and appears to have summered well and strengthened up. He'd been in training for more than a year, so he was probably over the top on his last run at Aintree. It depends on what he does over hurdles, but he could be going chasing.

Olofi (Fr) h124

4 gr.g Slickly (Fr) – Dona Bella (Fr) (Highest Honor (Fr))
2009/10 17m⁵ 16g* 16s³ 17s* 17d 16d⁴ Apr 8

It's fair to suggest the high-class miler Slickly achieved a deal more in his days on the track than he's managed at stud. Alain de Royer Dupre's Gris de Gris, a very smart performer around the same trip on the Flat in France, is comfortably the best of Slickly's offspring to have made the track so far, and those behind his career as a sire probably wouldn't have expected a National Hunt horse to be the next offspring capable of flying the flag. Olofi is the jumper in question, and he surely can't fail to enjoy a productive time of things in 2010/11 after setting such solid foundations over hurdles last season, his first campaign of racing under any code.

Olofi didn't achieve much on his debut, though Timeform's race-reader suggested he 'shaped as well as any behind the winner' on the day and it wasn't too long before he turned that potential into something more solid, namely a smooth win at Chepstow in October. Better followed, with Olofi's second success of his very light career following soon after at Cheltenham, but it was his last run, a good fourth to Orsippus in a Grade 1 juvenile hurdle at Aintree, that really marked Olofi down as the sort who'll excel this season, probably in handicap hurdles intitialy from a fair-looking mark. Olofi is also Flat-bred on the dam's side, but his stamina should stretch to two and a half miles, while it wouldn't be a surprise if connections seek to take advantage of the generous four-year-old chasing allowance should his campaign over hurdles not go as smoothly as is to be hoped. **T R George**

Tom George (trainer): He's fine. He'll probably start off in the 4-y-o handicap at Chepstow at the beginning of October over two miles. We're hoping he's going to progress as he's a very lightly-raced horse over hurdles, and if he doesn't we'll go chasing. He's a very quick horse and I think he's a two-miler.

Oscar Whisky (Ire) h143p

5 b.g Oscar (Ire) – Ash Baloo (Ire) (Phardante (Fr))
2009/10 F16s* 16s* 16v* 16g¹ Mar 16

Dai Walters, the man behind Britain's newest racecourse at Ffos Las in Wales, has made a big name for himself in his relatively short time as an owner, with Serabad, Grand Slam Hero and Special Envoy all carrying Walters' blue and white silks to big-race success. The last-named, a smart hurdler who chased home Inglis Drever in the Long Distance Hurdle at Newbury in his pomp, is the best Walters has owned as it stands, though that position is highly likely to be threatened, and even passed, by Oscar Whisky this season should all go well.

Two from two in bumpers, including a thrashing of several subsequent winners at Newbury on his reappearance, Oscar Whisky maintained his unbeaten record through his first couple of outings over hurdles, winning most impressively at the same track and again at Sandown, in the process fully earning his place in the field for the Supreme Novices' Hurdle at Cheltenham. Strangely, though, it could be said that Oscar Whisky's pre-Cheltenham grounding of four effortless victories left him short for the big day. Menorah, Get Me Out of Here and Dunguib, the three ahead of him on the day, had all come in for more intense preparations and, despite looking outstanding in condition the paddock, Oscar Whisky failed to jump with quite the same fluency as he'd done previously, though shaping with plenty of promise all the same.

He mightn't be an outside-the-box recommendation, but, with any further experience sure to benefit him and with the two-mile division lacking in top-class performers (apart from the same yard's Champion Hurdler Binocular), our hopes are high that Oscar Whisky can bridge the gap and develop into a serious contender to dethrone his stablemate come March. **N J Henderson**

Nicky Henderson (trainer): He's a very good horse. He's a two-miler—he's got buckets of speed—and I think he'll stay over hurdles this season.

Pasture Bay (Ire)   F98p

4 b.g Flemensfirth (USA) – Silver Oak (Ire) (Anshan)
2009/10 NR :: 2010/11 F16m² May 19

Incorporating once-raced bumper performers may be considered a shade profligate, and we have two this year, but both Storm Kirk and Pasture Bay shaped with abundant promise on their sole starts to date and their respective futures look very bright indeed. Furthermore, both hail from low-key and underrated stables, so there's every chance they'll offer more in the way of value when facing winning opportunities. That said, if Pasture Bay turns up in another Kelso bumper it's highly likely he'll be sent off a short price—though that's not to say he won't represent value, of course! In fact he was favourite for his debut in a field of fourteen there in May, and that despite facing a stable-companion who'd already shown a fairly useful level of ability. After being left with plenty to do, Pasture Bay finished with a flourish despite showing greenness and a Timmy Murphy ride mindful of his mount's inexperience, though he couldn't get to that stablemate Freddie Brown, still two and a quarter lengths down at the line, three quarters of a length ahead of next-time winner Mr Jay Dee. Out of an unraced half-sister to Grand National winner Silver Birch, it was most encouraging Pasture Bay showed the speed to cope with a two-mile bumper run on firmish ground and, with the experience gained and another summer on his back, he will surely get off the mark in a similar event next time, with better races on the horizon thereafter.
G A Charlton

George Charlton (trainer): He's a nice horse and is going nicely. He made a good start in a bumper won by another of our's who I also like a lot. Ray Green is a great man for planning and he'll do the planning. We'll keep him to bumpers for the time being just for experience, and if he turns out very good we may go for one of the good ones, possibly at Aintree. He will stay but he's got plenty of gears at the moment.

Peveril   h142

6 b.g Presenting – Starana (Fr) (Northern Crystal)
2009/10 20g* 21d* 19v* 20d⁴ Mar 19

It may have taken David Bass forty-one rides over thirty months to record his first winner, but there was little doubt by the end of the 2009/10 season that he had become one of the most promising conditionals in the country under the tutelage of Nicky Henderson. Those impressions have proved well founded in the 2010/11 season even at this early stage, Bass already reaching more than half his tally for the previous campaign by the time of writing and notching by far the biggest victory of his career to date in May's Swinton Hurdle on Eradicate. We expect a similarly progressive campaign from Peveril, the horse which provided the eighth of Bass's fifteen winners last season and gave him his first taste of real action at the Cheltenham Festival.

Useful in bumpers, Peveril was successful in novice events on his first three starts over hurdles, at Leicester in November and twice at Warwick in February. The form of both races at Warwick looks strong. The runner-up in the first of them, The Giant Bolster, went on to excel himself in Grade 1 company at both Cheltenham and Aintree, while another member of our 'Fifty', Court In Motion, gave him most to do on the second occasion. Subsequently sent off second-favourite for the Martin Pipe Hurdle at the Cheltenham Festival, Peveril's jumping let him down in his first attempt in handicap company, though he was far from disgraced in finishing fourth, just over seven lengths behind the winner Pause And Clause. Chasing will likely prove Peveril's game in time, when he should make a useful novice at least, but if kept over hurdles he can be expected to win handicaps from his current BHA mark of 140. **N J Henderson**

Nicky Henderson (trainer): He's not a flashy horse and he rather crept up on us last year, but he kept on getting the job done. He'll go novice chasing.

Prince de Beauchene (Fr)   c147p

7 b.g French Glory – Chipie d'Angron (Fr) (Grand Tresor (Fr))
2009/10 c24v² c24v c20v* Apr 3

The likes of Direct Route, Grey Abbey and Inglis Drever have long since departed the scene, whilst the mercurial Tidal Bay becomes more frustrating by the run, so the time is ripe for a new star to emerge at White Lea Farm. Howard Johnson may bemoan his lack of a leading light at present, but maybe Prince de Beauchene is the one who can capture big-race glory for the yard in 2010/11. He's a half-brother to the smart staying chaser Miko de Beauchene, a horse who numbers the Welsh National amongst his successes, and it's surely that sort of race and similar soft-ground staying handicaps that will be on the agenda for the lightly-raced seven-year-old.

A winning chaser in France, Prince de Beauchene was successful on the second of just two starts over hurdles in 2008/9, but it was when returned to chasing in the following season that his career took off. Prince de Beauchene pulled a very long way clear of the rest when a length second to Huka Lodge in a three-mile

Prince de Beauchene (white face) appeals as a very smart staying chaser in the making

handicap at Carlisle on his return before shaping much better than the result in the Peter Marsh at Haydock two months later, travelling best of all when a blunder at the twelfth rather put paid to his chance. He confirmed the promise of that run in no uncertain terms back over two and a half miles when winning the inaugural running of a valuable handicap at the same track. It's very difficult not to take an extremely positive view of what Prince de Beauchene achieved in beating fellow ex-French up-and-comer Salut Flo, jumping and travelling fluently and asserting from two out to beat that one three and a quarter lengths, the pair fully twenty-four lengths clear of third-placed Mister McGoldrick.

The 8 lb the handicapper has raised Prince de Beauchene for that success seems most unlikely to prevent him from playing a leading role in high-end handicaps when the ground is testing, and it will be some surprise if he doesn't have at least one such race under his belt come the season's end. Whilst many will be hoping Quwetwo will help get Howard Johnson and Andrea and Graham Wylie back on the big stage this season, we think it could be Prince de Beauchene who does more to see the good times returning to White Lea. *J Howard Johnson*

Howard Johnson (trainer): We like him, he's an improving horse. The heavier the ground the better. When he came over from France we thought he'd be a relentless galloper, but he's got speed too.

Prince of Pirates (Ire)   F112p

5 b.g Milan – Call Kate (Ire) (Lord Americo)
2009/10 F16d* :: 2010/11 F16d⁶ May 3

Every cloud has a silver lining. Just ask the connections of Milan, the winner in 2001 of the Great Voltigeur and St Leger and runner-up in the Breeders' Cup Turf for owners Michael Tabor and Mrs John Magnier who was forced into a premature career at stud after suffering a fractured cannon bone in his off-fore on his reappearance as a four-year-old. The top-class middle-distance performer could no longer ply his trade as a racehorse, but he's now making a name for himself in his new career. Apart from Bach and Craigsteel, no other recent addition to the National Hunt sires ranks has made the same impression as Milan, especially in National Hunt Flat races.

Irish trio Acey, Go All The Way and Mediolanum all impressed in reaching a useful level in bumpers last season, and pick of Milan's representatives in Britain was Prince of Pirates, who runs in the colours of Mrs John Magnier. Prince of Pirates made the perfect start to his career when winning at Kempton and, once again ridden by the owner's son, shaped much better than his sixth-of-fourteen position suggests in a good-quality race at the Curragh three months later. Prince of Pirates probably would have been battling it out with the principals had his saddle not slipped.

Not too many bring as high a level of bumper form to novice hurdling as Prince of Pirates, and, in excellent hands, there's no reason why he shouldn't go a long way as a novice hurdler. *N J Henderson*

Nicky Henderson (trainer): He's a very smart horse, I hope. He'll be running in novice hurdles and could be good.

Qaspal (Fr)   h137p

6 b.g Subotica (Fr) – Une du Chatelier (Fr) (Quart de Vin (Fr))
2009/10 16d 16d⁶ 16s⁶ 16d* 20v* 16d* Mar 13

It may be fair to say that we're boarding the Qaspal bandwagon a bit late in proceedings given he hit his sharp upward curve when encountering handicaps in February and promptly won three on the trot, the last of those the Imperial Cup at Sandown. But we're taking the view that what's gone before is merely the tip of the iceberg, with his stout pedigree sure to come into play at some stage.

Runner-up in a bumper at Gowran for Mags Mullins in 2008/9, Qaspal was subsequetly switched to Minehead and wasn't knocked about when little better than mid-field in a trio of winter novices last season. After that he really took off. Qaspal cruised home in a conditional jockeys event at Kempton on his handicap debut, and followed up seven days later over two and a half miles on heavy ground at Sandown. Qaspal took a big hike in the weights and a step up in class in his stride when beating stablemate Oldrik over two miles on his return to Sandown the following month, the manner in which he responded to pressure pointing towards the potential which remains as his stamina comes into play more.

Incidentally, Qaspal misssed the cut for the Coral Cup the following week where he would have bid for the big-money bonus. Whilst it must have been a blow to connections at the time, there is always the chance it will prove a blessing in disguise, plenty of horses having struggled to recover from such a tough ask.
P J Hobbs

Philip Hobbs (trainer): I'm not sure what we're going to do with him as he'll obviously have a much higher mark now. I imagine we'll start off over hurdles before looking at novice chasing.

Qroktou (Fr) ★   h122p
6 b.g Fragrant Mix (Ire) – Cathou (Fr) (Quart de Vin (Fr))
2009/10 21v^{pu} 19s^4 24d^2 24g^2 Apr 14

They say that in football management it's never as good the second (or, in some cases, third) time round. Just ask Howard Kendall (Everton), Kevin Keegan (Newcastle) or Terry Venables (Crystal Palace). If the same applies to horse racing, then the success of this publication could be in early jeopardy given the number of potential repeat offenders, but, in the case of second-chance 'Fifty' member Qroktou, it could hardly be said he's got lots to live up to, as had been the case with the aforementioned trio.

In short, Qroktou didn't come up to scratch when chosen last season. Felt capable of developing into a high-end novice hurdler at the start of the campaign based on the strength of his bumper form (won at Newbury prior to close second to Aiteen Thirtythree, conceding 7 lb), the sum total of his four timber starts was far from what might have been expected, with form figures of 'P422' hardly what the chairmen and investors behind the Horses To Follow Galacticos were after.

That initial underachievement does have a positive side, however. Qroktou is still a maiden, so placing him shouldn't be difficult, and it's always possible he'll slip through the public net rather when it comes to pricing him up. Plus, by the end of the season, there were clear signs Qroktou was really getting the hang of hurdling, chiefly when an improved second to Munlochy Bay in a competitive big-field handicap at Cheltenham on his final outing. Having jumped with far more fluency, Qroktou did much the best of those to race prominently in a well-run race, underlining not only that he's a stayer but one who's some way ahead of his opening mark, even without the very real prospect of further improvement this season. As expected, that Cheltenham race has already started to prove strong form, with Alderley Rover and There's No Panic, who were some way back that day, both having won since. It shouldn't be too long before Qroktou follows their lead. **P J Hobbs**

Philip Hobbs (trainer): He's been a massively backward horse who's taken a long time to actually hold condition in training. He ran very well at Cheltenham, that was a good performance, and every time he runs we're going in the right direction. Off the handicap mark he is now I'd imagine we'll start in a novice hurdle before possibly looking at fences.

Quinz (Fr)   h132 c116
6 b.g Robin des Champs (Fr) – Altesse du Mou (Fr) (Tin Soldier (Fr))
2009/10 c22d⁵ c24sᶠ c22vᵖᵘ 24g⁵ 24g* 24g Apr 9

Form figures over fences reading '5FP' may not instil confidence, but we certainly think it's worth keeping faith with the lightly-raced Quinz in 2010/11.

All three of Quinz's chasing efforts came at Newbury, a track that takes some jumping even for experienced chasers, so it's hardly unreasonable to forgive him his failures in hot novice handicaps won by Hey Big Spender, Far More Serious and Doctor Pat. Quinz's jumping did indeed look a sticking point, but those experiences shouldn't have been lost on him and his effort in the race won by the first-named was full of promise the odd mistake aside, travelling as well as any for a long way until fitness seemed to find him out.

An even more compelling argument for Quinz, though, comes in the shape of his exploits over hurdles once chasing had been shelved. Reverted to timber from a mark in the mid-teens, and back at Newbury, Quinz contested one of the hottest handicap hurdles of the season and emerged with credit in filling fifth behind Alfie Sherrin considering things didn't go his way. And better still was to come.

Less than a month later, Quinz put fully twenty lengths between himself and the runner-up in routing a big field at Kempton, showing himself a useful hurdler. That wide-margin success saw his BHA mark leap by 21 lb to 138, an admittedly rare rise but not an excessive one, so his potential to win races back over fences if getting his act together is there for all to see; his chase mark is only 2 lb higher than the one he defied with such authority in that handicap hurdle at Kempton.

P J Hobbs

Philip Hobbs (trainer): He's a big, strong horse who should be better over fences, and I think we'll have to go down that route anyway because of the handicap mark he's got. He stays well.

Quousko de L'Isop (Fr) ★   F108

6 gr.g Balleroy (USA) – Pointissima (Fr) (Point of No Return (Fr))
2009/10 F16m⁶ F16s* F16s* Feb 23

The sixth and final of the Hobbs-trained contingent in this publication. The big difference with this one is that Quousko de L'Isop is trained by Rachel Hobbs as opposed to being the fourth horse beginning with the letter 'Q' to appear for Philip. Rachel—no relation—is married to former National Hunt trainer Andy Hobbs, and she looks to have the horse with which to make her name in her own right. Quousko de L'Isop is a tall, scopey French bred, a half-brother to a winning French chaser out of a useful middle-distance performer. He endured an unfortunate debut when brought down at halfway in a bumper at Hereford in February 2009 and his mid-field run at Stratford three months later was all about building up his confidence on the back of that experience. It was at Warwick a further eight months on, when encountering soft ground for the first time a further eight months on that Quousko de L'Isop marked himself out as a good prospect, travelling powerfully in front and drawing away on the bridle to win by eleven lengths from subsequent hurdles winner Lion On The Prowl. Yet that was just a taster, as four weeks on he gave another authorative display of front-running when conceding weight away all round in a thirteen-runner event at Southwell, looking a class apart, the winning margin of three and a half lengths over Ben Cee Pee M having looked set to be a lot greater for most of the race. Connections will surely look to take advantage of his strong-galloping when he goes over hurdles, and it's easy to see him making hay from the front in a couple of novice events before posssibly going on to bigger and better things.

Mrs Rachel M Hobbs

Andy Hobbs (assistant trainer): He's done very well over the summer. We learnt last season that he really wants to get his toe in and he won't be running until we get the proper winter jumping ground, when we'll start off low key, and I imagine his target could end up as being something like the EBF Final. We schooled him over hurdles last year and he was mustard. We rate him very highly, as does Aidan Coleman.

Royal Chatelier (Fr) h93p

5 b.g Video Rock (Fr) – Attualita (Fr) (Master Thatch)
2009/10 F16v⁴ 24s 22d 20s⁴ Mar 31

For one who takes the eye in appearance and also has plenty to recommend him judged on pedigree, it might have been expected that Royal Chatelier would have made a far greater impact than he did in his first season. However, he will start off from a low mark in handicaps as a result, and he did show sufficient promise to make us think that he will be well up to taking advantage of it. If and when he does it will be for a new trainer, as Royal Chatelier was sold for £11,000 at Cheltenham in May and has left Charlie Longsdon's yard.

An encouraging fourth in a bumper at Towcester on his debut, Royal Chatelier ran his best race over hurdles when occupying the same position in a maiden at Hereford on his final start. There he finished just over fifteen lengths behind the progressive Flanagan, making gradual inroads without being subjected to an unduly hard race after the first three had gone clear around three out. It's likely that the tall, useful-looking Royal Chatelier will stay beyond two and a half miles. His full brother the fairly useful hurdler Olympian has form over as far as twenty-one furlongs, while Royal Chatelier is closely related to the top-class chaser Impek who was effective at up to three miles. ***Michael Blake***

Michael Blake (trainer): He's summered really well, probably been back in for about a month now and we've been doing plenty of cantering with him. He's a nice moving horse who needs a bit of cut in the ground. He will be aimed at handicaps and we think we can win races with him. He'll be running over two miles six furlongs and three miles on good to soft and softer probably.

Sang Bleu (Fr) h132p

4 gr.g Lavirco (Ger) – Formosa (Fr) (Royal Charter (Fr))
2009/10 F12g³ F13g* 18d* 16v² 16s* Feb 11

The five-year-olds who contest the Arkle Trophy at Cheltenham no longer receive a weight allowance from their elders, as did recent winners Well Chief and Voy Por Ustedes, but that's not to say one from that age group won't win it again despite that. Back in 1999 the five-year-olds Flagship Uberalles and Tresor de Mai finished first and second in the Arkle and would have done so even at level weights given how far clear of the rest they were. Maybe Sang Bleu will be the first five-year-old to win an Arkle without the aid of an allowance. Bred in France, as were Voy Por Ustedes, Tresor de Mai and the 1998 winner Champleve, Sang Bleu looks a first-rate prospect for novice chases and will win good races even if the Arkle does prove beyond him.

A half-brother to a winning hurdler/chaser around two miles Quarte out of a winning chaser who stayed two and a half miles, Sang Bleu is certainly bred to jump fences and couldn't be in better hands, while the ability he has shown in just three runs over hurdles to date suggests that he has what it takes to go far in his new career. Sang Bleu won a bumper and a juvenile hurdle for Guillaume Macaire in France before joining Paul Nicholas, for whom he has run just twice. On the first occasion Sang Bleu chased home another one of our `Fifty', Me Voici, in the Finale Juvenile Hurdle at Chepstow; on the second he gave 8 lb and a half-length beating to another French-bred, Stars du Granits, in a juvenile at Huntingdon. Sang Bleu would almost certainly go on to better things kept to hurdling, but it's over fences that he is going to make a big name for himself.
P F Nicholls

See trainer interview, page 78

Spirit River (Fr)   h151
5 b.g Poliglote – Love River (Fr) (Epervier Bleu)
2009/10 16s⁵ 17s* 16g 21g* Mar 17

The placement of novice chasers at Seven Barrows is never likely to be the easiest of operations given the ammunition it typically houses, but things could be made that bit more difficult in 2010/11. Both Finian's Rainbow and Spirit River are due to set out on their debut campaign over fences and they are very smart prospects, perhaps at the same sort of trip; while the pair are also both owned by Michael Buckley.

Spirit River and Finian's Rainbow took different paths in their first British season. The former had lost his novice status on his final outing for Guy Cherel in France, and he started off by finishing fifth to Get Me Out of Here in a Newbury handicap that worked out particularly well. Spirit River did his bit for the form when a highly impressive winner at Cheltenham the following month, leaving his rivals standing as he struck on turning in. After losing all chance of getting his revenge on Get Me Out of Here in the totesport Trophy—he was still travelling well close up when blundering three out—he was upped to two miles five furlongs in the Coral Cup at Cheltenham. In jumping slickly throughout Spirit River showed his Newbury

This Coral Cup win is unlikely to be the last big prize for Spirit River

mistake to be no more than a blip, and even if he was always close up in a race which wasn't run at the usual hectic pace, it would be wrong to conclude that he was anything but a worthy winner in beating Tullamore Dew four and a half lengths.

A tall, athletic and strong-travelling type, Spirit River looks just the sort to make his mark at a high level over fences. Finian's Rainbow still has some improving to do before he reaches the same level as his stablemate, but, either way, what's for sure is that both possess bundles of potential. *N J Henderson*

Nicky Henderson (trainer): He's not short of speed, but he won the Coral Cup over twenty one furlongs. He'll be going over fences in novice company.

Spot The Ball (Ire)   h80p

5 b.g Oscar (Ire) – Sudden Inspiration (Ire) (Good Thyne (USA))
2009/10 F16v² F16d⁵ 16s⁵ 19v⁵ 16sᶠ 16g⁶ Mar 8

Those of legal betting age in the 1980s and early-1990s will probably remember, or have played, Spot The Ball, a game featured primarily in newspapers in which entrants had to guess the position of a football that had been removed from a photograph, based largely on the location of the player or players in shot. Those of legal betting age in the early part of the twenty-first century are almost certainly going to recall the horse of the same name if his campaign in handicaps goes as smoothly as we believe it will.

The thinking for including Spot The Ball is as easy to explain as the rules of the game itself, and the man entrusted with putting the 'x' in all the right places this season, namely Jonjo O'Neill, knows exactly what's required to win multiple handicaps in a season. Spot The Ball has several draws. He's well bred, by Oscar out of a half-sister to useful hurdler/chaser up to two and a half miles To Your Honour; and then there's his handicap mark of 90, achieved after four low-key runs in maiden/novice hurdles and surely a severe underestimation of Spot The Ball's ability; he was fair in bumpers after all, chasing home Basford Bob at Uttoxeter on his debut prior to being set plenty to do at Ffos Las in a race won by Adams Island. Expect plenty of entries, and almost as many cheques in the post. ***Jonjo O'Neill***

Jonjo O'Neill (trainer): I hope he's just taking time to come to himself. He's a brilliant-looking horse and he should have learned a lot from what he did last season. If he can't win off a mark of 90 he's a bicycle, isn't he?

Storm Kirk F96

4 b.g Heron Island (Ire) – The Storm Bell (Ire) (Glacial Storm (USA))
2009/10 NR :: 2010/11 F16g* Apr 28

Finding underrated trainers is arguably as tricky a task as selecting the 'Fifty' itself when it comes to the annual task of compiling Timeform's Horses To Follow. With 'level-stake profit' the measure used to assess the success of the publication, choosing horses who could well go under the radar is essential, a consideration that is indelibly linked to the prestige of the trainers involved. Granted, Messrs Nicholls, Hobbs and Henderson will almost always be represented, but it's the likes of Alistair Whillans, undervalued handler of Storm Kirk, whose efforts can often prove the difference between a profitable campaign and a losing one. Whillans has long since been viewed by Timeform as a more capable trainer than he's given credit for—any doubters should look at his recent rekindling of such as Bill's Echo over jumps and Social Rhythm on the Flat—and he underlined his talents when Storm Kirk made a successful debut in a Kelso bumper having been backed into 7/2, the four-year-old overcoming greenness to forge away from his nine rivals.

In truth, it was little more than a toss-up for a place in this year's list between Storm Kirk and his year-older brother, the same connections' Storm Brig, but the fact the latter won an extra bumper is hardly going to help his price as he embarks on a career over hurdles and, what's more, Storm Kirk has the option of winning another race in bumpers under a penalty, something he'll surely do. If his pedigree is anything to go by, he could go a long way over jumps when the time comes, with his half-brother Herons Well one of the success stories of the early stages of the 2010/11 season. **A C Whillans**

Alistair Whillans (trainer): He's probably still babyish and green and may want another year before he's at his very best; he's still a head and a tail and hasn't really filled out yet. He'll have another couple of runs in bumpers before going hurdling at the end of the year and, between him and his brother (Storm Brig), I think he'll be the better one.

Swincombe Rock ★   h120

5 ch.g Double Trigger (Ire) – Soloism (Sulaafah (USA))
2009/10 16m 21v² 17v² 24d 21m* Apr 19

Robert and Sally Alner, who have now retired from training, will have many special memories on which to reflect. Cool Dawn's all-the-way win in the 1998 Cheltenham Gold Cup was surely the biggest high, but their achievements with dual Gold Cup-placed Sir Rembrandt and Racing Post Chase winner Super Tactics be far behind, nor for that matter can those involving gutsy Welsh National hero Miko de Beauchene. Swincombe Rock's success in a twenty-one furlong handicap hurdle at Kempton last season probably features a fair bit lower on any such list, though this big, chasing type, very much in the mould of so many of the Alners' best horses and now in the care of another Gold Cup-winning trainer, looks set to go a good way to emulating some of his old stablemates in 2010/11. Twiston-Davies went to £36,000 to secure the five-year-old, an amount that could well look a bargain if things go as planned, as it was only late in the latest campaign that Swincombe Rock was finding his feet, with his Kempton defeat of a subsequent winner in Prescelli coming in just his second handicap and on only his fifth start over hurdles in all. The positives don't end there, either. Both Swincombe Rock's physique and pedigree point to further marked progress—his dam, also trained by the Alners, came into her own only once switched to fences—while he's barely had his stamina tested to date, with his sole try at three miles a write-off thanks to a couple of uncharacteristic mistakes. Expect to see Swincombe Rock switched to fences sooner rather than later, but follow him regardless of the path he takes. **N A Twiston-Davies**

Nigel Twiston-Davies (trainer): We think an awful lot of him. He jumps really well and he'll be going novice chasing from his current mark.

Tara Royal
c125p

5 b.g Kayf Tara – Poussetiere Deux (Fr) (Garde Royale)
2009/10 F16s 16s³ 17v* 17s⁴ 20d* 20d :: 2010/11 c20f* May 8

David Pipe has David Johnson, Paul Nicholls has Andy Stewart and Jonjo O'Neill has J. P. McManus. Every top trainer benefits from the help of a main supporter, and the backing of Tim Leslie has certainly helped propel Donald McCain into the upper echelons of the National Hunt game in recent times. Last season marked another upturn in the fortunes of McCain and coincided with Leslie's most successful campaign as an owner, too, with twenty-four of the trainer's eighty-eight winners coming in Leslie's very familiar yellow, blue and grey silks. Notable highlights for the pairing included Peddlers Cross's wins at Cheltenham and Aintree, as well as a remarkable run of handicap successes for Overturn that continued into the early parts of this season, both on the Flat and over hurdles.

It's reasonable to assume, therefore, that the duo will take another step forward in 2010/11, and Tara Royal could be one of the younger brigade who leads the way. Purchased at the same sale as Peddlers Cross, Tara Royal took time to find his feet over hurdles, but his wide-margin win in a novice at Carlisle marked him down as a useful prospect, and a successful bow over fences at Haydock in the spring did nothing to alter that impression; not only did Tara Royal jump superbly for a chasing debutant, but he also quickened well clear of some above-average novices with little fuss until they closed him down on the run-in. A winning pointer, chasing was always likely to be Tara Royal's game, and an early switch to handicaps could well prove as rewarding as a season kept to novices.
D McCain Jnr

See trainer interview, page 67

Taste The Wine (Ire)
h103p

4 gr.g Verglas (Ire) – Azia (Ire) (Desert Story (Ire))
2009/10 16s² 16s⁵ 16d⁴ Mar 24

There are a number of reasons why Flat horses might not transfer all of their ability to hurdles. Whether it be through lack of stamina or size, an inadequate jumping technique or being unsuited by typically softer ground, there are many, many horses who fail to come up to expectations over timber every single season. Fortunately for us, Taste The Wine did plenty to show in three starts last season that none of those factors is applicable to this fair Flat performer; indeed he caught the eye on two outings either side of a stiff ask in the Adonis at Kempton. He came from an impossible position under hands and heels to finish rnner-up to the useful Orzare in a juvenile at Plumpton in February on the first occasion, and created another good impression when a sympathetically-ridden fourth to William Hogarth in a Warwick novice in March having again been left with lots to do.

Given this clear promise, an initial handicap mark of 96 looks sure to fall well within his realm, especially as there remains untapped potential with trips in excess of two miles likely to suit. A quiet campaign on the Flat this summer points to his being held back for hurdles, and a race or two seem sure to fall his way during the winter months. *J S Moore*

Stan Moore (trainer): He's a tough and genuine sort of horse who ran a couple of nice races last season and looks one for handicaps now. I think he'll stay up to three miles over hurdles. He'll win his races.

Time For Rupert (Ire) h166

6 ch.g Flemensfirth (USA) – Bell Walks Run (Ire) (Commanche Run)
2009/10 19g 24s* 24s² 24g² Mar 18

Those of us who earn our corn here at Timeform Towers could never be accused of rivalling brain surgeons or rocket scientists when it comes to mental acuity.

Time For Rupert is the only one to make a race of it with top-notch staying hurdler Big Buck's (noseband)

And so it may appear with the inclusion of the top-class Time For Rupert, who found only Big Buck's his superior amongst last season's staying hurdlers. But there's method here all the same. Time For Rupert is one of the toughest and most genuine performers around and did nothing but improve last season, culminating with his World Hurdle second, clear of the rest but unable to quite live with Big Buck's from the last. When you go on to consider his stature, strong, robust and just the sort to make a chaser, it's almost inconceivable he won't take high rank in the novice division in 2010/11, with the RSA Chase surely the race for him.

Before runner-up at the Festival, Time For Rupert had already shown his liking for the Cheltenham hill by winning a competitive handicap in December and then running Tidal Bay close in the Cleeve Hurdle despite conceding that one 3 lb. What gives him added appeal looking forward to the transition to fences is that he doesn't hail from one of the elite yards but that of the perfectly capable Paul Webber. As such, he hasn't been overbet in his career to date, even when holding outstanding claims, raising hopes that there may be some value about him even when contesting relatively simple tasks in novice company. He will stay beyond three miles and is proven on ground ranging from good through to soft.
P R Webber

Paul Webber (trainer): He's getting on very nicely. We've made the decision he will go chasing and his season will hopefully start off at the Cheltenham November meeting in the two-and-a-half-mile novice. Now they've put in the new novice chase over that trip at the Festival it could make the RSA a less gruelling race.

Tocca Ferro (Fr) ★   h120p

5 gr.g April Night (Fr) – La Pelode (Fr) (Dress Parade)
2009/10 16s³ 16d* 21d⁴ 16d Mar 13

Tocca Ferro's win in a maiden bumper at Wincanton on his only start in his first season had suggested that he was more about speed than stamina; and his performances over hurdles in his second emphatically underlined that point. Not only did Tocco Ferro fail to stay when tried beyond two miles, but even over that distance he left the strong impression that he will be seen to better advantage when given the opportunity to race under conditions less testing than those he has encountered so far, all of his runs having taken place on good to soft or soft ground.

A promising third in a maiden at Newbury on his hurdling debut, Tocca Ferro then justified favouritism in a novice at Southwell in January before finding twenty-one furlongs beyond him at Kempton. Back at two miles for his handicap debut, in the Imperial Cup at Sandown, Tocca Ferro shaped really well up against generally much more experienced rivals, finishing seventh of twenty-three to Qaspal. Once again he impressed with the way he travelled for much of the way, still on the bridle when joining the leaders before two out, but more patient tactics would have served him better in such a strongly-run race and his effort had begun to peter out even before he made a mistake at the last. Even so, Tocca Ferro shaped as though ahead of his mark and he will surely win a handicap this season when conditions are in his favour. His half-brother and dam both won over fences in France, and the strongly-built Tocca Ferro looks the sort who will also do well over fences when the time comes. **Miss E C Lavelle**

Emma Lavelle (trainer): He's lovely. He was sick at the end of last year, but he travelled so well in the Imperial Cup—he was cantering turning in and just didn't get home; he scoped full of mucus afterwards. He's had a really good summer and he looks great. He'll stay over hurdles because I think off 126 he's got a pretty lenient handicap mark.

Via Galilei (Ire) ★   h101p

5 b.g Galileo (Ire) – Manger Square (Ire) (Danehill (USA))
2009/10 17s⁶ 16g 16g⁶ 16m* Apr 19

What do Heathcote, Numide, Rob Leach, Shahrur, Verasi, Warm Spell and Wingman have in common? Answer, they've all been skilfully handled by leading dual-purpose trainer Gary Moore to scoop valuable handicap hurdles in recent years. Ask the same question next year and, with a bit of luck, we'll be able to add Via Galilei to that impressive list.

Via Galilei was a smart if quirky performer on the Flat for Jim Bolger, numbering on his CV a handicap win from a mark of 98, so a hurdles record of one odds-on win from four starts might be deemed something of a disappointment so far. Not to us, though, as we are well and truly of the opinion that Via Galilei's first season over hurdles won't bear any resemblance to his second.

Testing ground proved Via Galilei's undoing on his hurdling debut after he'd led on the bridle at one point and, having been ridden with an eye on the future in good-quality novices on his next two outings, he overcame the concession of a big head start to the second and third when opening his account at Plumpton on his final appearance. The relatively narrow margin that day patently masked the amount Via Galilei had to spare and, with that, his Flat form and his trainer in mind, we could be hearing a lot more of Via Galilei in handicaps at around two miles. A third totesport Trophy this century for Moore, perhaps? **G L Moore**

Gary Moore (trainer): He's had a break since we wasted our time at Royal Ascot. His run before that was very pleasing and he's come back good. He'll have another run on the Flat and, if he improves as I hope, he could be fairly well treated—a nice handicap hurdle prospect.

Wayward Prince   h144
6 b.g Alflora (Ire) – Bellino Spirit (Ire) (Robellino (USA))
2009/10 F16d² 21s² 24d* 25s² 24g* Apr 9

Trainer Ian Williams could not have been more enthusiastic when discussing Wayward Prince's prospects following the gelding's victory in the John Smith's Sefton Novices' Hurdle at Aintree in April. His enthusiasm was understandable given that Wayward Prince, a tall, useful-looking individual whose long-term future has always been over fences, had come out on top in a Grade 1 contest on just his fourth start over hurdles. `He is a proper chaser in the making. This is small fry, hopefully, in comparison to what he might achieve,' said Williams.

Following promising efforts when runner-up in a bumper at Sandown (behind another of the `Fifty', Megastar) and a novice hurdle at Ludlow, Wayward Prince readily landed the odds in a maiden at Doncaster before finishing a length second to Wymott in a Grade 2 novice at Haydock. Clearly progressing fast, Wayward Prince came in for support at Aintree and was one of only half a dozen in the fourteen-runner field at single-figure odds. The ground at Aintree was less testing than Wayward Prince had encountered previously, but a strong gallop ensured that the emphasis was firmly on stamina even so. That suited the patiently-ridden Wayward Prince, who still had over four lengths to make up on pacesetting Western Leader when moving into second at the last flight. Continuing to run on strongly, Wayward Prince hit the front late on the run-in to win by six lengths from Western Leader, who sadly broke down badly on his off-fore. Wayward Prince, who will stay beyond twenty-five furlongs, has raced only on good ground or softer and acts on soft. He's one to follow in staying novice chases this season, when the obvious long-range target for him is the RSA Chase at Cheltenham. ***Ian Williams***

Ian Williams (trainer): He's done very well over the summer. He's always had the look and build of a chaser about him and winning the Sefton Hurdle was a real bonus. It's quite likely that he'll go straight chasing and he'll be campaigned over three miles. His attitude has always been good and it will continue to hold him in good stead.

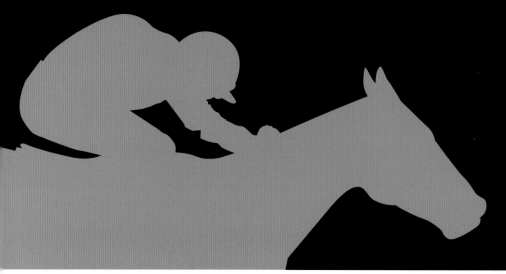

Araucaria (Ire)   F116

6 b.m Accordion – Native Artist (Ire) (Be My Native (USA))
2009/10 F18g* F16v² F18v* F16s² F17g⁴ Apr 9

The word Araucaria means different things to different people. To a botanist, Araucaria would immediately conjure up images of evergreen coniferous trees, a geographer may well point you towards the city in Brazil, while readers of the Guardian newspaper would turn to the crossword page. Here at Timeform, however, the only Araucaria we're interested in is the smart bumper performer trained by John Kiely.

The daughter of Accordion was successful twice at Punchestown last year, beating subsequent winner My Cool Lady by twenty-four lengths on the second occasion, but with a bit more luck she might well have won her other three starts as well. She stayed on very strongly, having been set a lot to do, when second to For Bill at Navan in November, was clearly inconvenienced by the way the race was run when filling the same position behind Shot From The Hip at Leopardstown and was still on the bridle when badly hampered on the home turn in the listed mares contest won by Big Time Billy at Aintree.

The undoubted ability she demonstrated last year isn't the only reason for thinking that Araucaria will do very well over jumps. She is well bred along jumping lines—from the family of Grand National winner Corbiere—and will stay at least two and a half miles, while she's an imposing sort physically, too. Plus, her trainer, John Kiely, has an excellent record with mares, having had the likes of Liss A Paoraigh, Black Queen, Clara Allen and Blazing Liss through his hands in recent times. All in all, Araucaria is a name well worth remembering. ***John E Kiely***

Arvika Ligeonniere (Fr)   h143p

5 b.g Arvico (Fr) – Daraka (Fr) (Akarad (Fr))
2009/10 F16s⁴ 20v* 16v² 24d⁴ 16g* Apr 23

The public backlash against high-flying City bankers is unlikely to be shared by Irish Champion trainer Willie Mullins, who is enjoying an increased patronage by enthusiastic American owner Rich Ricci, whose horses run in the pink silks of his wife Susannah. Ricci is one of the closest allies of Bob Diamond, who has been described by former Business Secretary Lord Mandelson as the 'unacceptable face

Arvika Ligeonniere looks every inch a chaser

of banking' and hit the headlines recently when appointed president of Barclays, as part of a company reshuffle which also saw Ricci promoted to Co-Chief Executive of both Barclays Capital and the firm's Corporate and Investment Bank. In truth, Ricci had hardly been short of funds to facilitate his equine hobby even prior to that new role, as he'd reportedly netted nearly £9 million from a shares payout earlier in the year. So much for the credit crunch!

Whatever the merits of 'casino banking', it is fair to say that Arvika Ligeonniere has represented a safe gamble for Ricci so far and seems sure to provide further returns on his investment over the coming months. Having finished runner-up on his only outing in France before joining current connections, the five-year-old quickly developed into a useful performer last season, winning a maiden hurdle at Fairyhouse in January and a minor novice hurdle at the Punchestown Festival in April. If anything, however, Arvika Ligeonniere created an even better impression when meeting with defeat on both starts in between. He impressed greatly with his jumping when a narrow second to the smart Summit Meeting back at Fairyhouse in February, shaping like the best horse for most of the way, which was also the case until his stamina ran out under rain-softened conditions when upped to three miles in the Albert Bartlett (Spa) Novices' Hurdle at

Cheltenham, eventually fading into fourth behind Berties Dream. He was dropped back in trip fully a mile for his smooth Punchestown success and may well prove best around two miles for the time being, whilst a switch to chasing promises to bring the very best out of this physically-imposing gelding. Indeed, an ante-post interest on Arvika Ligeonniere for the 2011 Arkle Chase probably wouldn't be the most reckless piece of speculation. *W P Mullins*

Bishopsfurze (Ire)   F119

5 b.g Broadway Flyer (USA) – Supreme Dipper (Ire) (Supreme Leader)
2009/10 F16v* F16g F16g* Apr 22

Willie Mullins has a strong hand in bumpers year after year and plenty of these horses graduate into top novice hurdlers. Fiveforthree is one such example, Cousin Vinny another, and there were shades of the latter horse when Bishopsfurze came from a seemingly impossible position to win at Fairyhouse on his debut last term. That display was sufficiently promising for his next start to be in the Champion Bumper at Cheltenham, but he didn't get a chance to show his true worth, meeting all sorts of trouble and nearest at the finish when seventh behind Cue Card. It took only a monthy for Bishopsfurze to make amends, in a competitive race at Punchestown. Ridden in closer touch than at Cheltenham, Bishopsfurze travelled comfortably and, little more than pushed out, came home one and a quarter lengths clear of Go All The Way, leaving the firm impression he could have pulled out more if needed.

A good sort physically, lengthy and useful looking, Bishopsfurze should take well to hurdles and, as he's from the same family as useful staying hurdler Time Electric, he'll almost certainly prove best at two and a half miles and beyond over timber.

There's obviously a way to go, but Bishopsfurze looks set to emulateg his stable-mate Quel Esprit, who landed the same Punchestown bumper before developing into a very useful novice hurdler the following season. *W P Mullins*

Galianna (Ire)   h103p

6 b.m Galileo (Ire) – Ann's Annie (Ire) (Alzao (Usa))
2009/10 16v^2 22s^F Jan 31

A crashing fall at the third last at Limerick in late-January clearly hasn't scared off connections of the mare Galianna, whose exploits on the Flat means she'll be an attractive commodity at stud even without pursuing a hurdling career. 'She's a seriously good hurdles mare in the making a beautiful novice prospect,' insisted trainer Pat Flynn after Galianna had romped home to a ten-length win on the Flat at Clonmel in May, a performance which underlined that she's now a useful performer in that sphere. A reproduction of that sort of form should ensure that she'll be a force in novice hurdles this winter, whilst the enhanced programme of valuable mares hurdles now on offer (both on British and Irish soil) is another reason why connections are clearly so keen to persist with her over timber.

Even without that Flat background, there has been plenty of promise in Galianna's two attempts over hurdles to date which suggest she'll pay her way in 2010/11. Her hurdling debut second in a two-mile maiden at Tramore was a perfectly satisfactory start, particularly as it came on very heavy ground—all of her best Flat form has come on good or firmer. In addition, she'd yet to be asked for her effort when suffering that fall at Limerick four weeks later, clearly travelling strongly under a patient ride at the time over a significantly longer trip. Galianna stays well on the Flat and is likely to stay much further than two miles over timber, though that's not to say she won't be up to winning races around the minimum trip, too. In short, she's unlikely to remain a maiden for much longer. *Patrick J Flynn*

Jetson (Ire) F113

5 b.h Oscar (Ire) – La Noire (Ire) (Phardante (Fr))
2009/10 F16v* F16v² Apr 4

'JETSON!!!!!!!!' That was the regular cry from Mr Cosmo Spacely (via the raucous tones of legendary voiceover artist Mel Blanc), who was the tyrannical boss of George Jetson in Hanna-Barbera's futuristic animated sitcom 'The Jetsons', a yell he'd often follow with the phrase 'YOU'RE FIRED'—though any possible plagiarism case against Alan Sugar could fall down on the fact Mr Spaceley uttered it first in 2062! Fortunately, it would appear Noel Meade hasn't had to resort to such aggressive tactics to get the best out of Jetson's equine namesake and, unlike the aforementioned president of 'Spacely Space Sprockets', it's most unlikely he'll have been dissatisfied with the gelding's performance at work to date. Two visits to the racecourse have yielded one win and a second place in bumpers, creating a good impression on both occasions. In truth, Jetson's debut success at Navan in February came in quite an ordinary affair, but the manner in which he quickened clear under testing conditions to land the odds demonstrated that he was an above-average prospect. The competition was much stiffer on his next start, again on heavy ground, at Fairyhouse's four-day Irish Grand National meeting, when Jetson was sent off at 8/1 in a field of nine, but he emerged as the best horse at the weights in chasing home the mare Our Girl Salley. He arguably should have won, too, as, having lost ground on the winner when taken wide entering the straight, he stayed on strongly and went down by less than a length.

Jetson hails from a family which has served the Meade stable very well down the years, including his half-brother Jered (by Presenting), who graduated from bumpers to become one of the leading novice hurdlers of 2007/8 (won four times) and is now a useful winning chaser. In addition, Jetson's dam La Noire was a half-sister to Meade's smart two-mile chaser Strong Run and top bumper performer Leading Run. The fact that both Strong Run and Jered have flattered to deceive under pressure suggests that greenness may not be the sole reason why Jetson didn't look 100% straightforward when initially coming off the bridle at Navan and Fairyhouse, but he saw things out well both times once the penny had dropped and any such quirks certainly shouldn't prevent him winning novice hurdles in 2010/11. Indeed, it is safe to say that Jetson, with no pun intended, is very much one for the future. ***N Meade***

Last Instalment (Ire)   F111p

5 ch.g Anshan – Final Instalment (Ire) (Insan (USA))
2009/10 F18v* Apr 5

There's often an element of guesswork involved when trying to rate wide-margin winners. And if the rout has occurred in an extended-distance bumper on heavy ground, contested largely by unraced horses, then the guesses can become even more vague. Step forward Last Instalment, who put twenty-seven lengths between himself and the runner-up when justifying strong favouritism at Fairyhouse in April. However, in our opinion, Last Instalment is worth all, and possibly a little more than, the rating he was given as a result of that wide-margin success and is very much one to follow in 2010/11.

The Fairyhouse race featured distances more akin to an Ironman contest, with literally furlongs separating the winner and the last horse home, so for Last Instalment to be still galloping on strongly under such attritional circumstances illustrates reserves of stamina and toughness rarely seen. His pedigree screams 'stayer' as well—he's a half-brother to a winning pointer and out of an Insan mare—and, prior to creating such a good impression at Fairyhouse, he won a maiden (also by a wide margin) on the second of his two starts in points. Hurdles rather than fences are likely to be on the agenda for Last Instalment in 2010/11 and he's sure to win his share in novice company when stamina is at a premium.
Philip Fenton

Loosen My Load can add to this Cheltenham win over the coming months

Loosen My Load (Ire)
h135 c133P

6 b.g Dushyantor (USA) – The Kids Dante (Ire) (Phardante (Fr))
2009/10 F16m* F16d* 16d* 16m² 16d* 16v⁴ 16g⁵ :: 2010/11 c20m*
May 18

Followers of this publication will be well aware of Loosen My Load as Henry de Bromhead's gelding justified his place in last year's edition by winning a Grade 2 novice at Cheltenham in November. He failed to build on that in two subsequent runs, but he was simply marking time over hurdles and we believe that there is considerably more to come from him over fences.

Indeed, he has already opened his account over the larger obstacles, impressively winning a maiden at Punchestown in May, in a race, coincidentally or otherwise, that his trainer had used to launch the chasing career of the subsequent Arkle winner Sizing Europe last season. Fitted with a tongue strap, Loosen My Load jumped fluently and needed only to be nudged out to overhaul the long-time leader after the last, proving himself at two and a half miles in the process but likely to prove at least as effective back around the minimum trip. Encouragingly, both the third and fifth from that race won next time out.

It is well worth pointing out that 2009/10 was Loosen My Load's first season of racing, so it is reasonable to believe that this big gelding will have strengthened up over the summer; in fact, it would come as no surprise if he were to continue to tread the same path as his aforementioned stablemate. ***Henry de Bromhead***

Magnanimity (Ire)
h139+

6 b.g Winged Love (Ire) – Mossy Mistress (Ire) (Le Moss)
2009/10 16s² F16s³ 16v* 19v² 16v³ 20v* 24g³ Apr 21

It was only late in the latest campaign that Magnanimity really started to fulfil his potential and 2010/11 should be even more productive if, as expected, he continues to go the right way. After making it second time lucky over hurdles in a maiden at Navan before Christmas, Magnanimity's progress stalled on both subsequent runs during the winter, but a short break seemed to work the oracle as he returned in the spring looking a different horse. A 10/1-success in a Grade 2 at Navan came his way first time back, beating the likes of British raider Frascati Park and Rigour Back Bob, and he might well have upheld form with the latter in a Punchestown Grade 3 just fifteen days later had conditions been more testing, Magnanimity doing all his best work at the finish to claim third faced with less testing ground than previously. Even so, that Punchestown third was a highly creditable effort, particularly as he was conceding weight all round, and the likelihood is Magnanimity will prove ideally suited by around three miles from now on.

With those promising foundations laid, the rangy Magnanimity seems likely to turn his hand to novice chasing this season and, if looks are anything to go by, he seems sure to do even better in that sphere—it is worth noting that he won his only point-to-point outing. His pedigree also adds weight to this theory, as he's a half-brother to prolific winning chaser Forest Dante, whilst his dam is a half-sister to the 2004 Grand National winner Amberleigh House. **_D T Hughes_**

On The Fringe (Ire) c119p

5 b.g Exit To Nowhere – Love And Porter (Ire) (Sheer Grit)
2009/10 c25g* Apr 21

There haven't been many hunter chasers who've made it into this publication down the years, even in interviews with trainers! Variety is apparently the spice of life, though, and such was the promise shown by On The Fringe last season that we felt it prudent to include him.

Like so many in Ireland, On The Fringe was first seen in public in the point-to-point field, finishing behind the subsequent bumper winners Crash and Last Instalment (who also features in this publication) on his first two starts before making it third time lucky in March. However, it was when On The Fringe made the switch to the racecourse proper that he gave the first real indication of his ability. He was the least experienced of the twenty-five that faced the starter in the Brian Price Memorial Champion Hunters Chase at the Punchestown Festival, but that didn't stop him from drawing clear from some of the best in the division, including Kilty Storm (runner-up) and Ballistraw (fourth), On The Fringe sealing victory with another bold jump at the last.

He appeals at the type that could well dominate in hunters, in Ireland at least, for the foreseeable future, but, as he is only five, there has to be a chance that On The

Fringe will be able to make his mark in open company, too, should connections follow that path instead. ***Enda Bolger***

Pandorama (Ire)   c149+

7 b.g Flemensfirth (USA) – Gretchen's Castle (Ire) (Carlingford Castle)
2009/10 c20d* c20s* c24d* Dec 28

Pandorama mightn't be a flashy sort like old stablemates Iktitaf, Harchibald and Go Native—in fact, he's every inch a strong galloper—but he's always been well-regarded by both his trainer and regular jockey Paul Carberry and this could be the season in which he really reaches his potential.

A one-time ante-post favourite for the Baring Bingham during his hurdling days, Pandorama wasn't seen after the turn of the year in his novice season over fences, though he still had a hugely successful campaign, winning all three of his starts, including a brace of Grade 1 events in December. Sent off favourite for the Drinmore Novices' Chase at Fairyhouse despite scraping home on his debut over

Pandorama (noseband) maintains his 100% record over fences with victory over Weapon's Amnesty (partly hidden)

fences, Pandorama justified the faith in him by accounting for Alpha Ridge quite readily, the manner in which he kept on suggesting a step up to three miles would be right up his street. The Knight Frank at Leopardstown over Christmas provided such an opportunity, and it was there that Pandorama confirmed himself a potential star of the staying ranks when rallying to beat subsequent RSA winner Weapon's Amnesty by a head in a thrilling finish. Unexposed when stamina is of the essence, Pandorama most likely has a good deal more to offer as a chaser and, having already accounted for one of his potential main rivals in what looks a fairly weak staying division in Ireland, he could mop up plenty of top graded races in his homeland in the coming season, especially when the mud is flying. **N Meade**

Paul Kristian   h104P F112p

7 b.g Overbury (Ire) – Farmer's Pet (Sharrood (USA))
2009/10 F18v* F16v* Jan 21

A horse who is rising eight and has made it to the track only four times isn't normally the sort who makes a horses to follow list, but an exception has to be made for Paul Kristian, such is the impression he has made when seen in public. He actually hit the headlines for all the wrong reasons on just his second start back in 2007/8, barely coming off the bridle when second to the now-smart chaser Let Yourself Go in a maiden hurdle at Limerick, understandably attracting the attention of the stewards as a result, his rider picking up a 50-day ban for his 'efforts'.

After twenty-one months off and a change of yards, going to Willie Mullins from Liam Burke, Paul Kristian returned in a bumper at Fairyhouse in December and showed no ill-effects from his spell on the sidelines, toying with his rivals before eventually being shaken up for a three-length win. Turned out the following month at Gowran, Paul Kristian scored in similarly striking fashion, cruising up early in the straight and picking up well when eventually asked, again value for much more than the bare winning margin implied.

Already a winner in points, and quite stoutly bred as an Overbury half-brother to three winning jumpers, including useful hurdler/chaser up to three miles Fleet Street, Paul Kristian will stay at least two and half miles over hurdles this term and has the added bonus of being able to start this campaign with his novice status intact, meaning he should be able to gain valuable experience in a couple of lesser races before stepping up in grade. To date, Paul Kristian has raced only on soft/heavy ground, and possibly wouldn't want anything much firmer given past problems. **W P Mullins**

The Midnight Club (Ire)   c142p

9 ch.g Flemensfirth (USA) – Larry's Peach (Laurence O)
2009/10 24s* c21s⁴ c22vF c24v³ c20v* c21g³ c25g³ Apr 20

There are't many nine-year-olds in training who look open to plenty more improvement. The Midnight Club does, however, and he should become a fixture in some of the top staying handicap chases this season on both sides of the Irish Sea. A graduate from the Irish pointing scene, The Midnight Club has stood up well to two busy novice campaigns and didn't take too long to translate his very useful hurdling form to fences during the latest one. That said, a solitary win in a two-and-a-half mile Clonmel maiden chase doesn't do him justice at all and there's definitely an air of unfinished business about him over the larger obstacles.

For the second year running, The Midnight Club acquitted himself well at the Cheltenham and Punchestown Festivals, finishing third in the Jewson (beaten four lengths by Copper Bleu) and the Champion Novices' (five and a half lengths behind stable-companion Kempes) respectively, doing his best work at the finish on both occasions. Very much a staying sort who finds plenty for pressure, he remains unexposed at three miles plus and acts well on soft/heavy going. The Hennessy Gold Cup at Newbury looks an obvious starting point, with a crack at one of the 'Nationals' a realistic hope for later on. *W P Mullins*

Interview
Donald McCain

It takes some trainers years to enjoy a Cheltenham Festival winner; many span an entire career without even getting so much as a sniff of one. Not Donald McCain, though, who tasted Festival glory in just his second full season at the helm of the Cheshire base he inherited from his legendary father, Donald Snr, when Whiteoak landed the inaugural running of the David Nicholson Mares' Hurdle. Whiteoak's big-price success might have been deemed a rare, rather flattering moment for the lesser lights in some quarters, but McCain could hardly have proven the doubters any more wrong. Wins on the biggest of National Hunt stages have continued to flow for McCain, including last season, courtesy of this term's Grand National hope Ballabriggs (Kim Muir) and McCain's Great White Hope Peddlers Cross (Neptune Novices' Hurdle) amongst others, establishing Donald Jnr as the leading National Hunt trainer in the North.

Despite such a lofty position, McCain confesses that, at this stage, he's just 'trying to improve the quality and will worry about numbers later,' but he does have the backing of a couple of powerful owners. The patronage of Trevor Hemmings certainly helped McCain establish his place towards the top bracket, but it is his more recently formed association with Tim Leslie, the man behind big-money buy Peddlers Cross, that has really propelled the level-headed trainer alongside the likes of jumps heavyweights Nicholls and Pipe. A few more have been purchased for Leslie this time around, leading McCain to say his main patron now has a bunch of 'really nice horses.'

The injury-enforced loss of stable jockey Jason Maguire isn't ideal with an eye on the yard hitting the ground running, but McCain stressed there was 'no great panic' and seems happy with his young team of understudies, who include Henry Brooke, John Kington and Josh Hamer, while he'll continue to use the likes of Graham Lee, Timmy Murphy and A. P. McCoy when they're available. What's more, according to McCain, Maguire's recovery 'couldn't be going any better,' saying he expects to see him back 'fairly early in the season.' Here's hoping, as otherwise McCain looks set fair to maintain his position at the top table, with the string he's assembled for this season surely his best yet.

Overturn (Ire) (h162) 6 b.g Barathea (Ire) – Kristal Bridge (Kris) 2009/10 16s⁴ 17s⁴ 16d³ 16m² 16m* 16s* 16g* 2010/11 16f² 16m* Jul 29 He'll have a break now, and whether we come back in the autumn for one run, or give him longer and bring him back after Christmas, we've not quite decided yet. There were a number of things behind his improvement. We tidied his wind up, though that was a minor thing, and we finally decided to let him loose to do his job as he liked doing it on the Flat, but quite how he got beaten off 100 at Doncaster I'll never know! I don't know whether he's just a good handicapper—he's very tough, very professional and has a great way of going—but he's rated 159 and you're not going to get into many handicaps off that mark. I would say Peddlers has got a touch more class, but I think we've got two genuine Champion contenders, really.

Ballabriggs (Ire) (c152) 9 b.g Presenting – Papoose (Ire) (Little Bighorn) 2009/10 24v³ c25s* c25d* c25g* Mar 18 This year is all geared around Aintree and the National, and we'll work back from there. He is still a novice over hurdles, so that will allow us to get a couple of runs into him. He didn't have leg problems prior to last season, he just hurt his back, and Mr Hemmings was patient, we treated

him and, touch wood, there's been no sign of it since. He's a big horse, and a fairly switched off horse, but he is a strong traveller and, if there is a doubt, it's that four and a half miles may just stretch him; he tied up at Cheltenham when he won there, though if you stop the race at the last he's bolted up and you wouldn't need to be so positive on him at Aintree. There aren't too many better jumpers in the yard.

The sure-footed Ballabriggs has Aintree on the agenda

Realmont (Fr) (h109 c149) 5 b.g Khalkevi (Ire) – Christina (Fr) (Olmeto) 2009/10 c20s² c20d³ May 24 Have you seen his form? He just got beat by Long Run one day giving him weight. He was bought from France last summer to stay over there and run in the big 4-y-o chase at Auteuil, but he got colic and fractured his pelvis. We got him back late last year and had him cantering again before we turned him away, and he's been back for three or four weeks now. I haven't done enough with him at home to know too much about him, but I wouldn't have thought he was a two-miler. He was one of the best three- and four-year-old chasers in France and is an exciting horse, though he's still a novice over hurdles and we'll probably go that route first.

Peddlers Cross (Ire) (148p) 5 b.g Oscar (Ire) – Patscilla (Squill (USA)) 2009/10 F16s* 17s* 21g* 20g* Apr 10 He's a horse we've always though highly of, and so did plenty of others before we got hold of him, and it's just nice to not make a mess of one; to go the way it did was magic. He's the best I've trained. I'm leaning towards either staying at two and a half miles or coming back in trip and going for the Champion. At the moment, I can't get into my head that he needs three

The unbeaten Peddlers Cross seems set to be kept to hurdles for the time being

miles, and we'll put chasing on hold for the time being as he's only five and has had just four runs over hurdles. Overturn is rated 8 lb higher than him at the moment, and they might have got that the wrong way round; the way he put his race to sleep at Aintree from the third last was most eyecatching and, until he's beaten, we don't know how good this horse can be. I don't think the top two-milers are stars, either, but you'd fancy him like mad in the Aintree Hurdle over further.

Wymott (Ire) (h137+) 6 b.g Witness Box (USA) – Tanya Thyne (Ire) (Good Thyne (USA)) 2009/10 20v² 22v* 24v² 25s* Feb 20 He won a Grade 2 at Haydock, beating Wayward Prince, but he had a small knock and we decided to miss the two big meetings. He's been schooling over fences for two years and, if you'd seen him jump, you'd see why we're excited about him. He could be a serious staying novice chaser this season, an RSA horse.

Any Given Day (Ire) (h136) 5 gr.g Clodovil (Ire) – Five of Wands (Caerleon (USA)) 2009/10 18g* 16m* 17d* 19g² 16g³ 16s² 21v⁵ 16 17d Mar 19 He's no oil painting, but he's just a tough, genuine horse who always does his best and likes going racing. I think he'll want two and a half miles on decent ground now and I will school him over fences - he's not very big but I think he has the heart for it.

Khachaturian (Ire) (c136) 7 b.g Spectrum (Ire) – On Air (Fr) (Chief Singer) 2009/10 c22g² c20g² c20gᵘʳ c24s* c22v³ c20v* c25g⁵ c25gᶠ Apr 9 He's a grand old horse. You have to be very positive with him, as otherwise he doesn't jump as well, but I thought he ran a hell of a race at Cheltenham, which wouldn't be his track. There's a big staying handicap in him somewhere—he's certainly earned it.

Fiendish Flame (Ire) (h133 c135) 6 ch.g Beneficial – Deenish (Ire) (Callernish) 2009/10 c16g* c21d² c16v³ c20d* c21g⁶ c20g³ Apr 17 He wasn't right at Kempton or Hereford and came back and won well at Musselburgh. We ran there to justify running at Cheltenham, but we shot ourselves in the foot, as he went up in the weights for doing it. He's probably a good handicapper, maybe just lacking a touch of class, and we'll stick between two and two and a half miles.

Fabalu (Ire) (h123p c134) 8 b.g Oscar (Ire) – Lizes Birthday (Ire) (Torus) 2009/10 c22v⁴ c25v³ c24v² c24v* c32g⁶ c26v* Apr 5 He's the one horse who might jump better than Ballabriggs! He's a smashing horse, I love him, so tough and genuine. He wasn't right early last season for some reason, but I think we should have beaten Door Boy at Newcastle and the ground was too firm for him at Cheltenham. He'll have one run, and then go to the Becher Chase; there's no reason to think he won't be an Aintree horse, and he does handle the mud very well.

Comhla Ri Coig (c130p) 9 b.g Sir Harry Lewis (USA) – Analogical (Teenoso (USA)) 2009/10 c20s³ c20v* Nov 29 He's a home bred - we trained his mother—and he's genuine. The softer the ground the better for him, especially having had another setback at Carlisle last season, but it could just be tough for him this year; he'll need to learn his job against handicappers. He may be a Welsh National horse in time, though.

Ernst Blofeld (Ire) (h129 c129) 6 br.g Flemensfirth (USA) – Estacado (Ire) (Dolphin Street (Fr)) 2009/10 c22v² c20v* c21s^F c20v² c24d* Mar 21 He's a grand horse, and still only six. He gets a trip really well and goes on soft ground, but he was a bit immature last season and possibly wasn't man enough when he ran it Cheltenham. He's actually a very good jumper—when he's made a mistake it's been down to being too switched off—and I could see him going well in those top staying handicap chases around Haydock.

Alegralil (h128) 5 b.m King's Theatre (Ire) – Lucy Glitters (Ardross) 2009/10 F17d* 16d* 19d* 16d 19g² 21s⁵ 18g^ur Apr 24 Things just didn't work out last season after a bright start, though the first run in a good race came as a shock to her system and I thought she ran a screamer down at Newbury on ground that was much too soft for her. She'll probably come back in that listed race at Wetherby in October, and we'll kick on from there with a view to going novice chasing at some point.

Cool Mission (Ire) (h128) 6 ch.g Definite Article – Mettlesome (Lomond (USA)) 2009/10 20v³ 19s* 20d* 24g² :: 2010/11 24g* May 13 He's another smashing horse, even though he doesn't show anything at home. He's genuine and he wants a big, galloping three miles, on ground that isn't too soft. It took a while for him to get to grips with jumping hurdles, but he seemed to jump small fences better and we'll be going over fences this winter; he's every inch a chaser.

Tara Royal (h127 c125p) 5 b.g Kayf Tara – Poussetiere Deux (Fr) (Garde Royale) 2009/10 F16s 16s³ 17v* 17s⁴ 20d* 20d :: 2010/11 c20f* May 8 When I went to the Cheltenham Sales two years ago, I wanted to buy Peddlers Cross and Tara Royal, and I came home with the pair of them! I might have been wrong trying to turn him into a three-miler, as he seems to have got sharper and sharper, and I may run him earlier in the year over two miles. Haydock was a fair prize, and he did everything really well; we switched him off, tried to educate him, and it was very impressive how he put the race to bed jumping the open ditch. He has a great attitude and, if you've got a mature novice like him, there's some good money to be had in the autumn.

Predictive (Fr) (h126) 7 gr.g Smadoun (Fr) – Dacca de Thaix (Fr) (Mont Basile (Fr)) 2009/10 20s² 20v* 22v* 18v³ 24g Apr 9 He goes on most ground and he's very tough and professional, He's got plenty of experience and he ran with credit at Kelso and Aintree. He'll go novice chasing, and I'd love to think he can turn into a Midlands National horse for Peter Douglas.

Double Hit (h116+ c124p) 6 ch.m Sir Harry Lewis (USA) – Grayrose Double (Celtic Cone) 2009/10 21d c16g* c21v² c20s² c22s* 24g³ Apr 16 She was a revelation (at Newbury)—Brian couldn't believe it was the same mare he'd ridden at Wincanton—but everything just clicked on the day. She's only tiny, but she's tough and honest and we might end up running her over hurdles as there are more races for mares.

Glenwood Knight (Ire) (h122) 7 ch.g Presenting – Glens Lady (Ire) (Mister Lord (USA)) 2009/10 20s³ 23s* 20v² Apr 3 He's a horse I've got an awful lot of time for. He's out of a sister to Papillon, by Presenting, and he's got the looks and the ability, but he is a bit fragile. He should for all the world have won the Fixed Brush Final at Haydock, as he was only about eighty per-cent fit and I told Jason (Maguire) to hang on to him; if he'd have had his way, he'd have pressed on at the top of the straight and sewn it up. My fault, but anything he did over hurdles he'll do twice as well over fences anyway—he's like Ballabriggs.

Glenwood Knight (centre) has to settle for minor honours here but should come into his own over fences in 2010/11

Palace Merano (Fr) (c119x) 7 b.g Antarctique (Ire) – Domage II (Fr) (Cyborg (Fr)) 2009/10 24s c24v c22v c19v c22s^6 c24d c22v^{ur} c30g* Apr 23 He got sent to me this season with a view to him making an Aintree horse one day. He's not an old horse, and gets the trip well, and you would hope that he'd keep improving at his age. He's a big, long-striding horse, and it's always nice to have Punchestown winners in the yard.

Edge of Town (Ire) (h118) 6 b.g Witness Box (USA) – Hackler Poitin (Ire) (Little Bighorn) 2009/10 19s^4 22v* 20v^3 24d* 25d^2 Mar 11 He gets three miles well and goes on most ground, and he's done extremely well over the summer. He couldn't jump hurdles for toffee, which is why we tried cheekpieces with him, but he is a big horse and I think it was just a lack of respect for the obstacles, as he's schooled over fences and jumped well. If he takes to it, he could be a really nice staying novice chaser.

Drill Sergeant (h116p) 5 br.g Rock of Gibraltar (Ire) – Dolydille (Ire) (Dolphin Street (Fr)) 2009/10 NR :: 2010/11 16g* Sep 5 I bought him at the sales in July. He's a horse I've always liked; he's just very tough, and he ran well at Royal Ascot this year. He's obviously had a lot of racing, but he's been safe enough schooling, not brilliant, which is how you'd expect a horse like him to be. I just thought, for the money paid, that he was good value—if he gets to grips with the job he could be a useful novice, and he made the perfect start at Worcester.

Tiger Maguire (Ire) (F110) 5 b.g Flemensfirth (USA) – De La Renta (Ire) (Oscar (Ire)) 2009/10 F17d^2 Mar 21 He's named after my stable jockey's father, a standing joke between him and my old man. He's a smashing horse, by Flemensfirth, and did his job very well in his bumper. He was very immature last season, a little bit nervous, but he loved the ground at Carlisle and he'll go hurdling.

Ebony River (Ire) (F94+) 4 b.g Alderbrook – Dishy (Ire) (Jurado (USA)) 2009/10 F17d^3 Mar 11 We went to Carlisle only for a nice education, as he's from the family of Fiendish Flame and Will Be Done, and I was really taken with his run; he travelled beautifully, and looked to have plenty of gears.

Pointers and Unraced Horses

Charminster (Ire) 4 b.g Broadway Flyer (USA) – Monteleena (Ire) Richie Harding, who rode Ballabriggs, recommended him to me. He won his only point—it wouldn't have been the strongest race and the ground was quickish—but he had a nice way of going and looked like winning by ten lengths until fiddling the last. He was an attractive horse at the sales, not overly expensive, and he'll run in a bumper before going over hurdles.

Dunowen Point (Ire) 4 b.g Old Vic (Ire) – Esbeggi He was going to win, cantering, when unseating in the point won last year by Peddlers Cross—he came from the same man, too. He's not a big horse, but he's strengthened up over the summer and does everything very nicely.

Lucky Landing (Ire) 4 b/br.g Well Chosen – Melville Rose (Ire) I wasn't familiar with the sire, other than he's a son of Sadler's Wells, but before the sales I'd done my homework on his point form and liked what I'd seen; he just got beaten by a couple of Gigginstown (Stud) horses. He's done really well over the summer—he's a big, strong horse now—and he's another interesting ex-pointer.

Railway Dillon (Ire) 5 b.g Witness Box (USA) – Laura's Native (Ire) His form doesn't stack up quite as well as the other pointers, but when he won his he did it in a similar fashion to Wymott and Edge of Town—he was the first off the bridle and just kept finding in what was a gruelling contest. It's alright having class, but you've got to want it as well and he looks tough. He'll go over hurdles, stepping up in trip quite quickly at the likes of Carlisle and Newcastle.

Russinrudi (Ire) 7 b.g Rudimentary (USA) – Lady of Grange (Ire) He's the biggest horse I've ever seen! I went into his box at the sales at Cheltenham and walked out saying he's too big, but we got him out and he was so light on his feet—I couldn't leave him alone then. He didn't run until he was six, but he ran twice as a seven-year-old in the space of a week and won two big-field points by long distances. Colin Motherway rode him in his points and said he's not a quick horse but has an engine and jumps and gallops.

Sine Mora 4 b.g Beneficial – Fashion House (Homo Sapien) He's a really likeable horse, by a sire I like. We nearly ran him at the end of last season, but we thought there was more benefit in backing off him and he's shown a good bit. It'll be bumpers and novice hurdles for him, but we can't overlook the fact that we want to keep him switched off, given his sire.

Interview
Paul Nicholls

If there were two things that could have been said with near absolute certainty before the start of this National Hunt season, they would have been that A P McCoy and Paul Nicholls would maintain their stranglehold on the Jockeys' and Trainers' Championships respectively. As we have seen with alarming regularity in recent months, a jockey is never far from an injury-enforced spell on the sidelines, so it's probably Nicholls whose bid for further glory in 2010/11 is the most watertight. The string he has assembled at Ditcheat appears to have more strength in depth than ever before, and the sheer number of horses he trains who are currently rated 140 and above dictates that big-race success will be as commonplace this season as it has been in years gone by. The likes of Kauto Star, Denman, Master Minded and Big Buck's have led the way in recent campaigns, but the yard is choc-full of younger horses who are coming through and in due course look all set to supercede their more vaunted stablemates.

In terms of riders, Ruby Walsh will again be picking up the plum rides in Britain and Ireland and, in his absence, the likes of Harry Skelton, Ian Popham, Ryan Mahon and Daryl Jacob can expect to be offered some excellent opportunities.

So a sixth successive title seems assured for Nicholls, but which are the horses who are going to do most to help him achieve it? Paul, who will be airing his thoughts exclusively on Betfair from October 8th, kindly took the time to run the rule over his string as things stand.

Kauto Star (Fr) (c191) 10 b.g Village Star (Fr) – Kauto Relka (Fr) (Port Etienne (Fr)) 2009/10 c24s* c24d* c26d^F Mar 19 He was a bit unlucky last year, after everything had gone right he made that mistake in the Gold Cup and that was the end of the race. We felt he was as good as ever, and that seems the case again now. He's come back in, looks great and has been working nicely, and I suspect he's no different to what he was twelve months ago. He appears to be ageless! The way he worked on Wednesday you'd say he was just as good as he ever was, but until he runs at Down Royal we won't know for sure. The signs are good, let's say that. It will be Down Royal, Kempton and Cheltenham. What I don't want to do is go and give him a really hard race when he's not fully wound up like I did last year.

Denman (Ire) (c181) 10 ch.g Presenting – Polly Puttens (Pollerton) 2009/10 c26d* c24g^{ur} c26d^2 c25g^4 **Apr 21** He really is in good form. He'll have entries for the Hennessy and the Betfair Chase and Paul (Barber) and I are going to have to sit down at some stage and decide where we'd like to go with him. I think Paul would quite like to have a go at the Hennessy because he's a sporting man and Denman always goes well at Newbury. But he's 8 lb higher than last year which is going to make life bloody hard with some exciting younger horses coming through, one in particular who'd look very good at the weights if Denman ran being What A Friend. It might make more sense to go and take on Imperial

Stable-companions What A Friend (noseband) and Denman will be back to tackle more big races

Commander in the Betfair Chase. We're in between a rock and a hard place in many ways. Neither Paul or I have any interest in running in the National.

Big Buck's (Fr) (h174+) 7 b.g Cadoudal (Fr) – Buck's (Fr) (Le Glorieux) 2009/10 24d* 24v* 24g* 24d* Apr 8 Another season hurdling and all things being equal he'll probably run in the four races he did last season, so that's Newbury, Ascot, Cheltenham, Aintree. I'm going to resist the temptation to enter him in the Hennessy until this time next year.

Twist Magic (Fr) (h131§ c168§) 8 b.g Winged Love (Ire) – Twist Scarlett (Ger) (Lagunas) 2009/10 c17s^3 c16s* c17s* c16g^{pu} c16g^{rtr} c16m^3 Apr 24 Won two Grade 1s last year and then disgraced himself which he was always going to do. He'll start off the season the same as last year. He runs in the Haldon Gold Cup and will then go for the Tingle Creek. He seems fine at the moment and, a bit fresher, I'm sure he'll be okay. It's just in the latter part of the season when he becomes a problem. I think he wants to miss Cheltenham and just go to right-handed tracks.

Neptune Collonges (Fr) (c168?) 9 gr.g Dom Alco (Fr) – Castille Collonges (Fr) (El Badr) 2009/10 NR It's great to have him back. The handicapper has actually dropped him to 164 which gives him a real chance if you look at his Gold Cup form. He'll have an entry in the Hennessy I suppose. I suspect he'll just need one run to sharpen himself up before he goes on anywhere. I need to sit down with John (Hales) and discuss it. He doesn't want the ground too deep or too quick now. He's had plenty of time and treatment and seems fine. He could be a right National horse.

Master Minded (Fr) (c165+) 7 b.g Nikos – Haute Tension (Fr) (Garde Royale) 2009/10 c16s* c16s^3 c17g* c16g^4 Mar 17 He's had a breathing op and seems in great form with himself and, no matter what I say or don't say, until he runs none of us are going to know. He'll probably run at either Cheltenham or Ascot before going to the Tingle Creek. I think to see the very best of him he wants softish ground. On form you'd have to say he is on the downgrade, and it's in the back of my mind that none of the family have trained on. He was so full on at five and good at six, if not as good, but he still looked very good when he won the Game Spirit last year. I don't know if he panics at Cheltenham or if he wasn't breathing, and until he's had a run or two we won't know. Harry Skelton rode him the other day and said he's as good as he's ever felt, but it's easy saying that at home, but it's encouraging all the same.

Celestial Halo (Ire) (h163) 6 b.g Galileo (Ire) – Pay The Bank (High Top) 2009/10 16d* 17s^2 16s^4 16g^4 20g^F Apr 10 He definitely goes chasing and he may have his debut at Exeter next month. He's schooled well; funnily enough he's never jumped a hurdle at home because he's always jumped baby fences, so we're hoping all that schooling will pay off. He'll either be very, very good because he jumps great, or he'll be too good and end up getting himself in trouble . . . he's a bit brave and bold. If he enjoys himself and puts it all together he could be very interesting.

Poquelin (Fr) (c161) 7 bl.g Lahint (USA) – Babolna (Fr) (Tropular) 2009/10 c20m* c20s^2 c21s* c21g^2 c20g^{ur} **Apr 9** He ran some good races last season bar the last one when he was over the top. He'll run in the Old Roan at Aintree in October before going for the Paddy Power, which will be hard but I can always claim off him. He has to go left-handed, which rules out the likes of Ascot and Punchestown and makes him that bit more difficult to place. The Ryanair will be his long-term target.

Noland (c160) 9 b.g Exit To Nowhere (Usa) – Molakai (Usa) (Nureyev (Usa)) 2009/10 NR He missed all of last year and is hard to train because he's fragile. If we can get him back right something like the Peterborough Chase would suit him, but we just need to be careful with him.

What A Friend (h127 c160) 7 b.g Alflora (Ire) – Friendly Lady (New Member) 2009/10 c26d^2 c24d* c25d* **Apr 8** He did what we wanted last season bar winning the Hennessy, but that didn't matter on the day! Won the Lexus, won at Aintree. This year his first run will be the Hennessy and from there we'll aim him for the Gold Cup. He's 159 so he could be well handicapped if we think he's a Gold Cup horse. He's undergone a breathing op so I hope that will improve him a bit. We always thought he'd need one, he's always made a bit of a noise at home and when Ruby got off at Aintree last time he said 'if you sort his breathing out he'll be a proper one.'

Tataniano (Fr) (h140+ c158p) 6 b.g Sassanian (USA) – Rosa Carola (Fr) (Rose Laurel) 2009/10 c17d* c16s* c18d^2 c16g* **Apr 10** He did nothing but improve really. The idea with him is probably to run in the Haldon Gold Cup or the Connaught Chase at Cheltenham before going to the Tingle Creek. I imagine we'll then give him a break before coming back for the Champion Chase. The only blip last season came at Newbury when I was running him to get him qualified for the Grand Annual. I knew he wasn't quite right and the ground was wrong, but I needed to get a third run into him. If you look at it now, he actually got a mark of 140 and is now rated 160, so he'd have been a certainty at Cheltenham, but the ground wasn't right and I took him out. If he had run and won there it would have been job done, but as it was we went to Aintree, the ground was right, and everyone got to see just how good he is. A blessing in disguise.

Taranis (Fr) (c153) 9 ch.g Mansonnien (Fr) – Vikosa (Fr) (Nikos) 2009/10 c25s* **Jan 30** We were obviously pleased to win at Cheltenham after he'd been off for so long. A little unrelated problem kept him off afterwards, but he's back in full work

The bold Tataniano can be added to his yard's already strong hand in two-mile chases

now. He'll have an entry for the Hennessy and Betfair Chase and clearly some of these horses are going to clash, but we want to go on and win another nice race with him because I think he's capable of doing that.

Chapoturgeon (Fr) (c151) 6 gr.g Turgeon (USA) – Chapohio (Fr) (Script Ohio (USA)) 2009/10 c20s^F c21s^4 c21s c16d^{bd} Apr 8 It never went right for him and he disappointed last season. He wouldn't have been too far behind Poquelin in the Boylesports if he hadn't stumbled when jumping the last. We're not all totally convinced he stays, so we might just drop him back in trip—the only time he ran over two miles last season he was bought down when going well—and see how we get on before stepping him back up. It's confusing because he did win the Jewson, even if he was very well handicapped then. He's had a breathing operation and it might be that has been at the root of the problem.

Niche Market (Ire) (c151) 9 b.g Presenting – Juresse (Ire) (Jurado (USA)) 2009/10 c25d c26d^3 c24v^5 c24g^2 c24g c36g^{pu} Apr 10 Obviously we're just learning about him but he strikes me as a horse who needs a lot of work, and we'll probably run him in the Hennessy before training him for the National.

Tricky Trickster (Ire) (c150) 7 b.g Oscar (Ire) – Pavlova (Ire) (Montelimar (USA)) 2009/10 27s^2 c24g*c26d c36g Apr 10 I couldn't get him right last autumn, but we're having a good run with him now. He'll have entries in all the good staying chases; wants a bit of cut in the ground obviously and we'll follow a route towards the National, with the Welsh National a possible target over Christmas.

Qozak (Fr) (h147p) 6 b.g Apple Tree (Fr) – Good Girl (Fr) (Vorias (USA)) 2009/10 17s* 19s⁶ 20vᵘʳ Feb28 Slightly disappointing last year I have to say. I probably ran him too quick after he won the first time and then he wasn't right when we ran him at Fontwell. He'll go novice chasing and we'll start small and see where we go from there. He's got a handicap mark over hurdles of 145 and I think that's high enough; he's probably more a 130-135 horse . . . not top division but he will win races in the middle. He's a big, rangy horse and chasing will be more his game.

The Nightingale (Fr) (c147+) 7 b.g Cadoudal (Fr) – Double Spring (Fr) (Double Bed (Fr)) 2009/10 c18s* c20s* c20d³ Apr 8 He really wants to go right-handed on soft ground. He could go to Down Royal and then possibly Punchestown. He has had problems but I think we ironed them out last year and he's fine at the moment.

Sanctuaire (Fr) (h145p) 4 b.g Kendor (Fr) – Biglique (Fr) (Staint Cyrien (Fr)) 2009/10 18d⁵ 18s³ 17v* 16g* 16d³ Apr 8 He wasn't the easiest to train when we first got him, but we've all been looking forward to this season, getting him into our routine and starting again from scratch. I'm very happy with him now and his first run will be in the Greatwood Hurdle. He wants a really well-run race where he can get a lead. That day will tell us a lot. He probably would have won the Triumph with that form, but we didn't even think about running him in it beforehand. He ran a bit too free at Aintree and it didn't quite work out, but I'm sure he'll put that behind him.

Definity (Ire) (h145+) 7 b.g Definite Article – Ebony Jane (Roselier (Fr)) 2009/10 NR He is an exciting prospect. He missed all of last year with a leg problem and will be back in soon and hopefully we'll go novice chasing. He's got the build, scope and pedigree to take well to fences and I hope he could take high rank.

Tchico Polos (Fr) (c144) 6 b.g Sassanian (USA) – Miss Saint Germain (Fr) (Pampabird) 2009/10 c19g² c18m* c17s* c16s³ c24dᶠ c20s² c16d* c20g² Apr 17 He's fine, he could go for the Haldon Gold Cup. He's probably not the best handicapped, but he'll run in all the top two-mile races and doubtless win us a good bit of prize money. He may go to Ireland with Kauto.

Picture This (Ire) (h139+) 7 ch.g Old Vic – Below The Wind (Gala Performance) 2009/10 24d⁴ 24v⁶ 24g* :: 2010/11 25f* May 8 He likes decent ground and I've got him ready to run in novice chases now so long as we can find the right ground for him. The only other thing if I couldn't find the right race is the £50,000 staying hurdle at Wetherby and I might look at that with him.

Woolcombe Folly (Ire) (c138+) 7 b.g Presenting – Strong Gara (Ire) (Strong Gale) 2009/10 c16d* c16g c16g* Apr 16 He was a bit unlucky—I shouldn't have run him in the Arkle. Won his two other starts and he'd be the type to run in all those good two-mile handicaps, and I'm sure he'll win one. He's a speed horse and remains with a lot of potential as a chaser.

Pepe Simo (Ire) (h138) 6 b.g Victory Note (USA) – Vallee Doree (Fr) (Neverneyev (USA)) 2009/10 NR We'll start him off in an ordinary beginners' chase, but I can see him developing into a really smart two-mile novice chaser. We bought him from Costello's, so he was jumping baby fences from when he was two and he's schooled well already this autumn. He was a smallish sort of horse last season, but he's grown and strengthened well over the summer. You could say he's looked quirky but I think he was babyish and he's much more the finished article now.

Pistolet Noir (Fr) (h138) 4 b.g Maille Pistol (Fr) – Black Et Or (Fr) (Noir Et Or) 2009/10 16g^3 16s* 17s^2 19s^2 16d 29d^3 Apr 8 I made a balls of it if you look strictly at the form book, but to be honest when we got him he was small and wiry, never jumped and had no enthusiasm . . . I thought I was doing something wrong, which I may have been, but then it clicked and I really fancied him at Aintree and he ran very well. I've got a different horse on my hands now; he's jumping, he's sweet so I'm hoping there will be a lot of improvement in him. He should be alright. We might start off in the Tote Silver Trophy at Chepstow and let him tell us where to go.

Royal Mix (Fr) (h137p) 4 gr.g Sagamix (Fr) – Princesse Irena (Fr) (Apple Tree (Fr)) 2009/10 16s* Nov 27 He won his only start last year and it's clearly good form. He was very hard to train afterwards as he was too lean and backward so we just roughed him off. He'll go to Cheltenham for a £50,000 4-y-o race in October and he'll tell us where we go with him from then on. He's a different horse now and giving him time was the best thing we could have done. I'm really excited about him.

Escort'men (Fr) (h137+) 4 ch.g Robin des Champs (Fr) – Escortee (Fr) (Cadoudal (Fr)) 2009/10 18d^5 17s^F 16s* 16g^6 Apr 9 He looked good when winning the Dovecote at Kempton and then I think he was just a bit too free on ground that wasn't as soft as ideal at Aintree. Obviously he's got quite a high handicap mark now, but he'll start hurdling before we have a think about we do. I'd be inclined to wait a year before going over fences.

Rivaliste (Fr) (c137) 5 b.g Robin des Champs (Fr) – Idomale (Fr) (Dom Alco (Fr)) 2009/10 c17d* c18d* c20s^2 c21g Mar 18 I think we'll go back to two miles with him. He's got loads of speed, and holding him up didn't suit him in the Jewson where he made lots of mistakes. He's a decent horse.

Take The Breeze (Fr) (c136+) 7 gr.g Take Risks (Fr) – Reine Breeze (Fr) (Phantom Breeze) 2009/10 c17s* c19v* c18v* c17v^3 c16d^4 c22v* c21g c25g3 Apr 9 We'll probably start him off in the Charlie Hall. I was amazed with his last run over three miles one at Aintree the last day, if he hadn't been interfered with at the second last he would have gone very close. He's versatile, you can run him over two miles on heavy ground or three miles on decent ground.

Michel Le Bon (Fr) (h135+ c135p) 7 b.g Villez (USA) – Rosacotte (Fr) (Rose Laurel) 2009/10 c24d* Nov 26 Due back in next month and he'll carry on his chasing career at Christmas. I'm not sure where we'll go with him, but I imagine graduation chases will suit him very well. I'll probably go low key like I did with What A Friend last year. He needs experience, but he could be really good.

Sang Bleu (Fr) (h133p) 4 gr.g Lavirco (Ger) – Formosa (Fr) (Royal Charter (Fr)) 2009/10 F12g³ F13g* 18d* 16v² 16s* Feb 11 A good novice chaser who'll probably run in the beginners chase at the Hennessy meeting. We'll start at two miles but he will want further, so I'm not sure whether he's an Arkle horse. He jumps well at home, you wouldn't get a better jumper, and I think the hurdles got in his way a bit last season.

Well-bred gelding The Minack looks a useful staying prospect

Ghizao (Ger) (h133+) 6 b.g Tiger Hill (Ire) – Glorosia (Fr) (Bering) 2009/10 F17m* F16s* 17s² 17s* 21g 16g Apr 10 He's had a breathing op during the summer. He had some good form early last season and probably just went over the top by the end as he'd been on the go for a long time. I still think he's capable of winning from his hurdle mark and after that we'll look to go chasing. The Greatwood at Cheltenham or Elite Hurdle at Wincanton will likely be for him. I think he's a two-miler, Ruby says he's got loads of speed, and I think he's going to be a great two-mile chaser.

The Minack (Ire) (h133) 6 b.g King's Theatre (Ire) – Ebony Jane (Roselier (Fr)) 2009/10 21v* 24s⁶ 21v* 20s* 24g Apr 9 Did well last year and he'll go novice chasing, starting off over two and a half miles before we step our way up to three miles. He loves soft ground and is from a family which points to him doing even better as a staying chaser. He's a half-brother to Definity and there would be nothing between them. I think they're both very good.

Watamu Bay (Ire) (h132) 7 b.g Sunshinie Street (USA) – Janzoe (Ire) (Phardante (Fr)) 2009/10 21v² 24s* 24v* 24d Mar 19 I suspect he's slow and wants soft ground; his form at Towcester tells you that. He jumps nicely and should win novice chases over three miles plus.

Pride of Dulcote (Fr) (c130p) 7 b.g Kadalko (Fr) – Quenice (Fr) (Quart de Vin (Fr)) 2009/10 c23d* Oct 21 He got a leg after he ran at Worcester last year, but is back in training now and will be ready to run in a graduation chase at Christmas. He's got the potential to go a long way judging by his hurdles form. The time off has done him the world of good, he was a bit leggy before but he's a different horse now. He's really grown up and strengthened, much more the finished article.

Toubab (Fr) (h130p) 4 gr.g Martaline – Tabachines (Fr) (Art Francias (USA)) 2009/10 17d³ 17s⁵ 16s² 2010/11 16f⁴ May 8 He's probably one of the best maidens in training, or I hope he is anyway! He'll start in a maiden hurdle and go from there.

Red Harbour (Ire) (h128) 6 ch.g Old Vic – Auntie Honnie (Ire) (Radical) 2009/10 21v³ 19g⁶ 19s² 20d* 21g⁵ Apr 17 Progressed well last year; I didn't get him quite right early on and then he was over the top by the time he ran at Ayr. But we won the race we wanted to win, so that's the main thing. He'll probably have one run over hurdles before going chasing.

Aiteen Thirtythree (Ire) (h125) 6 b.g Old Vic – Prudent View (Ire) (Supreme Leader) 2009/10 20s³ 24s² 24g² Mar 6 He was very backward after we put him in at the deep end early on last season, but he improved with each run. He'll run in a three-mile maiden hurdle at Chepstow in early October and unless he looks really, really smart I suspect we'll then go chasing. I think you'll see huge improvement in him when he jumps fences; we've always thought he was a good horse. I know he has a bit of a reputation, and now he has to go and prove he's a good horse rather than just doing it at home. He's more mature mentally now, and that's the biggest thing with him.

Al Ferof (Fr) (F125) 5 gr.g Dom Alco (Fr) – Maralta (Fr) (Altayan) 2009/10 F16d³ F16s* F16g* F16g² Mar 17 Very good horse. He won a point to point before running in bumpers and will want a trip. He jumps very well at home and I'm looking forward to starting him off in novice hurdles. We'll get him off over two and a half miles and see where we go from there.

Don't Turn Bach (Ire) (F123) 6 b.g Bach (Ire) – Bobbie Magee (Ire) (Buckskin (Fr)) 2009/10 F16v* F16d* F17g Apr 10 Disappointing on his only run for us, but he got fairly wound up and I suspect he was over the top. He wants very soft ground and a trip. He's not one you get over-excited about at home, but his form in bumpers in Ireland makes him look good.

Express Leader (h118) 7 b.g Supreme Leader – Karawa (Karinga Bay) 2009/10 20v³ 19s⁴ 23g² :: 2010/11 19d* May 6 He hasn't progressed as seemed likely after having a few problems. He's one for the smaller tracks around the West Country.

Kings Legacy (Ire) (h117p) 6 b.g King's Theatre (Ire) – Kotton (Fr) (Cyborg Fr)) 2009/10 17s* 19dᵘʳ Apr 8 Slightly disappointing that he decided to refuse the last day at Taunton when he would have won. He's still eligible to run in a novice hurdle before November and then he'll go chasing. I just hope he's not going to be one of those horses who doesn't fulfil his potential; he needs to improve.

Advisor (Fr) (h117+) 4 gr.g Anabaa (USA) – Armilina (Fr) (Linamix (Fr)) 2009/10 16s* 16s* 17d 16g Apr 17 He'd been on the go for a long time, including on the Flat, and I think he'd gone over the top by the end of last season, when the quicker ground was also no good to him...everything he's done has told us he wants it soft. He's had a breathing operation and I think he should win a good two-mile handicap hurdle.

Rock On Ruby (Ire) (F113+) 5 b.g Oscar (Ire) – Stony View (Ire) (Tirol) 2009/10 F16s4 F17s* F16g* Mar 6 He's alright, not the biggest in the world, but he jumps well. We'll aim low to start with and see how we progress. He needed a break after winning at Newbury so we just called it a day.

Rebel Rebellion (Ire) (F106) 5 b.g Lord Americo – Tourmaline Girl (Ire) (Toulon) 2009/10 F16d³ aF16g* F17g Apr 10 Big chasing sort who'll go novice hurdling this season I suspect. He's only five, will stay well and we like what we see so far.

The Reformer (Ire) (F104) 5 b.g Pilsudski (Ire) – Tinogloria (Fr) (Al Nasr (Fr)) 2009/10 F16m² Apr 19 He was beaten a head in a bumper at Kempton when he was very green. I would have thought we'll try and go one better before going over hurdles, but more than anything we're going to look after him because he'll make a good chaser in twelve months' time.

Poungach (Fr) (F102+) 4 b.g Daliapout (Ire) – Shalaine (Fr) (Double Bed (Fr)) 2010/11 F16g* He's a nice, young horse who won his only run in a bumper at Stratford in May. He's a chaser of the future and will have a light campaign this year.

Mr Hudson (Ire) (F101) 5 b.g Old Vic – Esbeggi (Sabrehill (USA)) 2009/10 NR He won a point for Richard Barber and then a bumper at Newton Abbot on his first start for us. He'll stay well in time and looks to have a good future.

Future Stars

Highlighting the talented trainers and jockeys who've escaped the attentions of the wider public can be as vital as identifying underrated horses. To that end, Timeform's experts have chosen five racing figures—three trainers and two jockeys—who look well worth keeping on side in 2010/11.

Lawney Hill

Name	LAWNEY HILL
Age	44
Base	Watlington, Oxon
First Full Licence	July 2005
First Winner	Bell Rock, Uttoxeter, 21/07/05*
Total Winners	44*
Best Season	18 (2009/10)
2009/10 Strike Rate	21.4%
Best Horse Trained	To Arms

also trained 9 winners as permit-holder and 6 on Flat

A trainer who went winless between October and March last term mightn't seem an obvious starting point, but it can pay to expect Lawney Hill to make a much better fist of things during the main body of this season. The transition from successful 'summer' jumps trainer to successful jumps trainer is one several have struggled with—even off-season stalwarts Peter Bowen and Tim Vaughan took time to make their name on the bigger stage—but the quality of Hill's string has never been higher and all the evidence points to a handler with all the necessary skills.

Hill's exploits in the early part of 2010/11 have been particularly impressive. From only seventy runners over jumps prior to September's ten-day National Hunt sabbatical, Hill had saddled fourteeen winners, only four down on the amount she mustered throughout 2009/10. What's more, another thirty-one of those she's sent to the races have been placed, resulting in over £65,000 in total prize money and a position well inside the top-twenty of the trainers' table. The quality of her string seems to be improving all the while, too. To Arms's win in a handicap hurdle at Southwell made him Hill's first ever horse with a Timeform rating in excess of 130, while multiple recent winner Mad Jack Duncan has looked every inch the sort to make his mark in some of the better staying handicap chases this season by winning three of his four starts since joining the yard from Alan King.

Trainer's Horse To Follow: I think **Fiveways** will be a nice horse; I'm very much looking forward to him. He'll be coming in a bit later after a minor setback, and he should be out in late-December, maybe the new year, but he's got a lot of potential and he's very tough. He'll be a novice hurdler this season, but I think we'll be looking at fences later on as he jumps well. He's quite a quirky, edgy horse, so we'll have to be careful, but on the racecourse he's totally different, very relaxed and always sticks his neck out when another horse comes at him.

Martin Keighley

Name	MARTIN KEIGHLEY
Age	36
Base	Moreton-in-Marsh, Glos
First Full Licence	October 2006
First Winner	Prince Dundee, Taunton, 08/01/07*
Total Winners	46*
Best Season	27 (2009/10)
2009/10 Strike Rate	16.3%
Best Horse Trained	Any Currency
	also trained 1 winner as permit-holder

Talk about the calm before a storm. Fourteen winners, spread over seven seasons, could hardly be considered a poor return for a trainer with few horses, but it can't have prepared many for the upturn in fortunes enjoyed by the upwardly-mobile Martin Keighley during 2009/10, the keen eyes at Timeform included.

A double at Towcester on April 27, courtesy of Badly Bruised and Wolf Moon, really started the Keighley ball rolling, and the latter in particular did plenty to establish the trainer as one to follow during the campaign. Wolf Moon added three more wins, including two at Keighley's local track, Cheltenham, and was joined in landing multiple successes for the stable by the likes of fellow Prestbury Park winner Benbane Head, Any Currency and Love of Tara, all of whom improved throughout the campaign and ended with Timeform ratings in excess of 120. The final totals made for impressive reading—twenty-seven winners, almost double his previous number combined, and a strike-rate of sixteen per-cent—and it should be a case of more of the same with the trainer this time around.

Trainer's Horse To Follow: I'm very excited about **Wolf Moon** going chasing. He's a real chaser in the making—he looks like one and he was a natural when we schooled him over fences last season. We said whatever he did over hurdles was a bonus—and he won two races over timber at Cheltenham—and there's just so much more to come from him. His attitude is so taking, as was the way he battled on up the hill at Cheltenham, and he could go quite high in the chasing ranks.

John Flint

Name	JOHN FLINT
Age	46
Base	Kenfig Hill, Bridgend
First Full Licence	February 2007
First Winner	Iris's Prince, Fontwell, 04/02/07*
Total Winners	25*
Best Season	17 (2009/10)
2009/10 Strike Rate	21.5%
Best Horse Trained	Fair Along
*also trained 8 winners as permit-holder and 14 on Flat	

It isn't quite up there with the likes of the Lampards (Frank Jnr and Snr), Broads (Stuart and Chris) and Mayweathers (Floyd Jnr and Snr) when it comes to offspring overshadowing their parent, but it's fair to say Rhys Flint made a much bigger splash than his father in his sporting field. Thanks largely to a fruitful association with Fair Along, a horse formerly in the care of his father, ironically, Flint Jnr established himself as a highly promising National Hunt jockey some time before father John had started to highlight his skills as a trainers.

The familial balance may soon be redressed, though, as Flint Snr has done plenty in recent times to put a number of rather stuttering years behind him. Having trained only ten winners until the start of the 2009/10 season, Flint made a real impression in recording seventeen successes in that latest campaign alone, operating at a strike-rate above 1 in 5 in the process. Flint's bread and butter has been improving those he's inherited from elsewhere— note Dawn At Sea, Changing Lanes and Bundle Up, for instance—and a promising start to 2010/11, featuring six winners, has him on course to smash his previous best once more.

Trainer's Horse To Follow: I do like **Mr Moneymaker**, who won first time out for us on the Flat. I think he'll eventually go over hurdles around the turn of the year and will be a nice one to follow. He'll want two miles and has schooled well.

Henry Brooke

Name	HENRY BROOKE
Age	19
Claim	7 lb
Minimum Weight	9-7
First Ride	Roman Bury, Market Rasen, 26/04/08
First Winner	Farmer Frank, Market Rasen, 16/05/10
Total Winners	4
Best Season	2010/11 (3)
Best Horse Ridden	Farmer Frank
Attached Stable	Donald McCain

With just three winners from little over fifty rides to say Henry Brooke's was at a fledgling stage would be something of an understatement. The nineteen-year-old has shown more than enough to us, however, to imagine his career is going to be one worth following, whilst the fact he's recently made the move to Donald McCain's powerful yard and taken out his conditional licence can only do his future prospects the power of good. Born in Yorkshire, Brooke spent a couple of seasons pointing whilst getting his embryonic career under Rules off the ground in a bumper at Market Rasen in late-2007/8. Based with Karen Walton, Brooke credits both the advice of Richie McGrath and the benefit of a stint riding out for Guillame Macaire in France for much of his development.

His first success between the flags came in April 2009, but it wasn't until May of this year to win his first race under Rules aboard Farmer Frank in a hunter at Market Rasen in May and he didn't have to wait long for another when driving home Marlborough Sound in a Hands and Heels race at Towcester later in the month. Brooke sees winning that series as a viable objective, and it surely is all the more so now he has based himself at Cholmondeley. Making the decision to join McCain and turn conditional wasn't an easy one, but it looks set to prove a good call judging by his first few weeks in the job, looking polished when riding his first winner for the yard on Tri Nations at Uttoxeter in September. It'll surely be just the first of a fruitful partnership.

Alex Voy

Name	ALEXANDER VOY
Age	20
Claim	7 lb
Minimum Weight	9-8
First Ride Flat	Woodsley House, Hamilton, 11/06/08
First Ride Jumps	Hurricane Warning, Perth, 3/07/08
First Winner	Strobe, Musselburgh, 1/02/09
Total Winners	16
Best Season	2009/10 (11)
Best Horse Ridden	Wild Cane Ridge
Attached Stable	Lucy Normile

It's fair to say that Scotland hasn't been the hotbed of young National Hunt jockeys in the same way Ireland has down the years. Peter Niven admittedly rode 1,000 winners whilst Ryan Mania and Wilson Renwick are currently making their way in the professional ranks, but these are rarities. It's to be hoped that Alex Voy can build on a very encouraging start to his career, which has seen him impress several observers here at Timeform and on the Northern circuit more widely, and show himself to be at the forefront of this small band.

Raised in Haddington, East Lothian, Voy grew up around horses though not specifically in racing, though the conviction to become a jockey set in during his early teenage years. After one ride on the Flat as an amateur, Voy took out his conditional licence and had his first ride over hurdles at Perth in July 2008. Further opportunities came his way when he made the move to the Perthshire yard of Alan and Lucy Normile later that season, and Voy's first winner came aboard Strobe at Musselburgh in February. Eleven winners from one hundred and thirty rides to a level-stakes profit was a highly encouraging return in 2009/10, with the highlight being a win on the Sue Smith-trained Leac An Scail in what was a valuable handicap chase by Hexham's standards. Voy continues to look increasingly effective in the saddle and strong in a finish, so it will be a major surprise if momentum doesn't mean even more impressive results follow in 2010/11, especially with the likelihood of more and more rides not just for the Normile's but as other trainers sit up and take notice too.

JURY

OVER £13,000 PROFIT IN FIRST 2 YEARS[*]

Brought to you by the expert Timeform panel.

It's the best verdict on the day's racing!

Find out more and view a list of **all bets** advised at **timeform.com/jury**

☎ **01422 330540**
🖱 **timeform.com/shop**

*Based on £50 per point at advised prices 10/09/08 – 31/08/10.

TIMEFORM
THE HOME OF WINNERS SINCE 1948

Ante-Post Betting

'Infuriating', 'frustrating' and 'plain unfair' are just some of the terms which can be used to sum up the perils of ante-post betting. Indeed, National Hunt history is littered with hard-luck stories for ante-post punters, a list which includes none other than the legendary Red Rum, who'd been a short-priced favourite for several weeks to claim his fourth Grand National win in 1978 only to miss the race after injuring a foot during one of his final pre-race gallops on the beach at Southport—an ironic turn of events given that his seaside base was often cited as the reason Red Rum remained sound for the bulk of his career. Fans of Spanish Steps, who was one of Red Rum's regular rivals at Aintree, were also very unlucky to do their money on the gelding in the ante-post book for the 1971 Cheltenham Gold Cup, when he was amongst the market leaders but wasn't declared for the big race due to an administrative slip-up. High-class hurdler Relkeel didn't prove anything like so durable as either Red Rum or Spanish Steps, yet plenty of ante-post punters still got their fingers badly burnt due to his non-appearances at the Cheltenham Festival during the 'nineties, notably late withdrawals from the Champion Hurdle in both 1995 (heat in tendon 24 hours beforehand) and 1997 (bad pelvic injury on last serious piece of work 48 hours beforehand). Even the latest renewal of the Champion Hurdle wasn't the most satisfactory of outcomes for ante-post backers, with supporters of runner-up Khyber Kim understandably miffed to be be beaten by a horse who'd been declared a non-runner on February 17th, only for a U-turn by his connections merely days before the big race. Even winning punters were left frustrated as the horse in question, Binocular, was tipped in these pages last year for the 2010 Champion Hurdle at 6/1, yet his SP on the day itself was 9/1!

Despite that backdrop, ante-post betting can still be a rewarding exercise and arguably possesses fewer risks since the advent of Betfair, with punters now having the option to lay off bets on the exchanges should their selection's odds shorten significantly during the build-up to the race. The latter policy, of course, rewards any speculative wagers on carefully-selected outsiders who progress well over the winter and this appeals as the best approach for the big races in 2010/11, rather than siding with the established market leaders. For example, Kauto Star is currently favourite in most lists for both the King George VI Chase (2/1) and the Cheltenham Gold Cup (5/1), yet there seems to be little value in either price given the aforementioned risks involved with ante-post betting, whilst it is also worth noting that this outstanding chaser is now rising eleven and is likely to be taking on a fresh set of rivals this winter. Imperial Commander, of course, emerged as a very serious rival to Kauto Star last season, going down by just a nose to him in the Betfair Chase at Haydock before taking his Cheltenham Gold Cup crown in March (Kauto Star looked held when falling four out), so his supporters could well be tempted by the 12/1 on offer about him for the King George VI Chase, particularly as there is very little between the pair in the ante-post market for the Cheltenham showpiece. Admittedly, Imperial Commander has flopped in the last two renewals of the King George, but he has had excuses on both occasions and it must be stressed that his defeat of Denman last March ranks amongst the best Gold Cup performances in the race's long history. However, it may pay to side with a couple of last season's leading novice chasers, **Punchestowns** and **Diamond Harry**, who both figure at much bigger odds than would have been the case had they not flopped in the RSA Chase at Cheltenham on their final 2009/10 outing. Lack of chasing experience is a plausible excuse for the

High-class hurdler Diamond Harry remains likely to do better over fences

geldings' Cheltenham flops, with Punchestowns also reported to have returned lame after losing a shoe that day. Both had looked top-class prospects when winning their previous two starts over fences, whilst their overall records make for very impressive reading—neither had finished outside of the first three prior to the RSA Chase. In addition, Punchestowns and Diamond Harry can boast a higher level of form over hurdles than the vast majority of horses who are sent chasing and seem sure to emerge as serious big-race contenders should they regain the winning thread on their return this autumn. Therefore, a small interest is advised on either Punchestowns (16/1 and 20/1) or Diamond Harry (33/1 and 25/1) for the King George VI Chase and Cheltenham Gold Cup, with even bigger odds typically available on Betfair.

The Willie Mullins-trained Mikael d'Haguenet was, of course, the first horse to defeat Diamond Harry over hurdles and remains a very exciting chasing prospect despite being forced to sit out 2009/10 due to a series of minor training setbacks. However, his suitability as an ante-post selection is compromised by the lack of an obvious big-race target—he currently figures in the ante-post lists for four Cheltenham Festival races (Arkle, RSA Chase, Queen Mother Champion and Gold Cup)! Different concerns apply to another of Ireland's leading chasing hopes, Joncol, whose connections have deliberately sidestepped the last two Cheltenham Festivals and seem unlikely to risk the giant gelding on anything other than testing ground, which rarely prevail at Prestbury Park on Gold Cup day nowadays. The Irish challenge for the Queen Mother Champion Chase is much more clearly defined, however, with reigning titleholder Big Zeb (a worthy ante-post favourite alongside dual winner Master Minded) heading a strong team that also includes the likes of Arkle winner Sizing Europe, 2010 runner-up Forpadydeplasterer, multiple Grade 1 winner Golden Silver and leading novice Captain Cee Bee. The last-named gelding arguably ranks as the best value at 16/1, but his lightly-raced profile must temper enthusiasm, as does the fact he burst a blood vessel on his most recent Cheltenham Festival visit.

Training problems have also proved a recurring issue so far for Ireland's leading Champion Hurdle hope Hurricane Fly, whose best price of 6/1 for hurdling's blue riband event seems rather stingy given that the gelding has been forced to sit out the last two Cheltenham Festivals due to injury. In addition, that quote doesn't appeal as particularly good value when compared to the 16/1 on offer about Solwhit, who was beaten just a neck by Hurricane Fly in a thrilling finish to the Rabobank Champion Hurdle at Punchestown in April and had actually come out on top on their only previous meeting earlier in the season. Solwhit is a proven Grade 1 performer (five wins

Solwhit (centre) gets the better of Hurricane Fly (right) and represents the best value amongst Ireland's Champion Hurdle contenders

already at that level) and can boast a more consistent record than most of his contemporaries. Admittedly, his sole below-par effort during the past eighteen months came in the 2010 Champion Hurdle, when he could manage only a one-paced sixth behind Binocular, but he clearly wasn't himself that day after suffering a late training setback (needed treatment after scoping dirty the week beforehand) and is well worth another try in the race. On a negative note, trainer Charles Byrnes has voiced concerns that Cheltenham may not suit Solwhit, but it is still worth chancing an investment on Solwhit for the Champion, particularly as his price is likely to shorten if he again tastes success in the trial races over the winter (thereby giving exchange punters the option to lay their bet off). Another Irish raider who is likely to prove popular in the 2011 Champion Hurdle ante-post betting is the Dermot Weld-trained Rite of Passage, who was one of the leading novice hurdlers of 2009/10, though owes his lofty place in the market (16/1) due to his surprise win in the Gold Cup at Royal Ascot in June. Weld, of course, isn't adverse to running his top Flat horses over hurdles—his Melbourne Cup winner Vintage Crop was a highly creditable sixth in the 1993 Champion Hurdle on just his third outing over timber—but it is probably best to reserve judgement on Rite of Passage until a final decision is made as to whether the gelding makes his own tilt at that Australian prize this November.

A better alternative from last season's crop of novices could come from the juvenile ranks, namely the Nicky Henderson-trained French import Soldatino, who is unbeaten in two starts on British soil, including the Triumph Hurdle at Cheltenham in March. Indeed, backing the Triumph winner in the following season's Champion Hurdle hasn't proved a bad policy in recent years, with Katchit winning the big one at 10/1 in 2008 (fellow five-year-old Punjabi was third at 25/1), Celestial Halo runner-up at 17/2 in 2009 (fellow five-year-old Binocular was a close third) and Zaynar third at 15/2 in 2010. As those results would suggest, there has been a higher standard of Flat recruits to the juvenile hurdling ranks of late which means the other leading four-year-olds from last season shouldn't be dismissed from Champion calculations at this stage, notably Sanctuaire and Alaivan. However, Soldatino makes the most appeal of this bunch and looks overpriced at 25/1 for the Champion, particularly as he looks open to a fair bit more improvement and seems sure to have the services of stable jockey Barry Geraghty (stable-companion Binocular, currently 3/1 favourite, is partnered by his owner's retained jockey Tony McCoy). In addition, it is impossible to overlook Henderson's impressive record in this race—he now has five wins thanks to See You Then (1985, 86 and 87), Punjabi (2009) and Binocular (2010), whilst the yard has also saddled a placed runner in four of the last ten renewals.

Henderson, of course, has saddled more Cheltenham Festival winners than any other trainer currently holding a licence and he has at least one represent-ative prominent in most of the ante-post markets already on offer for the 2011 meeting. In truth, there isn't much value to be found in these lists, especially in those for the meeting's top novice events over both hurdles and chases. The latter category is clearly fraught with danger, as the vast majority of horses quoted have yet to jump a fence in public, but anyone wishing to have an ante-post interest in this grade could do a lot worse than the 14/1 currently on offer about Tell Massini for the RSA Chase. Tom George's physically-imposing six-year-old tasted success in a maiden Irish point before joining present connections and was arguably the best staying novice hurdler of 2009/10 despite flopping at the Cheltenham Festival. A bacterial infection was to blame for Tell Massini's tame capitulation when favourite for the Spa Hurdle but, if anything, the result of that race merely enhanced his reputation as two of the first three home were horses he'd hammered earlier in the season. Two other horses he'd beaten convincingly when notching up a three-timer in 2009/10 were Chamirey and Reve de Sivola, who also boosted Tell Massini's form with fine placed efforts in the Pertemps Final and the Baring Bingham Hurdle respectively elsewhere at the Festival. Reve de Sivola went on to taste Grade 1 success at the Punchestown Festival and actually figures at shorter odds that Tell Massini in the RSA betting, despite the fact that jumping has proved far from his strong suit over the smaller obstacles. By contrast, Tell Massini impressed with his fluency last winter and seems sure to come into his own over fences. In addition, he seems certain to line up in the RSA Chase should everything go to plan, whereas plenty of the other names towards the head of this ante-post market have other possible Cheltenham Festival targets.

The biggest betting race of the year is the Grand National, though there usually isn't much room for manoeuvre in the ante-post market some seven months before the big race itself. That isn't strictly the case this time around, however, as Denman figures as the clear ante-post favourite in most firm's lists, yet will almost certainly miss the Aintree showpiece if recent murmouring from the Paul Nicholls camp is to be believed. As a result, several genuine National hopefuls figure at bigger odds than might have been the case, including Denman's stable-companion **Tricky Trickster**, who is widely available at 40/1. Tricky Trickster spent much of last winter at the head of the Grand National betting, particularly after his last-gasp victory over Niche Market (now also trained by Nicholls) after Denman had unseated in the AON Chase at Newbury. Things didn't go to plan after that win and he could manage only ninth in both the Cheltenham Gold Cup and Grand National, though he didn't enjoy much luck at Aintree (hampered by a couple of fallers) and could never land a serious blow as a result. On a positive note, previous experience of the National course increasingly seems an asset nowadays and Tricky Trickster took pretty well to the fences, whilst he clearly also has age on his side to develop into a National horse. The latter also applies to the Ferdy Murphy-trained Galant Nuit, who makes some appeal at 33/1, though he is reported at this stage as likely to wait until 2012 to make his Grand National debut. Instead, it could pay to have a small interest at 50/1 on **Maljimar**, who was making eye-catching headway from mid-division (tracking eventual winner Don't Push It) when falling at second Becher's in the latest National. Maljimar seems best fresh and trainer Nick Williams will almost certainly gear another light campaign around Aintree. Incidentally, the ambitious Williams was quoted as early as last winter with his plans to climb up the trainers' championship table in 2010/11: 'If you win the Champion Hurdle, the Gold Cup and the Grand National—that's Me Voici, Diamond Harry and Maljimar next season—you're bound to be in the top three.' Time will tell whether we were foolish to include only two of that trio in our ante-post suggestions but, for the record, the treble would come to 54,365/1 at this stage!

Ante-Post Selections

Diamond Harry *King George VI Chase (33/1) & Cheltenham Gold Cup (25/1)*
Punchestowns *King George VI Chase (16/1) & Cheltenham Gold Cup (20/1)*
Soldatino *Champion Hurdle (25/1)*
Solwhit *Champion Hurdle (16/1)*
Tell Massini *RSA Chase (14/1)*
Tricky Trickster *Grand National (40/1)*
Maljimar *Grand National (50/1)*

In Perspective

The daily reports of Timeform's representatives on the course form the basis of *Timeform Perspective*. Their observations, supplemented by those of Timeform's handicappers and comment writers, make *Timeform Perspective* thoroughly informative. Here are some key races from last season chosen from the Timeform Form-Book.

2238 Paddy Power Gold Cup Chase (Hcap) (Gr 3)   2½m110y (15)
(1) (161) (4yo+) £85,515

1982 *	TRANQUIL SEA (IRE) *EJO'Grady,Ireland* 7-10-13¹⁴⁸ AJMcNamara... 13/2 11/2f	1
1754 *	POQUELIN (FR) *PFNicholls* 6-11-1¹⁵⁰ RWalsh 12/1 4½ 2
1969 ⁵	HOLD EM (IRE) *WKGoldsworthy* 7-10-0¹³⁵ (s+t) JamieMoore... 20 14/1 2 3
3945 pu	BALLYFITZ *NATwiston-Davies* 9-10-11¹⁴⁶ PJBrennan............... 11/2 6/1 3½ 4
3213 ⁴	According To Pete *JMJefferson* 8-10-7¹⁴² PhilKinsella 10 9/1 5 5
4354 ⁴	Our Vic (IRE) *DEPipe* 11-11-9¹⁶¹ (h) DannyCook³ 25/1 6 6
2986	Il Duce (IRE) *MrsPRobeson* 9-10-7¹⁴⁵ (b) SPJones³ 40/1 7 7
1852	Tartak (FR) *TRGeorge* 6-11-5¹⁵⁴ SamThomas.......................... 18/1 24 8
4596 ²	Chapoturgeon (FR) *PFNicholls* 5-11-4¹⁵³ TimmyMurphy........... 13/2 7/1 f
86 ⁵	Tatenen (FR) *PFNicholls* 5-11-0¹⁴⁹ (t) ChristianWilliams ..... 10 12/1 ur
1852 ³	Knowhere (IRE) *NATwiston-Davies* 11-11-0¹⁵⁴ TMolloy⁵........... 20/1 pu
1420 *	Northern Alliance (IRE) *AJMartin,Ireland* 8-10-12¹⁴⁷ PCarberry..... 10/1 pu
91 *	Tarotino (FR) *AKing* 7-10-10¹⁴⁵ RobertThornton.................. 14 12/1 pu
1977 pu	My Petra *NJHenderson* 6-10-10¹⁴⁵ APMcCoy .... 16/1 pu
4356	I'm So Lucky *DEPipe* 7-10-4¹³⁹ (t) TomScudamore..................... 28/1 pu
1852 ⁶	Three Mirrors *FerdyMurphy* 9-10-1¹³⁶ GLee .... 33/1 pu

2.35race Mr Nelius Hayes 16ran 5m22.86

The first major handicap of the winter, typically featuring a host of second season chasers, several of them coming to the fore, including the authoritative winner, whilst others further back will prove bigger forces in similar events, conditions rather taking their toll this day with half the field failing to finish; the gallop was sound. **Tranquil Sea**'s novice season consisted of only 4 starts and he's only now coming of age, revealing himself a high-class chaser as he built on his recent Naas success with a similarly polished display here, looking a contender for the Ryanair at even this early stage, jumping superbly and giving a competitive handicap a markedly one-sided look, coming there easily going down the hill and no more than shaken up to put a seal on things from the last, winning with more in reserve; a tilt at some of the top 2m races this side of the Festival may also be worthwhile (speedy sort). **Poquelin** improved further on the face of things from 11 lb higher than when winning here last month, though his performance wasn't entirely convincing (had shown his best previously away from the mud), lapses in his jumping returning, getting well behind as a result, merely running through late having looked booked for more like sixth or seventh 2 fences out. **Hold Em** has lots of strong form, this the fourth time he's made the frame in a highly-competitive handicap, but that point also underlines his vulnerability to anything progressive, having no excuses this day, a mistake when in front at the second last just part of his package. **Ballyfitz** was a very useful novice prior to losing his way towards the end of last season, and returned to that level on the back of market confidence through the week, promising to do even better back over further (stays 25f), staying on to good effect after being outpaced; he could do with jumping better though (scrappy at times). **According To Pete** ran respectably on the back of a couple of Flat starts, making a couple of slight mistakes but found out by the drop in trip more than anything (will stay beyond 25f); he's had only 5 starts over fences, and shaped well from 3 lb higher than this when fourth in last season's Skybet at Doncaster. **Our Vic** is a long way off being the same horse he was in 2007/8, but this was at least much better than his 3 runs last season, going with enthusiasm in front and not giving in easily once headed; how much racing he'll stand is questionable, however, given the problems he's had (has bled). **Il Duce** is neither consistent nor genuine, but on his day he's capable of making an impact in these valuable handicaps (fourth in this from 3 lb higher in 2008), and, having left Alan King since last seen in January, he shaped as though retaining his ability, looking set to play a major part at the top of the hill, his absence possibly an issue in the end. **Tartak** was so tough last season that it's hard to believe there's not something bothering him at present, way below form on both starts this time around, his jumping again not what is was. **Chapoturgeon**'s facile Jewson win suggests this mark isn't all that harsh, but his jumping has let him down since, his fall at the eighth by no means his first mistake here. **Tatenen** impressed with his jumping when starting out last season but was anything but convincing on that score tried tongue tied here, blundering his way round, eventually unseating 3 out. **Knowhere**'s jumping is worse than ever and he just didn't seem interested here. **Northern Alliance** remains unexposed to a point, coming to this on the back of a career-best, just not himself here, his being hampered by Chapoturgeon's fall hardly a help. **Tarotino** earned his 15 lb rise at Bangor back in the spring, simply not in the same form here, markedly softer conditions a plausible issue, failing to jump anything like so well as he can, whilst those from his stable have tended to need a run to put them right this autumn, too. **My Petra**'s jumping has come unstuck in competitive handicaps the last 3 times she's run over fences. **I'm So Lucky** struggled in similar events at the backend of last season and was pulled up sharply on the final circuit returning. **Three Mirrors** sadly broke down fatally.

2390 Betfair Chase (Lancashire) (Gr 1) (1) (5yo+) 3m (18)
£112,660

3972*	KAUTO STAR (FR) *PFNicholls* 9-11-7 (t) RWalsh 8/11 4/6f	1
65 pu	IMPERIAL COMMANDER (IRE) *NATwiston-Davies* 8-11-7 PJBrennan 9/1	ns 2
4354*	MADISON DU BERLAIS (FR) *DEPipe* 8-11-7 (s) TomScudamore 15/2 6/1	24 3
3972 pu	Halcon Genelardais (FR) *AKing* 9-11-7 WayneHutchinson 20 18/1	1½ 4
2108 †	Notre Pere (FR) *JTRDreaper,Ireland* 8-11-7 (s) AELynch 7/2 4/1	24 5
4376 pu	Rambling Minster *KGReveley* 11-11-7 JamesReveley 66/1	dist 6
813 pu	Seymour Weld *CTPogson* 9-11-7 AdamPogson 200/1	dist 7

2.55race Mr Clive D. Smith 7ran 6m04.49

Another top-class renewal, and an epic duel between the Gold Cup and Ryanair winners, chinks in the remainder having been exposed fully 5 out in a race run at championship pace, Kauto Star pushed closer than for any of his previous 11 Grade 1 successes in a race where the balance changed several times in the straight, the photograph taking some time to decipher, with the narrow margin setting the scene for further pulsating clashes between the pair in the King George and Gold Cup later in the campaign. **Kauto Star** erased the memory of a subdued performance in 2008 as he lifted this prize for the third time in its 5-year history, landing his twelfth Grade 1 all told, and setting himself up for an attempt at equalling Desert Orchid's record of 4 King Georges, very much stamping himself as the one to beat again as he gained a hard-fought verdict over a rival who is likely to be his main threat at Kempton, this likely to put an edge on him if anything, travelling and jumping with his usual fluency, but hard at work 2 lengths down when Imperial Commander let him back in 3 out, holding a clear advantage after the next then joined at the last and having to dig deep to snatch the verdict on the nod (odds against on Betfair in the photo). **Imperial Commander** lifted both the Paddy Power and Ryanair at Cheltenham in 2008/9 but took his form to another level again on his first start since his disappointing effort at Punchestown in the spring, stamping himself as a tip-top chaser as he made Kauto Star pull out all the stops, looking to have that one at full stretch until his getting in tight 3 out cost him his 2-length advantage, digging deep to get back upsides at the last and looking to be just about shading it going to the line only to lose out on the nod, very much proving himself at 3m, promising to stay the Gold Cup trip in fact (has gained 5 of his 6 career successes at Cheltenham); he's been superbly handled through a light career so far and looks the main threat to Kauto Star's King George crown now, with suggestions that he's not so effective right-handed premature to say the least, his stable having been badly out of form when a remote sixth in that race last year. **Madison du Berlais** established himself as a top-class staying chaser in 2008/9, winning 3 of his 4 starts once cheekpieces had been applied, and should get back to that level with this behind him, tending to need a run to put him right, happier once he'd got to the front approaching the sixth here only to be left behind by the front 2 following errors at the last 2 in the back straight. **Halcon Genelardais** tends to be vulnerable in the top conditions races given the stamina test he needs, but has a good record in the Welsh National, placed under top weight in both renewals since his win, and will likely head there in form again, this no bad return considering those from his stable have been needing a run, sticking to his task having predictably been off the bridle from halfway, every chance with the third at the last. **Notre Pere** proved himself top class earlier in the year, seemingly not right 2 weeks on from his Down Royal fall here, his rider never truly happy from halfway, already in trouble when a mistake 5 out sealed his fate. **Rambling Minster** proved himself better than ever in staying handicaps last season, the second of his wins in a heavy-ground Blue Square Gold Cup here in February, and he should remain competitive back in that sphere from his current mark, having little realistic chance here, essentially hunted round in his own

time. **Seymour Weld**, who looks up against it in handicaps from a mark of 135, was well out of his depth on his first start for 5 months here, dropping through the field as early as the seventh having set off in front.

2533	Hennessy Gold Cup Chase (Hcap) (Gr 3) (174) (4yo+) £114,020	3¼m110y (21)
4354 [1]	DENMAN (IRE) *PFNicholls* 9-11-12[174] RWalsh	7/2 11/4f	1
4622 *	WHAT A FRIEND *PFNicholls* 6-10-4[152] SamThomas	7/1	3½ 2
2103	NICHE MARKET (IRE) *RHBuckler* 8-9-11[148] AndrewGlassonbury³	33/1	3¾ 3
3972	BARBERS SHOP *NJHenderson* 7-10-8[156] (s) BarryGeraghty	13/2	sh 4
1969	Gone To Lunch (IRE) *JScott* 9-10-3[151] SeamusDurack	16/1	6 5
3943 [6]	Kornati Kid *PJHobbs* 7-10-0[148] RichardJohnson	33/1	16 6
2108 [2]	My Will (FR) *PFNicholls* 9-10-9[157] NickScholfield	28/1	8 7
359 *	Snowy Morning (IRE) *WPMullins, Ireland* 9-10-2[150] PaulTownend	16 14/1	7 8
2103 [6]	Nenuphar Collonges (FR) *AKing* 8-10-0[148] (b) RobertThornton . 20 14/1	14 9
2108 [5]	Joe Lively (IRE) *CLTizzard* 10-10-7[162] GilesHawkins⁷	33/1	5 10
2108 [3]	War of Attrition (IRE) *MFMorris, Ireland* 10-10-6[154] NiallMadden .. 33/1	nk 11
2237 [6]	Chelsea Harbour (IRE) *ThomasMullins, Ireland* 9-10-0[148] (b) AELynch	66/1	1 12
1879 [3]	Cappa Bleu (IRE) *EvanWilliams* 9-10-0[148] (t) WayneHutchinson .. 12/1	1
1910	Offshore Account (IRE) *CFSwan, Ireland* 9-10-0[148] (t) DJCasey 40/1	ur
4376 *	Mon Mome (FR) *MissVenetiaWilliams* 9-10-13[161] AidanColeman. 40/1	pu
1990 [2]	Killyglen (IRE) *JHowardJohnson* 7-10-6[154] DenisO'Regan 15/2	pu
3401 [no]	An Accordion (IRE) *DEPipe* 8-10-4[152] (b+t) TomScudamore....... 28/1	pu
2238 [4]	Ballyfitz *NATwiston-Davies* 9-10-0[148] PaddyBrennan 16 14/1	pu
4376 [4]	State of Play *EvanWilliams* 9-10-0[148] PaulMuloney................ 12/1	pu

2.40race Mr Paul K Barber & Mrs M Findlay 19ran 6m39.59

A Hennessy to savour, Denman producing an outstanding performance as he defied a mark as high as 174 (some 13 lb higher than in 2007), emulating Arkle and Mandarin in becoming only the third dual winner, getting the better of an up-and-coming stablemate, with solid and established chasers filling the frame; the gallop was sound, though still few got into things as 3 of the first 4 raced handily, the runner-up the only one to come from further back. **Denman** failed to win during a troubled 2008/9, though proved himself every bit as big a force as he always was brought back this time around, giving upwards of 12 lb all round in the most competitive of handicaps with a performance that epitomised all he's about, jumping boldly close up and displaying an outstanding attitude when joined briefly by the runner-up approaching the last, battling back and powering away, reaffirming that he's certain to stay further should the opportunity ever arise (has been discussed for a Grand National bid in the past); now 5 wins from 5 at Newbury, he'll reportedly use the Aon as a springboard to Cheltenham this time around, and promises to mount a much bigger challenge to Kauto Star come March than he was able to the last time they met. **What A Friend** won 3 from 4 in his novice season, and whilst suffering defeat in the RSA he proved he can do it on the big stage returning, looking to have further depths to his ability too, though whether they can be unlocked remains to be seen, looking awkward in the past and unquestionably hanging fire once upsides Denman approaching the last here, ducking left, soon giving away the initiative. **Niche Market** was back to his best with a run behind him, 3 lb out of the weights on the day, ideally served by more of a test too, lacking the gears of the first 2 in the straight, though maintaining his own effort; the Welsh National looks a possibility for him, and Aintree remains realistic further down the line. **Barbers Shop** returned with a performance right up to his best, in cheekpieces for the first time, the trip seemingly not the problem it had appeared in the Gold Cup, rallying in fact as he missed out on third only narrowly; the Ryanair could still be his best long-term target, likely to avoid Denman and Kauto Star for one. **Gone To Lunch** is a thorough stayer, his standout effort having come on the only occasion he's had full use made of that, and, more than any of these, he strikes as a leading contender for the Welsh National, tough and reliable as he is, doing more than enough here to suggest he's in good order, sticking on after being shuffled back to a poor position around halfway. **Kornati Kid** is badly handicapped on the face of it, but there is better to come from him, in only his second season over fences and catching the eye on this return, failing to jump quite as he can, but still within himself leaving the back straight and not subjected to a hard time, finishing with a bit left to give; he should be fully effective at this sort of trip, though didn't stay 4m in last season's National Hunt Chase. **My Will** is reliable and shouldn't

be judged on this, in a difficult position as it went (held up and widest of all), still doing better than most from off the pace. **Snowy Morning** has returned from 6 months off in better form than this bare result indicates, going smoothly but too far back and in sixth when blundering at the second last, almost unseating and eased off; he'd been tongue tied for his last 5 starts incidentally. **Nenuphar Collonges** is lazy and doesn't jump well, so needs treating with a certain amount of caution, particularly with his mark dictating he contests competitive races more often than not. **Joe Lively** is too high in the weights, his Cotwold success last year standing way above anything else he's achieved, whilst it was disappointing to see him put in such a messy round of jumping here, given that's usually his key asset. **War of Attrition** is still a smart chaser on his day, proven with recent placed efforts in Ireland, but such competitive races as this are always likely to find him out, jumping sketchily here and folding quickly as the principals pressed on. **Chelsea Harbour** made too many mistakes again, the blinkers making no difference. **Cappa Bleu** perhaps isn't going to progress as first thought, already in trouble here when crashing out at the fifteenth. **Offshore Account** is a sound jumper all in all but paid the price for a bad mistake at the first on this occasion. **Mon Mome** has bigger seasonal targets, primarily a follow-up bid in the Grand National, whilst the Welsh equivalent is less than 4 weeks away, and this first outing since his shock win at Aintree (100/1) will sharpen him up, looking and shaping as if the run was needed. **Killyglen** will need to improve to win a handicap, but he did shape better than the end result, still going smoothly approaching the straight and stopping so sharply that there must have been a problem; his jumping was rather scrappy. **An Accordion**'s problems seem to have got the better of him, this only his second start since winning the William Hill Trophy at Cheltenham in 2008, running as if amiss on both occasions, too. **Ballyfitz's** jumping lets him down when there's pressure on, making several mistakes here and always struggling as a result. **State of Play** has a good record when fresh, this first start since his Grand National fourth disappointing, albeit not persevered with for long.

KEMPTON Saturday, Dec 26

2929	William Hill King George VI Chase (Gr 1) (1)		3m (18)
	(4yo+) £114,020		

2390 *	KAUTO STAR (FR) *PFNicholls* 9-11-10 (t) RWalsh	8/15 8/13f		1
2390 3	MADISON DU BERLAIS (FR) *DEPipe* 8-11-10 (s)		dist	2
	TomScudamore	10/1		
2533 4	BARBERS SHOP (FR) *NJHenderson* 7-11-10 (s) BJGeraghty	14/1	1	3
2531 pu	Nacarat (FR) *TRGeorge* 8-11-10 SamThomas	25/1	3½	4
2390 2	Imperial Commander (IRE) *NATwiston-Davies* 8-11-10		23	5
	PJBrennan	8 13/2		
2740 3	Albertas Run (IRE) *JonjoO'Neill* 8-11-10 APMcCoy	25/1	5	6
2740 2	Tartak (FR) *TRGeorge* 6-11-10 DenisO'Regan	25/1	2½	7
2789 ro	Our Vic (IRE) *DEPipe* 11-11-10 (b) TimmyMurphy	40/1	17	8
1978 3	Ollie Magern *NATwiston-Davies* 11-11-10 TMolloy	100/1	1	9
2734 4	Sandymac (IRE) *GLMoore* 9-11-3 AndrewGlassonbury	200/1	8	10
2740 *	Deep Purple *EvanWilliams* 8-11-10 PaulMoloney	14 17/2		pu
2381 2	Master Medic (IRE) *RH&MrsSAlner* 8-11-10 RobertWalford	33/1		pu
2740 5	Racing Demon (IRE) *MissHCKnight* 8-11-10 GLee	100/1		pu

3.05race Mr Clive D. Smith 13ran 6m07.01

A representative field, for all it lacked Denman, headed by the winner for the last 3 years Kauto Star but also including winners in 2009 of the Ryanair, the Bowl at Aintree and the Charlie Hall, as well as 3 that had been placed in this race previously; all bar one of that sextet was well below form but that was chiefly due to the searching pace that was set by Ollie Magern and Nacarat, one with which only Kauto Star was truly able to cope, his outstanding performance not only the best in this race in the last 40 years but surpassed in Timeform's experience over jumps by only Arkle and Flyingbolt. **Kauto Star** produced a stunning, near-perfect performance, the best of his already stellar career, his ability to cope so much better than his rivals with the searching gallop and the supreme accuracy of his jumping hallmarks of a truly outstanding chaser, the way he sauntered clear in the straight to win with seemingly a good deal left likely to live long in the memory of all those fortunate enough to witness it, this fourth straight King George success equalling Desert Orchid's tally, and in terms of performance bettering the form shown by the horse that made this race his own; so far as the Cheltenham Gold Cup is concerned, Kauto Star already has the best performance in that race in the last 40 years to his name and if he is on song—and there have been few more genuine and reliable horses in the history of the sport—he will be virtually impossible to beat, his supposed vulnerability to Denman on soft ground a red herring. **Madison du Berlais's** position owed much to his and his rider's perseverance, seemingly not at his best, looking to be going nowhere in the back straight (tending to hang under pressure) but plugging on dourly to take second on the run-in, a bit flattered to beat the pair behind him on the day. **Barbers Shop**, again in cheekpieces, ran his best race yet, though even back at 3m he didn't finish the race so strongly as he might have done, giving chase to the winner after 3 out only to lose second after the last; he's well worth a try over short of 3m again and races like the Ascot Chase and the Ryanair would be worth considering. **Nacarat** set the race up and deserved to finish second, showing his true form for the first time this season, getting all bar the winner in trouble a long way out with a bold display of jumping in front but having nothing left in the straight, a mistake at the last when still pressing for second also taking its toll; this course clearly suits him well and a run under presumably top weight in the Racing Post Chase might be an option rather than alternatives in conditions events. **Imperial Commander** surely wouldn't have got close to Kauto Star whatever on this occasion but his chance was effectively gone when making a bad mistake at the second, nearly unseating his rider and never on terms after, making another error at the fifth, his finishing effort saying a fair bit for his resolution; if it doesn't come too soon then the Cotswold Chase might be a pre-Festival option for him. **Albertas Run** hasn't come close to the form of his second to Kauto Star in the 2008 running in 7 outings since, struggling towards the rear at halfway on this occasion. **Tartak** shaped better than the distances indicate, travelling more comfortably than most early on the final circuit and jumping better than he had previously this season before being left behind after 6 out; he may be of interest at a more realistic level next time. **Our Vic** is nothing like the horse that was second to Kauto Star in the 2007 running, struggling with the pace soon after halfway. **Ollie Magern** helped ensure a true test but his exertions predictably told and he was left well behind in the last mile. **Deep Purple** clearly wasn't himself and was later reported to have bled. **Master Medic** was up considerably in trip but was essentially outclassed rather than outstayed, labouring before the eleventh and plugging on in around sixth when he seemed to have a problem and pulled up sharply before 3 out. **Racing Demon** looks completely out of sorts.

3012 Lexus Chase (Gr 1) (5yo+) £83,784   3m (17)

2533²	WHAT A FRIEND PFNicholls,GB 6-11-10 SamThomas	11/2	1
2685*	MONEY TRIX (IRE) NGRichards,GB 9-11-10 DNRussell	14/1	½ 2
2701*	JONCOL (IRE) PaulNolan 6-11-10 APCawley	7/2	1¼ 3
2390⁵	Notre Pere (FR) JTRDreaper 8-11-10 (s) AELynch	5/1	14 4
2383⁴	Schindlers Hunt (IRE) DTHughes 9-11-10 RLoughran	16/1	4½ 5
2383³	Voy Por Ustedes (FR) AKing,GB 8-11-10 RobertThornton	13/2	½ 6
2701³	J'Y Vole (FR) WPMullins 6-11-5 DJCasey	25/1	15 7
2701¹	Aran Concerto (IRE) NMeade 8-11-10 DJCondon	14/1	pu
2680⁵	Cane Brake (IRE) TJTaaffe 10-11-10 (s) JLCullen	25/1	pu
46⁴	Cooldine (IRE) WPMullins 7-11-10 PaulTownend	10/3f	pu
2701²	In Compliance (IRE) DTHughes 9-11-10 PWFlood	14/1	pu

1.25race Mr Ged Mason & Sir Alex Ferguson 11ran 6m33.40

A slightly below-par renewal of this Grade 1 chase and the fact that it went for export for the fifth time in 7 years was further confirmation, if it were needed, of the current dearth of talent in this department in Ireland; that said, Cooldine had a legitimate excuse for his poor showing and Joncol was arguably a bit better than the bare form; the pace steadied a bit mid-race but was sound overall and it turned into a test of stamina. **What A Friend** paid a handsome compliment to Denman who gave him 22 lb in the Hennessy and, though he carried his head a bit high, looked far more resolute than has often been the case in the past, under pressure turning for home but finding plenty to lead halfway up the run-in; he's a sound jumper and may still have more to offer provided his temperament continues to hold up (this only his sixth start over fences), but his earlier run at Newbury does show how much he needs to improve to trouble his more illustrious stable-companion if lining up for the Gold Cup in March, not to mention Kauto Star. **Money Trix** improved again to keep up his record of never having been out of the first two when completing, jumping as well as he has ever done over fences, ridden more patiently than usual and staying on strongly from 2 out to very nearly snatch an unlikely victory; he will reportedly head back here in February for the Hennessy, and more testing ground could aid his chances of going one better given that stamina looks his strong suit. **Joncol** was helped by the rain which fell in the 23 hrs after the original post time but possibly paid the price for attempting to match strides with Notre Pere, leading narrowly when losing momentum with his only notable error 3 out and holding a clear advantage rounding the home turn, only to drift right on the run-in having jumped that way at the last; this effort merely underlines that he isn't yet up to Gold Cup class (still only 6) but that won't stop him running a big race in the Hennessy back here in February. **Notre Pere**'s Punchestown win in April is probably best treated with a pinch of salt but this has to go down as another sub-par effort following on from his dismal display at Haydock; he led or disputed the lead, jumped well apart from a mistake at the sixth, but was off the bridle 4 out and couldn't go with the main protaganists from 2 out; it will be interesting to see what weight he is allotted for the Grand National. **Schindlers Hunt** jumped better than last time but merely kept on from mid-field without threatening; his return to form last season coincided with the fitting of a tongue tie so it is somewhat surprising that he hasn't worn one since returning from his summer break. **Voy Por Ustedes** seemed to just about get this trip in the King George last year but it was a different story in these more testing conditions as, having closed onto the heels of the leaders after 3 out, he had nothing left from the next; he was looked after when his chance had gone and will presumably be aimed at the Ryanair Chase at the Festival. **J'Y Vole**'s lacklustre effort can't be blamed entirely on a lack of stamina as she never looked like landing a blow at any stage; she was held up again, jumped soundly apart from going right 5 out, but failed to make any significant impression thereafter. **Aran Concerto** may not have fully recovered from the heavy fall he took last time, beaten well before stamina became an issue, already detached when pulled up before 6 out; he is obviously hard to train and it looks a case of back to the drawing board with him now. **Cane Brake** finished third in this last year but was a spent force a long way out this time, eventually pulled up before 2 out. **Cooldine** took a long time to settle in mid-field, was in trouble 4 out and was going up and down on the spot before being pulled up early in the straight; this run was clearly too bad to be true and he was subsequently reported to be coughing post race; he won 3 times over fences last season including the P. J. Moriarty here and the RSA Chase at Cheltenham before finishing fourth to Rare Bob at Punchestown in April. **In Compliance** is unlikely to stay this far when conditions are like this and wasn't subjected to a hard time after his chance had gone 3 out, pulled up before the last.

4118	Spinal Research Supreme Nov Hdle (Gr 1) (1) (4yo+) £57,010		2m110y (8)
3672 2	MENORAH (IRE) *PJHobbs* 5-11-7 RichardJohnson	12/1	1
3557 *	GET ME OUT OF HERE (IRE) *JonjoO'Neill* 6-11-7 APMcCoy	11/2 9/2	hd 2
3469 *	DUNGUIB (IRE) *PhilipFenton, Ireland* 7-11-7 BTO'Connell	10/11 4/5f	1¾ 3
3665 *	Oscar Whisky (IRE) *NJHenderson* 5-11-7 BJGeraghty	11/1	2 4
3629 *	Flat Out (FR) *WPMullins, Ireland* 5-11-7 PaulTownend	20/1	6 5
3326 5	Spring Jim *JRFanshawe* 9-11-7 FelixdeGiles	80/1	2½ 6
3341	Fiulin *EvanWilliams* 5-11-7 PaulMoloney	100/1	½ 7
3778 1	Vino Griego (FR) *GLMoore* 5-11-7 JamieMoore	50/1	nk 8
3785 5	Far Away So Close (IRE) *PaulNolan, Ireland* 5-11-7 DNRussell	100/1	½ 9
3369 *	Blackstairmountain (IRE) *WPMullins, Ireland* 5-11-7 RWalsh	11 12/1	nk 10
3640 3	Hollins *MickyHammond* 6-11-7 JasonMaguire	250/1	nk 11
3425 *	Dan Breen (IRE) *DEPipe* 5-11-7 TomScudamore	25/1	3½ 12
3486 2	Dream Esteem *DEPipe* 5-11-0 DannyCook	100/1	4 13
2925 5	Cootehill (IRE) *NATwiston-Davies* 6-11-7 PJBrennan	66/1	8 14
3934 5	Takestan (IRE) *PatrickOBrady, Ireland* 7-11-7 JCullen	200/1	3 15
3200	Chain of Command (IRE) *WJGreatrex* 7-11-7 WayneHutchinson	100/1	½ 16
3594 3	Mister Wall Street (FR) *FerdyMurphy* 5-11-7 GLee	200/1	4 17
3341 2	General Miller *NJHenderson* 5-11-7 AndrewTinkler	25/1	ur

1.30race Mrs Diana L. Whateley 18ran 3m56.53

A Supreme Novices' that had centred around one horse for virtually all the build-up, several likely contenders scared off and running later at the meeting, so the field was lacking a little depth, the absence of good Flat horses who'd made into promising hurdlers particularly notable, and physically, with the exception of no more than half a dozen, including the first 3, these were as ordinary a bunch as has contested this race in a long time; the pace was little more than steady and the outcome turned on speed and tactics, and though the 4 with the best form chances came clear, that was by not nearly so far as they might have done in a truly-run race, several of those behind likely to have been flattered in showing marked improvement, the overall form no more than average for the race. **Menorah** won the day essentially through speed and tactics, his rider atoning for Ascot with a sharp move up the inside 2 out (rather put off at that flight by the wandering Dan Breen), which made the difference, all out to hold on after taking the last 2 lengths to the good; the second and third have at least as much potential for open company next season, but he looks a top prospect for novice chases if sent down that route instead. **Get Me Out of Here** confirmed he's a smart novice for all he met with his first defeat, going down only narrowly on the day and promising to improve past the winner going forward, making up some 2 lengths on his rival from the last (again hung left) after that one had got first run turning in; he'd have been better suited by a truer test promises to stay beyond 2m, likely to make a chaser when the time comes, too. **Dunguib** remains a really bright prospect, the best in this field, despite a first defeat over hurdles, simply undone by overconfident tactics in a race which didn't go his way tactically, dropped out again and taken wide (not entirely fluent on occasions too), sitting further off a steady pace than the other principals and having too much ground to make up on some smart rivals after 2 out, keeping on but no impression after the last; he'll be a short price to gain compensation at Punchestown and whether he is kept to hurdling or goes novice chasing next season he is likely to be a force to be reckoned with in either sphere. **Oscar Whisky** doesn't have quite the physique of the first 3 (though he was outstanding in condition) and came up that bit short with his sights raised, but he has it in him to make a better fist of things another day, at 2m or further, at least if able to brush up his jumping, errors at both the fifth and 2 out counting against him, maintaining his proximity from the last. Flat Out appeared the stable's second string but fared the better of the pair, promising more still when his stamina is drawn out, outpaced 2 out after being well placed but sticking on back through runners late, despite a mistake at the last; he's a lean sort. **Spring Jim** looked an optimistic contender at this level but he appeared to show a useful level of form, on a par with his Flat ability, hitting 3 out and some way off the pace but keeping on well in the straight; it remains to be seen whether this form is reliable, however, and it's sure to have an effect on his handicap mark. **Fiulin** was again highly tried but appeared to show a useful level of form, in keeping with his Flat record, well placed to the fore, rather losing

his place going to 2 out but running back through late in the day, underlining the fact he'll be suited by further. **Vino Griego** ran close to form in face of his stiffest task yet and again didn't obviously do much wrong, further off the pace than ideal 3 out and just staying on; it could well be that he's becoming more straightforward, and he was one of the better types physically (looked in top condition), likely to make a chaser. **Far Away So Close** is one of the more interesting for the future of those behind the first 4, having scope physically and shaping as if having more ability than he's shown, raising his game away from soft/heavy going for the first time, still travelling strongly held up in a poor position when unsettled by a mistake 3 out and taking time to get going again, staying on at the finish; he's bred to be effective beyond 2m and has potential as a novice chaser for next season. **Blackstairmountain** had been impressive on his hurdling debut but the bare form of that left him with a lot of improvement to make to figure here and he wasn't up to the task, dropping away quickly before the last; he was an unimpressive type, not an obvious one to go on progressing. Hollins faced a very stiff task and appeared to run above himself, albeit in a falsely-run race, behind 3 out too before picking off some of the beaten horses; it's to be hoped the handicapper doesn't take a literal view. **Dan Breen** remains with potential at a lower level for all this test proved beyond him, leading 3 out but showing his inexperience when running around on his approach to the next and soon brushed aside. **Dream Esteem** was flying too high, pulling hard in rear after being hampered at the first too; she lacks scope. **Cootehill** has had his limitations exposed several times against top novices, limited potential as far as handicaps go too, though this was a tame effort even so, dropping out once headed 3 from home. **Takestan** was unlikely to be competitive at this level, though his hard-trained appearance (not surprising given how much racing he's had this season) suggested he won't necessarily run to his best even back at the right level. **Chain of Command** was out of his depth. **Mister Wall Street** is a fair novice, but this was unrealistic, mistakes counting against him, too. **General Miller** unseated at the first.

4119 **Irish Independent Arkle Challenge Trophy Chase** 2m (12)
(Gr 1) (1) (5yo+) £85,515

2942 *	SIZING EUROPE (IRE) *HenrydeBromhead,Ireland* 8-11-7 AELynch	6/1		1
2665 *	SOMERSBY (IRE) *MissHCKnight* 6-11-7 RobertThornton	4/1	¾	2
3593 ³	OSANA (FR) *EJO'Grady,Ireland* 8-11-7 (s) AJMcNamara	14/1	1¾	3
3428 ³	Mad Max (IRE) *NJHenderson* 8-11-7 PCarberry	25/1	2¾	4
2953 *	Riverside Theatre *NJHenderson* 6-11-7 BJGeraghty	7/1	3½	5
3652 *	Quiscover Fontaine (FR) *WPMullins,Ireland* 6-11-7 PaulTownend	22/1	5	6
1757 *	Kangaroo Court (IRE) *MissECLavelle* 6-11-7 JackDoyle	22/1	¾	7
3447 *	Captain Cee Bee (IRE) *EPHarty,Ireland* 9-11-7 APMcCoy	3 5/2f	4	8
3447 ²	Fosters Cross (IRE) *ThomasMullins,Ireland* 8-11-7 DNRussell	50/1	2½	9
3428 ²	I'm Delilah *FerdyMurphy* 8-11-0 GLee	25/1	8	10
3232 ²	Sports Line (IRE) *WPMullins,Ireland* 7-11-7 RWalsh	15/2	17/2	nk 11
3428 *	Woolcombe Folly (IRE) *PFNicholls* 7-11-7 NickScholfield	25/1	4½	12

2.05race Ann & Alan Potts Partnership 12ran 3m52.87

An average Arkle in terms of historical standards, indicative of the 2m novices as a whole, the form looking some way shy of the Queen Mother standard at present; the gallop made for a true test and the the first 4 had it between them going to 3 out, a few of the others closing up only late. **Sizing Europe** remains with potential beyond what he's achieved so far, his best hurdles form in advance of this, whilst he's still unbeaten 5 races into his chasing career, his jumping standing up well to this sterner test than for his graded wins in Ireland (all small fields); in excellent shape for this first start since Boxing Day (goes well fresh), he travelled strongly close up throughout, quickened clear on the bridle after Mad Max's blunder 2 out and found enough under pressure up the hill despite being reeled back gradually, putting his weak-finishing past over hurdles behind him. **Somersby**'s progress as a chaser continues apace, stepping up to the mark in face of much his stiffest test yet here, and he's likely to go higher still, ready for 2½m on this evidence, or at least a stiffer test kept around this trip, taking a while to find his stride as the tempo increased heading to 3 out and reeling

the winner in gradually from the second last, still strong at the finish; his jumping is excellent and he has age on his side compared with the other principals. **Osana** produced a bigger performance with cheekpieces fitted, getting closer to Sizing Europe than at Leopardstown on Boxing Day, though still some way short of the best of his hurdles form, having every chance as things went and never looking a likely winner for all he dug in; he is a fluent jumper. **Mad Max** comes with warnings, his career having been stop-start for a reason (has had breathing problems), but this is an indication of his vast ability should it all one day click, improving on anything he'd achieved before despite making a mess of the second last when in front and still travelling well, albeit with Sizing Europe looming, rallying but with no chance after; it's hard to know where he'd have finished, but he's worth at least as much credit as Osana. **Riverside Theatre**'s jumping wasn't so convincing as it had been in 2 chase wins pre-Christmas, and he was behind with the situation accepted at the top of the hill before running through beaten rivals late in the day, his performance not especially easy to weigh up, though after only 3 appearances over fences it certainly shouldn't be suggested that we've necessarily seen the best of him yet (yet to race beyond 2m). **Quiscover Fontaine**'s wins in Ireland came in comparatively weak races and he came up short with his sights raised, albeit on vastly different ground (won bumper on good), not entirely fluent and never getting beyond mid-field. **Kangaroo Court** has come up short both times on the big stage, well beaten in last year's Supreme and now here, bettering his 2 wins on the face of it but making several mistakes and struggling in rear by the ninth, no more than closing up late, albeit promising to benefit from a return to 2½m as he did. **Captain Cee Bee**'s problems that led to his lengthy absence before this season are clearly not behind him, a broken blood vessel explaining his weak finish here, though his jumping let him down before that, anyway, as it had on his previous Grade 1 assignment. **Fosters Cross** is a useful chaser, but he's seemingly exposed with it, well beaten by both Sizing Europe and Captain Cee Bee on his previous 2 outings, and as such his sights need lowering, his consistency sure to stand him in good stead at a realistic level. **I'm Delilah** has developed fast since beaten from a mark of 110 on her chasing debut, and there will be other days for her, clearly not herself here, looking sluggish from the early stages as she was taken on for the lead. **Sports Line** wasn't himself, very edgy in the preliminaries (sweating) and folding quickly after hitting 3 out, having still been on the bridle in touch going to that fence; he'd reportedly failed to settle since travelling across. **Woolcombe Folly**'s jumping didn't stand up to this much stiffer test than at Doncaster (suffered schooling fall previous week), always on the back foot as a result of mistakes; he'd had just one previous try over fences, though, and may still do better in calmer waters.

4121	**Smurfit Kappa Champion Hdle**		2m110y (8)		
	Challenge Trophy (Gr 1) (1) (4yo+) £210,937				
3433*	BINOCULAR (FR) *NJHenderson* 6-11-10 APMcCoy	8 9/1			1
2790*	KHYBER KIM *NATwiston-Davies* 8-11-10 PJBrennan	7/1		3½	2
3644²	ZAYNAR (FR) *NJHenderson* 5-11-10 (s) AndrewTinkler	9 15/2		2½	3
3235⁴	Celestial Halo (FR) *PFNicholls* 6-11-10 (b+t) RWalsh	8 7/1		2½	4
2928²	Starluck (IRE) *AFleming* 5-11-10 TimmyMurphy	12 14/1		ns	5
3235¹	Solwhit (IRE) *CharlesByrnes,Ireland* 6-11-10 DNRussell	7 6/1		6	6
3204*	Medermit (FR) *AKing* 6-11-10 RobertThornton	10 11/1		¾	7
3569²	Jumbo Rio (IRE) *EJO'Grady,Ireland* 5-11-10 AJMcNamara	50/1		4½	8
3776*	Punjabi *NJHenderson* 7-11-10 BJGeraghty	13/2 15/2		1¼	9
2928¹	Go Native (IRE) *NMeade,Ireland* 7-11-10 PCarberry	4 11/4f		hd	10
2264	Raise Your Heart (IRE) *MsJoannaMorgan,Ireland* 7-11-10 JCullen	100/1		nk	11
3807*	Won In The Dark (IRE) *MissSJHarty,Ireland* 6-11-10 GLee	40/1		19	12

3.20race Mr John P. McManus 12ran 3m53.59

An eagerly anticipated Champion, even more so than usual given the twists and turns of the division throughout the season, and it went beyond expectations to a large extent, Binocular's performance the best in the race since Rooster Booster in 2003, and there's no reason to question the result; Celestial Halo ensured a good gallop, immediately stringing them right out, and it eased only briefly mid-race (time around 3 seconds faster than the Supreme), whilst those immediately behind are solid and established high-class hurdlers; Hurricane Fly was the only notable absentee. **Binocular** belatedly produced the top-class performance he'd promised last season, putting his disappointing start to this campaign (his connections had initially ruled him out of Cheltenham after Sandown) behind him in the best possible way, and, now clearly right back to himself, he could easily be a dominating force in the 2m division, certainly judging by the style of this, and he is only a 6-y-o; he travelled and jumped with all of the enthusiasm that had been lacking in the Fighting Fifth and Christmas Hurdle, picking his way through the pack with ease and displaying a sharp turn of foot when asked to hit the front 2 out, the emphasis on speed almost certainly bringing out the very best in him; it was perhaps a wise decision by connections to keep him away from the paddock until very late, as consequently he wasn't so edgy as usual in the preliminaries (still slightly warm/on toes). **Khyber Kim** has developed more than any of these this season, backing up his 2 wins here towards the end of last year with this excellent effort up again in grade, and he should have his day at this level at some stage, his performance good enough to have won some recent runnings of this; whilst Binocular was too strong he in turn stood out from the remainder, cruising through from the rear as that one had, and maintaining his proximity after the last for all he was never going to get there. **Zaynar** is a high-class hurdler, though one who looks ideally suited by further than 2m, certainly when conditions aren't testing, seemingly having his limitations exposed here, likely aided by the gallop, also a positive ride and the reapplication of cheekpieces (which he'd worn previously only when winning Triumph), lacking the gears of the first 2 from the second last: the 2½m Grade 1 at Aintree could well be on his agenda. **Celestial Halo** has failed to show his best in 2 starts since the turn of the year, though this certainly wasn't as flat as he'd been at Leopardstown, doing too much if anything as he went enthusiastically in front with blinkers applied, battling as usual once headed 2 out, too. **Starluck** has established himself as a very smart hurdler this season and may yet do better still, long striking as one ideally suited by a sharp track, looming up with typical menace approaching 2 out here, failing to see things out fully up the hill yet still achieving more than previously. **Solwhit** is bound to bounce back and win more top races, with a defence of his Aintree Hurdle presumably on the agenda, clearly not himself on the back of an interrupted preparation here (reported to have scoped dirty last week). **Medermit**'s defeat of Punjabi in January was rather devalued by that one's performance here and, whilst there's no doubting his status as a very smart hurdler, that's probably as good as he is, found wanting as things really took shape from 2 out. **Jumbo Rio** is a smart hurdler but he's not up to this standard, by no means discredited in the circumstances. **Punjabi** has failed to find the form that saw him lift this last season in 4 starts this winter, Medermit confirming superiority over him from Haydock here, acknowledging that neither were fully on their game. **Go Native**'s season has been a success overall, his 2 Grade 1 wins establishing him amongst the elite 2-milers, and there's no doubt he wasn't himself this day, knocked back by mistakes at the first 2 flights and never really going with the same zest as usual. **Raise Your Heart** had been out of sorts on the Flat in Dubai as recently as 12 days ago and made no impression in face of this very stiff task back over hurdles, his appearing to run close to form potentially misleading. **Won In The Dark** falls short

amongst the best, though something must have been wrong for him to fare so badly.

4123	David Nicholson Mares' Hdle (Gr 2) (1)		2½m (10)
	(4yo+ f+m) £50,697		
459	QUEVEGA (FR) *WPMullins,Ireland* 6-11-5 RWalsh	13/8 6/4f	1
3301 ¹	CAROLE'S LEGACY *NJHenderson* 6-11-0 AndrewTinkler	20/1	4½ 2
3010 ¹	VOLER LA VEDETTE (IRE) *ColmAMurphy,Ireland* 6-11-5		1¼ 3
	BJGeraghty	5/2 9/4	
3429	Amber Brook (IRE) *NATwiston-Davies* 9-11-0 PJBrennan	33/1	3½ 4
3196 ²	Easter Legend *MissECLavelle* 6-11-0 AColeman	14 11/1	½ 5
3343 ¹	Arctic Magic (IRE) *WSKittow* 10-11-0 TJO'Brien	33/1	10 6
122 ⁶	Aura About You (IRE) *PaulNolan,Ireland* 7-11-0 APCawley	28/1	1½ 7
3873 ³	Alasi *PRWebber* 6-11-0 WTKennedy	100/1	3 8
3628 ⁵	No One Tells Me *MrsJHarrington,Ireland* 5-11-3 (s) RMPower	16/1	sh 9
3429	Argento Luna *OSherwood* 7-11-3 SPJones	33/1	1½ 10
3795 ¹	Sway (FR) *JonjoO'Neill* 4-10-11 APMcCoy	10 9/1	1½ 11
3429 ³	Pepite de Soleil (FR) *PFNicholls* 6-11-0 RobertThornton	33/1	17 12
3429 ¹	Zarinava (IRE) *MrsJHarrington,Ireland* 6-11-5 PaulMoloney	25/1	9 13
3486	Princess Rainbow (FR) *JennieCandlish* 5-11-0 AlanO'Keeffe	20/1	2 14
3823 ²	Just Beware *MissZCDavison* 8-11-0 (s)		28 15
	GemmaGracey-Davison	200/1	
3808	Here Comes Sally (IRE) *PaulPierce,Ireland* 10-11-0		dist 16
	SWFlanagan	100/1	
3557	Stravinsky Dance *NJHenderson* 5-11-5 (b) MrsSWaley-Cohen	50/1	pu

4.40race Hammer & Trowel Syndicate 17ran 4m45.69

A race that invariably has limited depth despite there being plenty of runners and Quevega didn't have to reproduce the very smart form of her runaway success of a year earlier to gain her second Festival win; Stravinsky Dance raced in a clear lead but was ignored by the main pack, the overall pace no more than fair, with things taking shape from 3 out. **Quevega** quashed any doubts over her well-being having been unraced since last May (suffered injury behind), not having to show quite her sparkling best but looking to have that sort of performance in her as she took this race decisively for the second successive year, getting into contention easily approaching the third last and quickly gaining control after the next; she'll be very hard to beat if kept to mares races. **Carole's Legacy** ran up to the best of her chase form back over hurdles, faring a deal better than she had in this race last year, closer up throughout than the pair she split and succumbing to Quevega's turn of foot more than anything; she's yet to try 3m in this sphere and may do better still given the chance. **Voler La Vedette**'s defeat of Go Native may not be solid, by she's probably a smarter mare than this suggests, free through the early stages and taking a while to warm to her jumping too, almost certainly beaten on merit by Quevega all the same after having her chance 2 out. **Amber Brook** was back on her game after a couple of flat efforts, ridden more positively than often and sticking to her task without being a major threat to the first 3. **Easter Legend** has still to reveal her all on this evidence, sure to have been challenging for a place had she not blundered when getting into things going strongly at the second last, losing ground and momentum and not unduly knocked about as she rallied late. **Arctic Magic** will be better off back in handicaps, running respectably here without ever looking like mixing it with the principals, albeit with plenty to do having been short of room when others from the back made a move. **Aura About You** was third in this race in 2009 but had been off since early-May and was let down by her jumping, mistakes finally taking their toll from 3 out. **Alasi** had no chance in this grade, showing improvement on the day if anything, the return to further suiting as expected. **No One Tells Me** had a lot to find with Voler La Vedette alone, twice having been well beaten by her this season, and she wasn't discredited, going with enthusiasm close up in the main group (wearing cheekpieces) and taking over briefly before 3 out. **Argento Luna** will likely show herself in form down in grade again, not up to this task and spared a hard race once beaten. **SWAY**'s jumping will have to improve considerably if she's to match her useful French form, a first-flight mistake a sign of things to come and never really travelling as a result.

4132 Neptune Investment Management Nov Hdle 2m5f (10)
(Baring Bingham) (Gr 1) (1) (4yo+) £57,010

3201 *	PEDDLERS CROSS (IRE) *DMcCain,Jnr* 5-11-7 JasonMaguire..... 6 7/1	1
3005 *	REVE DE SIVOLA (FR) *NickWilliams* 5-11-7 DarylJacob 9 15/2	1½ 2
3626 *	RITE OF PASSAGE *DKWeld,Ireland* 6-11-7 MrRPMcNamara..... 4 7/2f	3¾ 3
3503 *	Summit Meeting *Mrs.JHarrington,Ireland* 5-11-7 RMPower......... 10/1	¾ 4
3668 *	Finian's Rainbow (IRE) *NJHenderson* 7-11-7 BJGeraghty 11/2	¾ 5
3792 3	The Giant Bolster *DGBridgwater* 5-11-7 RJGreene 200/1	nk 6
3557 3	Manyriverstocross (IRE) *AKing* 5-11-7 RobertThornton............. 12 11/1	8 7
3469 3	Some Present (IRE) *ThomasMullins,Ireland* 7-11-7 DNRussell.. 20 14/1	11 8
2993 *	Baily Rock (IRE) *MFMorris,Ireland* 7-11-7 MartinFerris 100/1	12 9
3343 pu	Quartano (GER) *WJGreatrex* 7-11-7 WayneHutchinson............. 100/1	1¼ 10
3818 *	Gus Macrae (IRE) *MissRebeccaCurtis* 6-11-7 (t) TomScudamore 50/1	13 11
3174 *	Ghizao (GER) *PFNicholls* 5-11-7 TimmyMurphy................... 20/1	8 12
3161 *	The Knox (IRE) *JHowardJohnson* 7-11-7 DenisO'Regan......... 28/1	8 13
2218 3	Consulate (IRE) *JFEdwards* 6-11-7 MrDEdwards.................. 200/1	23 14
3367 4	Hollo Ladies (IRE) *NMeade,Ireland* 5-11-7 PCarberry 40/1	7 15
3236 2	Quel Esprit (FR) *WPMullins,Ireland* 6-11-7 RWalsh................ 5/1	
2912 3	Sleepy Hollow *HMorrison* 5-11-7 DougieCostello 100/1	rc

2.05race Mr T. G. Leslie 17ran 5m02.59

An up-to-standard renewal for all it didn't quite match up to the one Mikael d'Haguenet won 12 months earlier, the established runner-up giving a guide to its worth, and several remain with the potential to reach a very smart level in time; the pace was fair, certainly better than in the Coral Cup, and the fact the first 3 were never far away is just coincidental, Manyriverstocross the only notably unlucky one, that one all but unseating when hampered badly by Quel Esprit's departure at the second. **Peddlers Cross** has passed each test with flying colours so far, finding more by the run as he's worked his way to Grade 1 level, posting a smart and also solid performance here after his Haydock form had been difficult to gauge, looking a most exciting prospect, bearing in mind his build and pedigree suggest he should flourish when chasing, whilst he has an excellent attitude too; the longer trip was firmly in his favour amongst stronger opposition, in touch travelling strongly throughout, his jumping typically impeccable, and finding loads for pressure after the second last having initially been passed quite readily by the placed pair. **Reve de Sivola** is more experienced than most novices, certainly in terms of big races, contesting graded events on all 8 starts since his debut, and his proximity gives the form an extremely solid look, particularly as his jumping wasn't quite the hindrance it's been at times, acknowledging minor mistakes 5 out and 3 out, looking set to take some beating when taking over between the last 2 flights, unable to quite match the winner in the end but underlining his good attitude as he rallied; there has to be a chance 3m will bring more out of him. **Rite of Passage** remains the type to win top races at some stage, potentially the best of these going forward in fact, not fluent and shuffled back 4 out as things were beginning to take shape, getting back into contention easily out wide 2 flights later only to be fended off by a couple of stronger stayers in the finish, seeing the trip out all the same; the 2½m event at Aintree could suit him. **Summit Meeting** proved himself a very useful novice given a second try in graded company, clearly not right on his first, potentially better still in fact, coming from much further back than the first 3 having been caught in the early interference and strong to the finish, the longer trip seeming to suit. **Finian's Rainbow** could well have a smart performance in him if persevered with over hurdles, raising his game further on his second try at Grade 1 company, leaving the impression the trip was an absolute maximum for him too, having travelled at least as well as the first 3 until after 2 out; he's very much a novice chaser to look forward to next season. **The Giant Bolster** has just an ordinary novice win to his name so far, but clearly has a deal more ability than that suggests, out-running his odds by some way here, acknowledging he might prove flattered to some extent having been ridden more to obtain the best possible placing as opposed to getting involved in the battle. **Manyriverstocross** will be a bigger player in Grade 1 novice company another day, Thornton almost out of the side door as he was badly hampered by Quel Esprit's fall at the second, dropping to rear, deserving credit for getting back into contention at all, still there 2 out (not fluent) before the running he'd already done told on him up the hill. **Some Present** is a useful novice, placed 3 times in graded company, but he's essentially exposed now, at a level some way short of the principals here, too, shaping as though still in form on the day from a poor position, spared a hard race once clearly held. **Baily Rock** has proved reliable this season, winning 4 times, including 2 handicaps, but had little chance in this grade. **Quartano** had his limitations exposed in the Challow earlier in the season and was never a threat here. **Gus Macrae**'s bumper form and previous 2 hurdles outings marked him down as a useful prospect and perhaps this was just a case of too much too soon, the trip remaining likely to suit back in calmer waters; he again jumped fluently in the main. **Ghizao** shaped better than the result and remains with scope for improvement, not bred for this longer trip and patently failing to see it out having made smooth progress from the back approaching the second last, a slight mistake there enough to see him capitulate. **The Knoxs**'s defeat of Wymott at Newcastle has been endorsed by that one's subsequent Grade 2 success and he remains with long-term potential, this seemingly coming too soon in his development, still relatively green. Consulate is established as just a fair novice, something of a vanity runner here. **Hollo Ladies** was hampered by the faller at the second but didn't jump well enough himself, anyway, always behind; his Grade 1 win at Leopardstown in December remains a huge stand-out in his record. **Quel Esprit**'s early departure took something away from the race as a whole, diving through the second flight and taking something of a kicking on the ground as he hampered several others. **Sleepy Hollow** faced by far his stiffest task yet but was in the process of running a big race when running out through the rail at the second last, still in front at the time for all several were taking aim.

4133 RSA Chase (Gr 1) (1) (5yo+) £85,515   3m110y (19)

3470²	WEAPON'S AMNESTY (IRE) CharlesByrnes,Ireland 7-11-4 DNRussell			1
			8 10/1	
3669*	BURTON PORT (IRE) NJHenderson 6-11-4 APMcCoy	10 9/1	7	2
3562*	LONG RUN (FR) NJHenderson 5-11-3 MrSWaley-Cohen	5/2 11/4	sh	3
3669²	Knockara Beau (IRE) GACharlton 7-11-4 JanFaltejsek	20 16/1	½	4
3435*	Punchestowns (IRE) NJHenderson 6-11-4 BJGeraghty	9/4 2/1f	16	5
3680*	Little Josh (IRE) NATwiston-Davies 8-11-4 PJBrennan	28/1	15	6
3572³	Chasing Cars (IRE) MrsJHarrington,Ireland 8-11-4 RMPower	50/1	5	7
3811*	Citizen Vic (IRE) WPMullins,Ireland 7-11-4 RWalsh	10 12/1		f
3554*	Diamond Harry NickWilliams 7-11-4 TimmyMurphy	6 5/1		pu

2.40race Gigginstown House Stud 9ran 6m13.52

Rarely can a championship race at this Festival have promised so much and delivered so little, the winner putting up a convincing performance, though with practically none of his serious rivals close to their best, many let down by their jumping, the form some way short of what Cooldine and Denman had achieved in winning this in recent years; the pace was nothing out of the ordinary, which meant most were still in contention despite their mistakes until relatively late. Weapon's Amnesty gained a second Festival success in as many years as he added to last season's Spa Hurdle, jumping much better than of late back at 3m, conditions possibly also a help on that score, impressing with the way he travelled and quickening away into the straight, winning with something to spare; he's open to further improvement under the right conditions and his record here means he becomes a plausible Gold Cup candidate, though he'll have to step up a good deal further if he's to realise that goal. Burton Port confirmed himself a smart novice for all he lost his unbeaten record, though he made rather harder work of things than might have been expected, his placing owing something to his rider's perseverance, and the under-performance of others, recovering from his mistakes on the long run to 3 out, and taking second only late after being outpaced again after that fence; he could well benefit from being freshened up, though probably still lacks the potential of some of those he beat here. Long Run was second best on the day, just losing that position to a more strongly-ridden rival on the post, but that was still a let down, 5 serious errors taking their toll; he still

has a very bright future, and the King George will surely be on his agenda for 2010/11. Knockara Beau largely avoided the mistakes which had littered his performance at Ascot, showing a smart level of form, likely flattered to beat some of those he did but showing a good attitude all the same as he ran back through after losing his place completely following a bad mistake 4 out; the Scottish National could be worth a try with him. Punchestowns remains a high-class prospect for all he didn't shine here, a setback the previous week having put his participation in doubt for a time, whilst his jumping was sticky on occasions and he reportedly ripped a front shoe off and returned lame behind. Little Josh seemed out of his depth as much as anything, dropping out from the fourth last having typically made a couple of mistakes; saying that, his jumping has shown signs of improvement of late. Chasing Cars's participation looked optimistic to say the least and he never threatened, his jumping failing to stand up to the demands of the course, soon left behind as the race began in earnest. Citizen Vic dictated the pace and was still in with every chance when he fell fatally 2 out. Diamond Harry was ill at ease from before halfway (on toes/sweating beforehand), showing his very best form on softer going previously, though perhaps inhibited by his attitude as much as anything; his jumping was by no means as bad as at Newbury, though he still isn't entirely convincing on that score.

4134 Seasons Holidays Queen Mother Champion Chase (Gr 1) (1) (5yo+) £182,432   2m (12)

3364*	BIG ZEB (IRE) ColmAMurphy,Ireland 9-11-10 BJGeraghty	10/1		1
2666²	FORPADYDEPLASTERER (IRE) ThomasCooper,Ireland 8-11-10 APMcCoy	6	2
		10/1		
3430*	KALAHARI KING (FR) FerdyMurphy 9-11-10 GLee	9/2	3¼	3
3558*	Master Minded (FR) PFNicholls 7-11-10 RWalsh	5/6 4/5f	½	4
3671*	Oh Crick (FR) AKing 7-11-10 WayneHutchinson	66/1	2¾	5
3364²	Golden Silver (FR) WPMullins,Ireland 8-11-10 PaulTownend	33/1	22	6
3197⁴	Well Chief (GER) DEPipe 11-11-10 (s) TimmyMurphy	33/1	¾	7
3558²	Mahogany Blaze (FR) NATwiston-Davies 8-11-10 (b) PJBrennan	66/1		1
3197*	Twist Magic (FR) PFNicholls 8-11-10 RobertThornton	15/2 8/1		pu

3.20race Mr Patrick Joseph Redmond 9ran 3m51.14

Substandard showings from the Paul Nicholls-trained pair left a depleted field by championship standards, particularly that of

Master Minded, though Big Zeb produced a top-class performance nevertheless as he saw off last year's Arkle winner with authority, one more than worthy of winning this prestigious event; the gallop made for a good test. **Big Zeb** finally delivered the top-class performance he'd long promised, shining for the first time in Britain after 2 previous flops, aided by Master Minded's underperformance but most convincing in his own right, jumping with a deal more fluency than on previous visits and tanking throughout, sealing matters between the last 2 fences and just kept up to his work; he'll be the one to beat at Punchestown on this evidence, acknowledging Master Minded and/or Twist Magic have the potential to put up more of a fight. **Forpadydeplasterer** has established himself as a high-class chaser in his first season outside novices, runner-up in the best 2 2m chases of the season so far, a deal more superior to Kalahari King here than he'd been in last year's Arkle, no match for an on-song Big Zeb having gone from the front (not always fluent) but battling all the same. **Kalahari King** failed to quite produce all his Doncaster handicap success had promised, unable to go with the same fluency and snatching third only at the death; he should show himself in a better lightly at Aintree and/or Punchestown (has won at both Festivals), though whether he's up to troubling the likes of Big Zeb remains to be seen. **Master Minded** looked somewhere near his best in the Game Spirit but came up some way short of comfirming that impression against top-quality opposition, failing to go with quite the same zest as usual and in trouble fully 3 out, even losing third near the finish; his connections were quick to point out that his very best form has come on going softer than good, but for our money he's got something to prove now. **Oh Crick** isn't quite up to this level and ran as well as could be expected, matching his third in the

Victor Chandler, though it was only very late on that he made up ground, potentially a shade flattered as a result. **Golden Silver**'s defeat of Tranquil Sea shortly after Christmas reads well but hasn't jumped fluently enough on either start since, left behind from 2 out here. **Well Chief** had his day when successful here earlier in the season but is essentially some way below the best nowadays and never seemed happy after a couple of early mistakes; he was wearing cheekpieces, incidentally. **Mahogany Blaze**'s jumping has become a major issue, worse if anything with blinkers back in use of late, getting no further than the fifth here. **Twist Magic** had been a deal more convincing previously this season, everything going wrong here though, rather bolting to post (missed his place in the parade) and already under pressure when blundering 4 out, something possibly amiss.

4137	**Weatherbys Champion Bumper**	2m110y
	(Standard Open NHF) (Gr 1) (1) (4, 5 and 6yo) £34,206	

```
3252 *  CUE CARD CLTizzard 4-10-12 JoeTizzard ................... 40/1       1
3560 *  AL FEROF (FR) PFNicholls 5-11-5 RWalsh ................. 8/1    8  2
3474 *  FRAWLEY (IRE) JohnEKiely,Ireland 5-11-5 BJGeraghty .. 16 14/1  8  3
1683 *  Tavern Times (IRE) ThomasMullins,Ireland 6-11-5 DNRussell 15/2 13/2 1½ 4
2937 2  Megastar GLMoore 5-11-5 JamieMoore ................... 25/1      hd 5
3639 *  Dare Me (IRE) PJHobbs 6-11-5 RichardJohnson ....... 20 18/1  sh 6
3737 *  Bishopsfurze (IRE) WPMullins,Ireland 5-11-5 PaulTownend .. 20/1  1¼ 7
3573 2  Sheer Genius (IRE) JohnJosephMurphy,Ireland 5-11-5
          EFPower ................................... 100/1           ½ 8
3560 2  Made In Time (IRE) MissRebeccaCurtis 5-11-5 (t) APMcCoy .. 25/1 1¼ 9
3752 *  Bubbly Bruce (IRE) WHarney,Ireland 6-11-5 AJMcNamara .. 50/1 hd 10
3560 4  Back At The Ranch (IRE) PMPhelan 5-11-5 ColinBolger .. 150/1 nk 11
2944 *  Elegant Concorde (IRE) DKWeld,Ireland 5-11-5
          MrRPMcNamara ................................ 8 10/1         hd 12
3114 *  Up Ou That (IRE) WPMullins,Ireland 5-11-5 DJCasey ..... 33/1  5 13
2384 *  Dunraven Storm (IRE) PJHobbs 5-11-5 TJO'Brien ......... 33/1 hd 14
2818 2  Super Villan MBradstock 5-11-5 MattieBatchelor ...... 150/1 1¾ 15
3783 5  De Forgotten Man (IRE) MKeighley 5-11-5 WarrenMarston .. 100/1 1½ 16
3560 3  Carpincho (FR) MrsSJHumphrey 6-11-5 CharlieHuxley ... 80/1 1½ 17
2971 *  On His Own (IRE) JHoward&Johnson 5-11-5 DenisO'Regan .. 40/1 ns 18
3219 *  Hidden Universe (IRE) DKWeld,Ireland 4-10-12 PJSmullen . 11 16/1 1½ 19
3813 *  Shot From The Hip (GER) EJO'Grady,Ireland 6-11-5
          MrJPMaguire ................................ 11/2        3¾ 20
3488 2  Basford Bob (IRE) JennieCandlish 5-11-5 AlanO'Keeffe .. 100/1 2½ 21
3121 *  Shannon Spirit (IRE) THogan,Ireland 5-11-5 MissNCarberry . 16 14/1 10 22
2832 *  Drumbaloo (IRE) JJLambe,Ireland 6-11-5 RobertThornton .. 8/1 14 23
3695 *  Day of A Lifetime (IRE) WPMullins,Ireland 5-11-5 MrPWMullins . 10/1 4½ 24
5.15race Mrs Jean R. Bishop 24ran 3m48.48
```

A race dominated by Irish stables over the years but their challenge this time wasn't up to its usual strength and British-trained horses filled 4 of the first 6 places, the home team containing the best types physically, too; the winner's performance looks well up to standard, the runner-up having ensured a proper test at the trip. **Cue Card** is clearly a very bright prospect for next season, sure to do well over hurdles, having the ability to travel strongly and a good turn of foot, impressing with the way he made ground through the field from the rear 5f out and joined issue on the bridle into the straight, still green (edged left) when shaken up to lead over 1f out but quickening right away; he's an athletic sort and along with Megastar stood out in terms of condition beforehand, and though the Irish team clearly wasn't up to its usual standard (and several didn't have the best of runs) it would be unwise to underrate his performance, the handful of British-trained winners of this race including 2 hurdlers of considerable merit in Dato Star and Monsignor, he being the first 4-y-o to win the race since Dato Star too. **Al Ferof** was the form pick and in beating the rest convincingly he matched his Newbury effort, wisely having plenty of use made of him and still travelling strongly in front into the straight, lacking the winner's turn of foot though; he's by a strong stamina influence and will be suited by further than 2m over hurdles. **Frawley**, bred for the Flat, emerged best of the Irish contingent, suited by less testing conditions and slightly better than the result after meeting trouble in running as he made ground going well towards the straight; he would be a speedier type than the majority of the Irish-trained runners in this field, and whether he can confirm superiority when the mud is flying remains to be seen. **Tavern Times** had won on good going back in the autumn and at least matched that form under similar conditions here, likely to have improved on it too with anything like a clear run, having a wretched time as he tried to make ground in the last 5f, staying on well once in the clear; he may well be a contender for the Champion INH Flat at Punchestown and should win races over hurdles next season. **Megastar** was the best type in the paddock and has a bright future over hurdles next season, sure to win races, winner of a race at Sandown that worked out really well and

better than the result in going close to that form here, travelling well in rear only to be blocked in and forced to switch wide at the top of the hill, doing well to make as much ground as he did after that. **Dare Me** had been off a long time before his reappearance and wasn't able to build on that effort a month on, on less soft ground as well, but he has plenty of potential as a jumper, still to fill out fully. **Bishopsfurze**'s debut form wasn't easy to pin down but he confirmed himself a useful prospect for next season under very different conditions, doing well the way the race went to finish as close as he did, propping in rear at the top of the hill and then hampered as he made ground up the rail towards the straight, staying on to be nearest at the finish; he was the pick of an ordinary Irish team in terms of physique and may well prove the best of them as a hurdler, sure to stay beyond 2m. **Sheer Genius** did best of the 3 maidens and seemed to improve a fair bit, possibly due to the less testing ground than he'd raced on previously, still well back 4f out but staying on; he could well fill out over the summer and would have some potential as a jumper, judged on pedigree as well. **Made In Time** finished a bit further behind the runner-up than he had at Newbury and while he was perhaps a little better than the result, paying for trying to press the leader down the hill, he essentially had no excuses; he's well related and is likely to have a future as a jumper next season. **Bubbly Bruce** did well to run creditably under circumstances which probably weren't ideal, hampered as he stayed on from well off the pace over 3f out, likely to need more of a test of stamina when he goes over jumps; he was one of the better types among the Irish-trained runners. **Back At The Ranch** confirmed his form behind the runner-up last time, looking much more a stayer than might be expected from his pedigree, rallying after losing his place completely coming down the hill; he lacks physique somewhat, so whether he will transfer this useful level of ability to hurdling is debatable. **Elegant Concorde** is better than the result indicates, plugging on when badly hampered on the inside rail 2f out and unable to recover, and may yet be able to improve in this sphere, though in the longer term his lack of scope may well hinder his prospects of reaching a high level as a jumper. **Up Ou That** looks on the weak side at the moment and couldn't cope with a much more demanding task than he faced on his debut, failing to settle and weakening 3f out; he may yet have more to offer. **Dunraven Storm** proved too green, uncoordinated as he tried to make ground down the hill and unable to make any further progress into the straight; he's the type that ought to make a jumper next season. **Super Villan** had plenty to find on form, one of the 3 maidens in the field, and was under pressure in rear 5f out; he might have been seen to better advantage on softer going and his physique suggests more a chaser than a hurdler of the future. **De Forgotten Man** lacked the speed on less testing ground and in better company to land a blow, though he has shown enough to suggest he will be of interest as a novice jumper next season. **Carpincho** couldn't match his form against the runner-up from last time, ridden along at the top of the hill and soon losing his position; he has shown enough this season to think he'll be competitive in ordinary novice hurdle company next season. **On His Own** had been bought for £240,000 out of Oliver McKiernan's stable after his impressive bumper debut and certainly looks the part, but he didn't show to advantage over a shorter trip on firmer going, dropping away fairly swiftly after chasing the pace to the top of the hill; he probably has potential in the longer term, over further and on softer ground. **Hidden Universe** might

well need softer ground than he encountered here but he's nothing much on looks and may not have won much of a race on his debut anyway; it would be no surprise to see him raced on the Flat before his attentions are turned to hurdling, so a better idea of his ability should be apparent by the autumn. **Shot From The Hip** has probably got quite a bit of ability, the ground perhaps against him, though he wasn't helped by the minimal assistance he received, taking charge early on and then veering left and right as his exertions told, causing interference to several rivals into the straight. **Basford Bob**'s form looked short of the standard required and he was only briefly out of rear division, though carried wide at the top of the hill as he tried to make ground; he's not a bad type and had shown fairly useful ability previously, so he is likely to be of interest when he goes over jumps. **Shannon Spirit** was nothing much on looks and failed to make an impact in this better company, losing his position coming down the hill. **Drumbaloo** had been well backed the previous week but the drying ground was plainly all against him and he was struggling a long way from home; he may yet make up into a decent jumper given time, softer going and a distance of ground. **Day of A Lifetime** failed to impress in appearance, and came up some way short of what he'd promised in soft ground at Fairyhouse, failing to settle, which might well have brought about a problem with his tack, certainly proving hard to steer as he ran wide at the top of the hill.

4161 **Ryanair Chase (Festival) (Gr 1) (1) (5yo+)** £142,525   2m5f (17)

3671 2	ALBERTAS RUN (IRE) JonjoO'Neill 9-11-10 APMcCoy	14/1 1
2789 *	POQUELIN (FR) PFNicholls 7-11-10 RWalsh	11/4f 4½ 2
3570 *	J'Y VOLE (FR) WPMullins,Ireland 7-11-3 DJCondon	28/1 ns 3
2929 pu	Deep Purple EvanWilliams 9-11-10 PaulMoloney	16 11/1 5 4
3558 4	Voy Por Ustedes (FR) AKing 9-11-10 (b) RobertThornton	14 9/1 6 5
3110 *	Scotsirish (IRE) WPMullins,Ireland 9-11-10 PaulTownend	20/1 5 6
2929 3	Barbers Shop NJHenderson 8-11-10 (s) BJGeraghty	11/2 4 7
2293 *	Jack The Giant (IRE) NJHenderson 8-11-10 AndrewTinkler	25/1 5 8
3812 *	Tranquil Sea (IRE) EJO'Grady,Ireland 8-11-10 AJMcNamara	5 11/2 2 9
3197 2	Petit Robin (FR) NJHenderson 7-11-10 PCarberry	14 16/1 3½ 10
3671 1	Planet of Sound PJHobbs 8-11-10 RichardJohnson	14 11/1 9 11
3472 3	Schindlers Hunt (IRE) DTHughes,Ireland 8-11-10 PWFlood	12/1 u1
2701 ur	Barker (IRE) WPMullins,Ireland 9-11-10 DJCasey	33/1 pu

2.40race Mr Trevor Hemmings 13ran 5m11.54

A worthy Grade 1 for all it tends to fall short that bit short of Champion Chase/Gold Cup standard in terms of form, this looking a strong renewal too, the rejuvenated Albertas Run producing a top-class performance in getting the better of some solid and high-class opposition; the pace was slower than for the 2 handicaps at the trip, still making for a fair test though, things taking shape from the third last. Albertas Run's enigmatic ways are impossible to dispute, but he's top class on his day, this second Festival success in 3 years (landed RSA Chase in 2008) testament to that, going with a lot more zest away from softish ground for the first time since his Ascot win in November and willing under strong pressure as he held off the placed pair from 2 out; he'll presumably head for the Bowl at Aintree next, a race he was third in last year, but all will depend on his mood. Poquelin confirmed his status as a high-class chaser, having every chance after travelling/jumping exuberantly in touch though, no match for the top-class winner, likely to have struggled to hold off the third too but for hemming her in rounding the final turn; he's likeable. J'Y Vole has bloomed all of a sudden since the turn of the year, establishing herself as a very smart chaser at Gowran and then here, looking second best at the weights this time, her rider's attempt to challenge up the inside of Poquelin turning in rather costing her that position (held in). Deep Purple's Charlie Hall and Peterborough wins were easy to pick holes in but he's clearly very smart all the same, not quite up to this task but giving a good account of himself, sticking on after being tightened up when weakening on the approach to 2 out. Voy Por Ustedes is no longer the top-class chaser of previous seasons, the blinkers perhaps indicative of waning enthusiasm, though if that was the case they had the desired effect, going with relish for a long way, coming up short under pressure, though. Scotsirish falls short at the top level, by no means discredited here, plugging through from the back without mounting a serious challenge. Barbers Shop has held his form well in top company overall, third in the King George when last seen, but this was disappointing, jumping stickily and never seeming entirely happy as a result. Jack The Giant shaped as though retaining plenty of ability after 17 months off the track with ligament trouble, travelling as well as any to 4 out and weakening only after a mistake at the next, the trip possibly an issue having raced mainly around 2m, though rustiness looks the most likely cause. Tranquil Sea has had an excellent season, his 3 wins including the valuable Paddy Power handicap here earlier in the season, but he just wasn't on his game this day, only briefly looking a threat before stopping quickly 4 out. Petit Robin is best around 2m, and went smoothly to a point, though he again showed a tendency to make mistakes, his jumping falling to pieces in fact in the second half of the race. Planet of Sound's jumping is becoming an increasing concern, this round littered with minor errors, folding after the thirteenth; he was reported to have suffered a breathing problem. Schindlers Hunt seemingly isn't as reliable as he was, a sloppy round of jumping holding him back this day, making several mistakes even before unseating at the twelfth. Barker was highly progressive after joining this yard mid-way through 2008/9 but seems to have developed a problem with his jumping, badly let down by it the last twice.

4162 Ladbrokes World Hdle (Gr 1) (1) (4yo+) £148,226   3m (12)

3006*	BIG BUCK'S (FR) PFNicholls 7-11-10 RWalsh 4/5 5/6f		1
3342²	TIME FOR RUPERT (IRE) PRWebber 6-11-10 WTKennedy 16/1	3¼	2
3181²	POWERSTATION (IRE) EamonO'Connell,Ireland 10-11-10	11	3
	AJMcNamara 33/1		
3006²	Karabak (FR) AKing 7-11-10 APMcCoy 8 15/2	½	4
3588⁶	Ebadiyan (IRE) PatrickOBrady,Ireland 5-11-10 JCullen 66/1	½	5
3181⁴	Oscar Dan Dan (IRE) ThomasMullins,Ireland 8-11-10 PCarberry.. 80/1	2½	6
3342¹	Tidal Bay (IRE) JHowardJohnson 9-11-10 DenisO'Regan 8/1	½	7
3470⁵	Cousin Vinny (IRE) WPMullins,Ireland 7-11-10 PaulTownend 25/1	3	8
3342 pu	Lie Forrit (IRE) WAmos 6-11-10 CIGillies 40/1	12	9
3342	Fair Along (GER) PJHobbs 8-11-10 (s) RPFlint 50/1	4	10
3342³	Katchit (IRE) AKing 7-11-10 RobertThornton....................... 18 14/1	11	11
3588*	War of Attrition (IRE) MFMorris,Ireland 11-11-10 (s) DNRussell.... 20/1	4½	12
3204⁴	Cape Tribulation JMJefferson 6-11-10 PhilKinsella...................... 50/1	25	13
3058*	Sentry Duty (FR) NJHenderson 8-11-10 BJGeraghty 12/1	pu	

3.20race The Stewart Family 14ran 5m49.27

A Festival that had seen several expected stars fail to fulfil expectations finally drew a performance worthy of the meeting, for though those apart from the favourite didn't have the form to win an average running, Big Buck's himself is one of the best we've seen in this division and underlined the point with plenty to spare; the time was fractionally slower than for the Pertemps Final, indicating the relatively steady pace set, the race developing after 3 out. **Big Buck's** confirmed himself by some way the top staying hurdler around in winning a second World Hurdle in ready fashion, the much-discussed so-called flat spot failing to materialise as he cruised through the race and joined the leader on the bridle before the last, the only slight alarm coming after a slight mistake there, soon firmly in control after; only the return of Punchestowns or Kasbah Bliss to this sphere seems likely to do much to threaten his total dominance of the division for the forseeable future, and a follow-up success in the Liverpool Hurdle at Aintree looks very much on the cards. **Time For Rupert** will be a leading candidate for RSA Chase honours at the 2011 Festival, a smashing chasing prospect on looks, and now a top-class hurdler after 2 seasons of endless progress, running his best race yet in finishing clear of the remainder here, always well placed and having most in trouble as he kicked on 2 out, unable to properly get Big Buck's off the bridle but battling hard as the pair galloped clear. **Powerstation** added to his excellent record at the Festival by finishing third in this for the second year running, finding plenty as he stayed on, for all he was never a threat to the first 2; he'll presumably take his chance at Punchestown next. **Karabak** is a high-class staying hurdler, and still not fully exposed, failing to fire on his big day here, the false gallop likely a factor in that, failing to bring his stamina into play, whilst he made a couple of mistakes too, including 2 out as he was being asked for his effort; his physique suggests he's likely to be best kept over hurdles. **Ebadiyan** was a smart hurdler coming into this but seemed to run above himself all the same, a prominent ride likely a help, flat out fully 3 out as the race began to develop, the trip clearly no issue this time as he sustained his gallop; he wouldn't be an obvious type for chasing and may well continue to struggle for winning opportunities kept to hurdling. **Oscar Dan Dan** ran to form in the end, though didn't look the most straightforward, getting behind even before the pace really picked up and just running through beaten horses after 2 out; he's exposed as a hurdler and needs substandard fields to be fully competitive at this level. **Tidal Bay** was closely matched with the second on Cleeve running, reiterating what a rogue he is, not applying himself at all and just running past beaten horses after jumping 2 out in last place. **Cousin Vinny** had a choice of 4 options at the meeting but wasn't likely to be up to the task in any of them, failing to make an impact returned to hurdling and stepped up to 3m for the first time, not fluent and ridden 3 out, beaten before stamina became an issue. **Lie Forrit** may well need softer ground to be seen to best advantage, and is one of few of those behind the principals with some pretentions to better, not so well served by the run of the race either (had also been edgy beforehand), struggling once the pace increased and behind when blundering 2 out; his tendency to make the odd mistake would need to be ironed out if he's to make a significant impact switched to fences next season. **Fair Along** has been below par on all 3 starts since Wetherby, going with little zest here, flat out 3 from home and left behind at the next. **Katchit** couldn't add to his excellent Festival record, ridden to make ground before 2 out only to wilt in the straight, reportedly returning lame; he's not easy to place these days. **War of Attrition**, making his first appearance at the Festival since winning the 2006 Cheltenham Gold Cup, was soon put in his place after going enthusiastically in front until 2 out, not up to this class as a hurdler. **Cape Tribulation** has been campaigned exclusively in graded races this season but might have been better taking his chance in a handicap or 2, not up to this level over 3m for the first time this season, never in contention; he isn't an obvious chaser on looks or pedigree. **Sentry Duty** is far from certain to stay 3m, though just didn't seem in top form on just his second start of the season anyway, sweating at the start and pushed along as early as the seventh, soon behind.

CHELTENHAM Friday, Mar 19

4171 JCB Triumph Hdle (Gr 1) (1) (4yo) £57,010   2m1f (8)

3781¹	SOLDATINO (FR) *NJHenderson* 4-11-0 BJGeraghty	11/2 6/1		1
2235²	BARIZAN (IRE) *EvanWilliams* 4-11-0 (v) TJO'Brien	20 14/1	1¾	2
3690⁴	ALAIVAN (IRE) *EJO'Grady,Ireland* 4-11-0 AJMcNamara	9/2	7	3
3462¹	Carlito Brigante (IRE) *GordonElliott,Ireland* 4-11-0 DNRussell	4 7/2f	3¼	4
3328²	Barwell Bridge *WJGreatrex* 4-11-0 TimmyMurphy	20 16/1	3¼	5
3719¹	Gilded Age *AKing* 4-11-0 RobertThornton	28/1	¾	6
3947¹	Blazing Buck *AWCarroll* 4-11-0 LeeEdwards	100/1	10	7
3860	Puzzlemaster *HMorrison* 4-11-0 TomScudamore	150/1	1¾	8
2785¹	Olofi (FR) *TRGeorge* 4-11-0 PJBrennan	11 10/1	8	9
3785³	Pittoni (IRE) *CharlesByrnes,Ireland* 4-11-0 PCarberry	12 9/1	4	10
3195¹	Advisor (FR) *PFNicholls* 4-11-0 RWalsh	7 8/1	¾	11
3873¹	Troubletimestwo (FR) *AWCarroll* 4-11-0 AFreeman	100/1	½	12
3489⁴	Blue Nymph *JJQuinn* 4-10-7 DougieCostello	50/1	12	13
2952⁹	Westlin' Winds (IRE) *CREgerton* 4-11-0 MrOGreenall	10/1	12	14
3690⁶	Pebble In A Pool (IRE) *AndrewOliver,Ireland* 4-10-7 (s) DJCondon	200/1		ur
3337⁵	Investissement *EvanWilliams* 4-11-0 PaulMoloney	66/1		pu
1231²	Rupestrian *TimVaughan* 4-11-0 RichardJohnson	40/1		pu

1.30race Mr S. Munir 17ran 4m04.91

Overall a rather substandard Triumph compared to some strong renewals in recent years, and yet another race at the meeting in which plenty ran below expectations, largely due to the searching gallop set by Barizan which, like a Triumph of old, drew the emphasis firmly onto stamina, the winner proving a stouter stayer than the ex-Flat runners in the field, posting a performance little better than that achieved by Sanctuaire in winning the Fred Winter in the process; in terms of physique they weren't a prepossesing lot either, and it's unlikely many will make a significant impact next season. **Soldatino** built on his Adonis success, showing himself a smart juvenile, picking up strongly in the straight after tracking the favourite for much of the way, still 5 lengths down on the long-time leader but closing fast when handed the initiative by that one's mistake at the last, the outcome likely to have been very close but for that given how that rival stuck on again; he's reportedly unlikely to run again this season and was given quotes afterwards for next season's Champion Hurdle but for all that his obscure pedigree isn't a stout one as French non-thoroughbreds go this was an old-fashioned Triumph, won by the stoutest stayer, and it will be surprising if 2m proves his optimum trip in the longer term. **Barizan** excelled himself on his first start since the autumn and would have gone very close indeed had he not blundered at the last, only 5 lengths up and seemingly flagging at the time (had been 16 lengths clear 2 out) but sticking on really well again once regaining his momentum; he had a tough race and might struggle to be at his peak at Aintree, though would clearly be a leading candidate in the Anniversary if over this. **Alaivan** seemed undone by the emphasis on stamina, travelling smoothly under a patient ride for a long way but unable to sustain his headway going to the last; his lack of size tempers enthusiasm slightly for his prospects beyond this season, but if there is a good 2m hurdler in this field then it is likely to be him, and he will presumably get the chance to cement his reputation at Aintree and/or Punchestown. **Carlito Brigante** has better efforts than this behind him already, likely in front of him too, travelling well under a waiting ride, but still back in the pack with it to do when the winner and third got away in pursuit of the long-time leader, seeing the race out thoroughly as he sustained his effort, just no chance of getting there. **Barwell Bridge** proved himself a useful juvenile with his sights raised, probably capable of improving further too, left with a bit too much to do 2 out, keeping on without being knocked about unduly in the straight, though also carrying his head awkwardly, which tempers enthusiasm a little. **Gilded Age** continued his progress and may yet have more to offer, his effort rather petering out in the straight as he edged left, suggesting this searching test stretched his stamina; he was one of the better types and might well make an impact in handicaps next season. **Blazing Buck** faced a stiff task and did well to match his previous form, given that he was ridden more prominently than most, once more proving himself more of a stayer than his Flat form indicated, better as a hurdler than he was in that sphere too, despite his lack of size. **Puzzlemaster** belatedly showed form more in keeping with what he'd done on the Flat, going nowhere after a blunder 3 out but keeping on steadily; whether this proves a reliable guide to his merit is not certain, though heavy going and poor jumping might excuse his previous efforts. **Olofi** was the best type in the field and has a future as a novice chaser next season, clearly not at his best on this first start since December though, closer to the pace than most and paying for that as he weakened 2 out. **Pittoni** was well below form on less testing ground than previously, off the bridle by halfway; he was one of the better types and may have more to offer back on soft/heavy going. **Advisor** had proved himself a fairly useful hurdler in 2 unbeaten starts previously, this clearly not his running, struggling in rear from 3 out, though it's doubtful whether he'd have been a factor in

the finish anyway. **Troubletimestwo**'s form looked well short of what was required and he couldn't cope, struggling as early as the third. **Blue Nymph** was highly tried on her third start over hurdles and soon began to labour after a blunder in rear at the fifth; she was the biggest in the field and her Flat form suggests there could be more to come as a hurdler back at a realistic level, perhaps over further. **Westlin' Winds** was well below his previous progressive form, faced with a searching test of stamina, paying for racing prominently as he dropped right out approaching 2 out; he was one of the better of the Flat types in the field and may yet get back on track in calmer waters. **Pebble In A Pool** is clearly temperamental and was already behind when she tried to refuse and unseated at the third. **Investissement** found this much too searching a test at just the second attempt over hurdles and was in rear until pulled up. **Rupestrian** had done well early in the season and clearly wasn't himself following 7 months off, acknowledging the task he faced, behind when pulled up before the last.

4173 Albert Bartlett Nov Hdle (Spa) (Gr 1) (1) 3m (12)
(4yo+) £57,010

3588⁴	BERTIES DREAM (IRE) *PJGilligan,Ireland* 7-11-7 AELynch	33/1	1
3575°	NAJAF (FR) *PFNicholls* 5-11-7 TimmyMurphy	25/1	6 ²
3677³	KENNELL HILL (IRE) *WKGoldsworthy* 8-11-7 (t) JasonMaguire	66/1	8 ³
3503²	Arvika Ligeonniere (FR) *WPMullins,Ireland* 5-11-7 DJCondon	28/1	13 ⁴
3889 ᵖᵘ	Possol (FR) *HDDaly* 7-11-7 RichardJohnson	28/1	7 ⁵
4132 ᶠ	Quel Esprit (FR) *WPMullins,Ireland* 6-11-7 RWalsh	6 11/2	4 ⁶
3536°	Silver Kate (IRE) *DMRichards* 7-11-0 AColeman	16 14/1	5 ⁷
3746²	Premier Victory (IRE) *THogan,Ireland* 6-11-0 (t) JCullen	33/1	18 ⁸
3300°	Chartreux (FR) *DEPipe* 5-11-7 TomScudamore	28/1	22 ⁹
3226°	Watamu Bay (IRE) *CJMann* 7-11-7 DarylJacob	66/1	5 10
3341°	Restless Harry *RDickin* 6-11-7 HenryOliver	172 8/1	
3469²	Fionnegas (IRE) *WPMullins,Ireland* 6-11-7 DJCasey	16/1	uᴿ
3330°	Bostons Angel (IRE) *MrsJHarrington,Ireland* 6-11-7 (b) RMPower	50/1	pu
3375²	Cappa Bleu (FR) *EvanWilliams* 8-11-7 PaulMoloney	20 18/1	pu
2998°	Enterprise Park (IRE) *WPMullins,Ireland* 6-11-7 PaulTownend	10 11/1	pu
2828°	Shinrock Paddy (IRE) *PaulNolan,Ireland* 6-11-7 APCawley	172 8/1	pu
2788°	Tell Massini (IRE) *TRGeorge* 6-11-7 PJBrennan	7/2 10/3f	pu
3542³	The Betchworth Kid *AKing* 5-11-7 RobertThornton	16/1	pu
3109°	The Hurl (IRE) *MFMorris,Ireland* 7-11-7 APMcCoy	25/1	pu

2.40race Half A Keg Syndicate 19ran 5m55.38

An up-to-standard renewal in terms of the figures, but it lost plenty of depth as the market leaders failed to fire, save for Restless Harry that is, who was a close third when falling at the last; the pace was good, making for an attritional test on worsening ground, the principals all ridden patiently. **Berties Dream** held his form well in good company around 2½m and relished this test as he sprang something of a surprise, the depleted field making his task easier no doubt, but he still saw off a pair who themselves had been placed in Grade 1 company, despite mistakes at the last 2 flights, typically digging deep; it's seemingly undecided whether he'll stay over hurdles or go chasing next season, though he's not the most substantial with fences in mind. **Najaf** had been workmanlike on his British debut but showed much more like his smart French form with his sights raised, shaping better than the winner in many ways, easing alongside the long-time leader between the last 2 flights and seeming to be outstayed as much as anything at this markedly longer trip, for all he just about saw it out; he's not an obvious chaser on looks with a view to next season, though that's proved no barrier for several others from his stable in the past. **Kennel Hill**'s useful level of ability isn't in doubt, this the fourth time this season he's made the frame in a graded event, but he remains one to swerve as a betting proposition no matter what the opposition, consenting to run on only late here and veering right as he did so. **Arvika Ligeonniere** is very much the type to make a name for himself over fences next season, both bred and built to thrive over the larger obstacles, and shaping like a smart gelding for a long way here until his stamina gave out, looking a potential winner as he tanked up to the leaders approaching the second last only to empty; there could still be a good novice hurdle in him this spring. **Possol** reportedly suffered a problem with his back at Doncaster, but failed to fire again back over hurdles a fortnight on, putting up relatively little fight as things began to take shape 3 out, below the form he'd shown when winning twice in this sphere in the autumn. **Quel Esprit** is best judged on the useful form he's shown in Ireland, a 2-day turnaround following his early departure in the Baring Bingham reason

enough to forgive this, finishing weakly in comparison to how he'd travelled up until 3 out. **Silver Kate** will almost certainly bounce back, this her first blip since her hurdling debut, not fluent on a couple of occasions as the race was taking shape and spared a hard race once the principals had broken away. **Premier Victory** is a useful mare, but more still is needed in Grade 1 company, acknowledging she wasn't seen to best effect here anyway having forced the pace. **Chartreux** was disappointing given the impression made at Ffos Las, that form endorsed by several of those behind too, though it's still very early days in his career, green in comparison to most of these, and he's worth another chance to build back in calmer waters. **Watamu Bay**'s Towcester novice win has worked out well but this was a step too far for him, struggling a long way out; he looks an out-and-out stayer. **Restless Harry** is a useful and likeable novice, his fall at the last rather unfortunate given he was squeezed between the first 2 and lost sight of the hurdle, battling at the time for all he'd been passed, though his jumping hadn't been entirely fluent up to then, anyway; he will make a chaser, his size pointing to him being better in that sphere if anything, whilst his attitude should stand him in good stead, too. **Fionnegas** is a very useful novice, beaten only by Dunguib in a Grade 1 in Ireland last month, but he wasn't able to repeat that at this longer trip, a brief effort petering out after 2 out, held in fourth when unseating after interference at the last. **Bostons Angel** is unlikely to stay this far, but that wasn't the problem on the day, not looking enthusiastic after mid-race mistakes, the blinkers perhaps having less effect a second time. **Cappa Bleu**'s chase form leaves him with scope to improve in this sphere but he shaped as if amiss here, weakening quickly; he'd been tongue tied previously. **Enterprise Park** had been highly progressive hitherto, winning all 3 starts in Ireland, and something clearly wasn't right, hitting the third and pulled up soon after. **Shinrock Paddy**'s jumping didn't stand up to this stiffer test in a larger and more competitive field, making several minor errors before halfway and never on terms; he's already a Grade 1 winner, though. **Tell Massini** remains a good prospect given the impression he'd made earlier in the season, one sure to make a chaser, clearly not right returning from over 3 months off, travelling strongly at the top of the hill only to go out quickly 2 from home. **The Betchworth Kid** is best judged on what's gone before, bumped after a mistake at the second, and reportedly struck into/losing a shoe. **The Hurl** should bounce back, holding his form well in Ireland prior to this, and it was simply a case of him being out of his depth here.

4174 totesport Cheltenham Gold Cup Chase (Gr 1)   3¼m110y (22)
    (1) (5yo+) £270,798
2929⁵ IMPERIAL COMMANDER (IRE) *NATwiston-Davies* 9-11-10 1
           PJBrennan 8 7/1
3556 ᵘᶠ DENMAN (IRE) *PFNicholls* 10-11-10 APMcCoy 4/1   7 2
3678⁶ MON MOME (FR) *MissVenetiaWilliams* 10-11-10 AColeman 50/1   23 3
3340² Carruthers *MBradstock* 7-11-10 MattieBatchelor .... 33/1   sh 4
3472² Cooldine (IRE) *WPMullins,Ireland* 8-11-10 PaulTownend ...... 9 10/1   ¾ 5
2797 ¹ Calgary Bay (IRE) *MissHCKnight* 7-11-10 GLee 50/1   8 6
2693⁵ My Will (FR) *PFNicholls* 10-11-10 NickScholfield 80/1   12 7
4376⁵ Cerium (FR) *PaulMurphy* 9-11-10 DNRussell 200/1   10 8
3556 ᵘ Tricky Trickster (IRE) *PFNicholls* 7-11-10 BJGeraghty .... 14 12/1 dist 9
3743 Mr Pointment (IRE) *PaulMurphy* 11-11-10 KWhelan .... 250/1 dist 10
2929 ¹ Kauto Star (FR) *PFNicholls* 10-11-10 (t) RWalsh 4/5 8/11f   1
3.20race Our Friends in the North 11ran 6m43.75

A Festival which produced a succession of unexpected results and at which plenty of the star names underperformed had one last trick up its sleeve in the eclipse of Kauto Star, the best chaser in more than 40 years, whose bid for a third Gold Cup ended on the floor, but that failed to stop this being a race of rare quality, a tremendous duel between 2 top-notch horses resulting in one of the best-ever performances in this great race, the first 2 drawing a long way clear after 3 out; the early pace wasn't so strong as anticipated but it had picked up by halfway and ensured this was a proper test of stamina, a test worthy of the Blue Riband of steeplechasing. **Imperial Commander**'s narrow defeat by Kauto Star at Haydock suggested he'd made further

progress since his Ryanair win last season and, back at a track where he has such a fine record (6 wins now), he showed the extent of it, producing a performance even better than Kauto Star's in winning this race last year, beating an even stronger Denman than that horse had for all he didn't do it by quite so far, impressing with his jumping, always travelling well, clearly going better than the runner-up 4 out and getting on top once in the straight, ridden to extend his advantage after the last; he's a year younger than both his chief rivals and as such ought to be regarded as favourite for next year's renewal at this stage, and with the novices looking to have plenty to prove a second Gold Cup might well be his next March; the Bowl at Aintree was reportedly nominated as a possible target nearer to hand. **Denman** finished second in the Gold Cup for the second successive year, producing a better performance than when he'd landed the race in 2008 this time around, going with plenty of zest up with the pace but not quite so comfortable as the winner from 4 out and unable to match that one in the straight; he'll reportedly have the Grand National as his principal target next season, but surely couldn't be discounted if he makes a fourth appearance in this race, while a third Hennessy really would be something; beforehand he failed to take the eye, looking nowhere near so well in himself as he did before the Hennessy, but his appearance on that occasion is the exception rather than the rule with him. **Mon Mome** will go to Aintree on the back of a career-best performance, one that puts him amongst the picks of the weights as he attempts to become the first dual Grand National winner since Red Rum; he sweated up at the start and got a long way behind on the second circuit, nearly 20 lengths off the fifth 3 out and still 10 lengths down on third at the last, his stamina very much kicking in at that point though, flying up the hill to snatch third. **Carruthers** really is a splendidly genuine and enthusiastic chaser, racing with zest and jumping solidly in front, not up to going with the front 2 from 3 out (where he blundered) but responding to pressure to get back past the fifth after the last, only to be nailed for third on the line; he was one of the joint youngest in the field and may well have a bit more to offer, particularly back on more testing ground. **Cooldine** ran his race back at the scene of last season's RSA Chase success, and his effort opened the door for better still another time, not seeming himself beforehand but perked up when racing, getting into third after 3 out only to tie up late on; he would seem not to have had the ideal season in terms of preparation, and might well step up on this at Punchestown. **Calgary Bay** was the pick of the paddock and acquited himself well in face of a stiff task, failing to settle and making a few uncharacteristic mistakes but still travelling well 5 out and in contention for the minor placings until late, this trip seemingly a maximum for him; he might well have a bit more to offer still, with Aintree likely to suit him if he takes his chance in one of the graded races there. **My Will**'s performance didn't have quite the promise that his fifth last season did, though it was more encouraging than his last run had been, going on late after getting behind on the final circuit; he'll presumably look to improve on last year's Grand National third next. **Cerium** hadn't been seen since finishing fifth in last season's Grand National and, looking in need of the run, was left well behind on the final circuit; his Aintree effort was all the more creditable as he suffered a fracture to his skull during the race but whether he gets the chance to do better next month is in the balance, well down the order to get a run this time. **Tricky Trickster** looked as well as any beforehand but his performance suggested

he hadn't got over his run at Newbury, facing a stiff task but lacklustre nevertheless, not helped by an early mistake; whether 3 weeks is long enough to get him back thriving for the Grand National remains to be seen. **Mr Pointment** had left Paul Nicholls for £18,000 at the end of last season and looked nothing like the smart chaser he has been on his day, sweating up and edgy beforehand and soon toiling after uncharacteristic mistakes. **Kauto Star** position as the outstanding chaser around remains unquestioned, little having happened since to doubt the merit of his King George win, though a surprising return of jumping problems denied him the chance of a third Gold Cup, never travelling that well after a bad mistake at the eighth, hard at work in fifth when he took a heavy fall 4 out, unlikely to have troubled the first 2 but thankfully seemingly none the worse; he will be 11 by the time of the next Gold Cup, old for a winner of this race in the modern era, but will presumably have just 2 runs in the meantime, and a fifth King George might well see him return here as favourite next March.

4532 BGC Partners Liverpool Hdle (Gr 1) (1)   3m110y (13)
(4yo+) £57,010

4162 *	BIG BUCK'S (FR) PFNicholls 7-11-7 RWalsh	3/10f	1
3795 2	SOUFFLEUR PBowen 7-11-7 TomO'Brien	14 16/1 2¾	2
4173 5	POSSOL (FR) HDDaly 7-11-7 RichardJohnson	33/1 1¼	3
4162	Tidal Bay (IRE) JHowardJohnson 9-11-7 BrianHughes	15/2	4
4160 5	Kayf Aramis NATwiston-Davies 8-11-7 PaddyBrennan	25/1 11	5
3676 3	Bouggler MissECLavelle 5-11-7 (s) JackDoyle	16 12/1 8	6
3777 pu	Wolf Moon (IRE) MKeighley 7-11-7 WarrenMarston	66/1 dist	7

2.00race The Stewart Family 7ran 6m21.22

In terms of a Grade 1 race (formerly Grade 2) Big Buck's faced little in terms of opposition after Time For Rupert's withdrawal and needed to be nowhere near his best to extend his unbeaten run to eight, making relatively hard work of beating a pair of smart but exposed ones in second and third; Possol and Kayf Aramis set a steady pace, winding things up only heading into the back straight on the final circuit. **Big Buck's** is in a league of his own amongst the staying hurdlers, highlighted by the fact that he was able to win this for the second year running despite being nowhere near his best, in nothing like the mood he was at Cheltenham 3 weeks earlier, needing strong driving from 3 out, though still comfortably on top at the finish; he'll be back on song after a break and will continue to be extremely hard to beat. **Souffleur**'s limit seems to have been more or less reached but he's producing it regularly again after his injury trouble and should win lesser graded events than this, up against it with Big Buck's, even with that one not firing fully, especially with a hold-up ride not ideal in a steadily-run race. **Possol** is as good a hurdler as he is a chaser after all, confirming as much 3 weeks after a hard race at Cheltenham, while his attitude here couldn't be faulted, either, finding extra for strong pressure in fact, albeit having disputed the steady pace. **Tidal Bay**'s initial resurgence switched to hurdles has come to a swift halt, failing to apply himself fully both in the World Hurdle and here, though the steady pace does give some excuse for one held up last; he's entirely unpredictable. **Kayf Aramis** is sure to bounce back, long since tough and reliable, and this is the second year running he's failed to show his form at this meeting, fading gradually in the straight having disputed the pace. **Bouggler** has held his form by and large but is error-prone, his jumping worse than usual with cheekpieces fitted and paying the price with a very weak finish (close up until blundering 2 out). **Wolf Moon** has taken a wrong turn since his early-season progress, all not seeming well with him the last twice, for all he was out of his depth here.

4534 totesport Bowl Chase (Gr 1) (1) (5yo+) £86,520   3m1f (19)

3012 ³	WHAT A FRIEND *PFNicholls* 7-11-7 RWalsh	11/4 5/2		1
4174 ⁴	CARRUTHERS *MBradstock* 7-11-7 MattieBatchelor	11 10/1	3¼	2
3780 ²	NACARAT (FR) *TRGeorge* 9-11-7 APMcCoy	4/1	13	3
4174 ⁶	Calgary Bay (IRE) *MissHCKnight* 7-11-7 GrahamLee	14/1	8	4
4174 °	Imperial Commander (IRE) *NATwiston-Davies* 9-11-7 PaddyBrennan	5/4 11/8f		ur

3.10race Mr Ged Mason & Sir Alex Ferguson 5ran 6m26.97

A race which had been upgraded to Grade 1 turned out to be a substandard renewal, Imperial Commander in nothing like his Gold Cup form while none of the remainder, including What A Friend, were entirely convincing, either; the pace was just fair to halfway, Nacarat and Carruthers disputing, things beginning to develop fully when the favourite unseated at the fourteenth. **What A Friend** is undoubtedly a high-class chaser, now a dual Grade 1 winner, and any doubts that remained regarding his temperament have to be disregarded for the time being; nonetheless, he's unlikely to ever mix it with the very best, an on song Imperial Commander included in that, and things very much fell into his lap on the day, the only one of these kept fresh for this (all 4 rivals had run in the Gold Cup 20 days earlier) to start with, while it was only after mistakes from the second and third 2 out that he swept past, looking in trouble to that point. **Carruthers** will land a big prize sooner or later, and it will be well deserved given his consistency; he underlined his cracking attitude turned out quickly after the Gold Cup, taken on in front and not jumping so well as he can yet still battling under pressure in the straight. **Nacarat** is best when allowed to dominate, but Carruthers prevented him from doing so this day, and that perhaps led to a sloppier round of jumping than usual; he still travelled like a winner for much of the way and went a couple of lengths clear briefly after 3 out, but a blunder at the next proved to be the final straw, having no more to give after that. **Calgary Bay** failed to impress with his attitude in the novice at this meeting last season and again turned in a rather moody effort, jumping slowly at the ninth and eleventh and never on terms. Imperial Commander showed just what he's capable of in the Gold Cup, but he wasn't in anything like that sort of form less than 3 weeks on, jumping badly and already in serious trouble when unseating after diving at the fourteenth; his record shows that he is clearly at his best when fresh.

4549 John Smith's Melling Chase (Gr 1) (1) 2½m (15)
(5yo+) £99,768
What should have been the sixth last fence was omitted due to a stricken horse

4161 *	ALBERTAS RUN (IRE) *JonjoO'Neill* 9-11-10 APMcCoy 15/2 8/1	1
4134 2	FORPADYDEPLASTERER (IRE) *ThomasCooper,Ireland* 8-11-10 3¼ 2 DavyRussell 4/1jf	
3671 *	MONET'S GARDEN (IRE) *NGRichards* 12-11-10 1¼ 3 RichardJohnson 7 15/2	
4177 5	Tartak (FR) *TRGeorge* 7-11-10 DenisO'Regan.......................... 16 14/1 ¾ 4	
4134 f	Mahogany Blaze (FR) *NATwiston-Davies* 8-11-10 (b) 11 5 PaddyBrennan.......................... 33/1	
4161 4	Deep Purple *EvanWilliams* 9-11-10 PaulMoloney.......................... 9/1 4½ 6	
4134 5	Oh Crick (IRE) *AKing* 7-11-10 RobertThornton.......................... 25 16/1 1¼ 7	
4161	Jack The Giant (IRE) *NJHenderson* 8-11-10 BarryGeraghty..... 14 12/1 dist 8	
4134 3	Kalahari King (IRE) *FerdyMurphy* 9-11-10 GrahamLee 7/2 4/1jf	f
4161 ur	Schindlers Hunt (IRE) *DTHughes,Ireland* 10-11-10 (v) f PaddyFlood.......................... 18 16/1	
4161 2	Poquelin (FR) *PFNicholls* 7-11-10 RWalsh 6 7/1	ur

3.10race Mr Trevor Hemmings 11ran 4m54.34

A coming together of the first 2 from the Ryanair and second and third from the Champion Chase made for a competitive and very solid Grade 1 event and, though Kalahari King's early departure took something away, it certainly lived up to its billing, Alberta's Run producing another top-class effort to follow up his Cheltenham win; Monet's Garden ensured matters were truly-run. Albertas Run has to be treated differently now, recording back-to-back Grade 1 wins within just a few weeks, and it may be that he's ground dependent as much as anything, all of his big performances since winning the SunAlliance on good to soft having come on good; he was close to the strong gallop throughout, though the stern test at the trip was in his favour as much as any (stays 3m), and he kept finding more after taking over turning into the straight, if edging left slightly. Forpadydeplasterer is impossible to knock too much because of his immense consistency, this a match for his improved effort in the Champion Chase, and he will have another big day somewhere down the line; nevertheless, there was a hint here as to why he has so many more seconds on his CV than wins, breezing into second place 2 out (looked the winner) only to continually hang left under pressure, maintaining his proximity without going through with it fully after the last. Monet's Garden retains all of his ability and enthusiasm as a 12-y-o and, though unable to confirm Ascot superiority over Alberta's Run, he comes out of this full of credit, highlighting all of his positive attributes as he jumped boldly in front and rallied gamely once passed; he's been campaigned carefully over the past 2 seasons and may well have one more year in him as a result. Tartak shaped as if on his way back in the Grand Annual and, pitched in deep, he produced a career-best effort at the meeting where he was successful as a novice in 2009, and it was in spite of a clumsy round of jumping; he's not certain to back this up again, though, given the way his season's gone. Mahogany Blaze has long since been exposed as not good enough for this sort of level but gave his running, no threat but keeping in touch until the run-in. Deep Purple flopped when turned out quickly in the King George earlier in the season and, though not faring so badly this time, he may well have been feeling the effects of his fourth in the Ryanair. Oh Crick isn't easy to place, facing a stiff task in Grade 1s and too high in the weights for handicaps, though he does seem at his best around 2m nowadays, weakening from 3 out here. Jack The Giant shaped as if amiss turned out quickly after returning from a lengthy absence. Kalahari King is a sound jumper on the whole, his second-fence exit forgivable in the wider picture. Schindlers Hunt fell fatally at the third. Poquelin confirmed his step up from handicaps with a very good second at Alberta's Run in the Ryanair and must have taken more out of himself there than the

122

winner, very laboured here and well held when unseating 4 out; his best form has all come at Cheltenham.

4563	John Smith's Maghull Nov Chase (Gr 1) (1)	2m (12)	
	(5yo+) £62,711		

3332	2	TATANIANO (FR) *PFNicholls* 6-11-4 RWalsh	10/3	1
4119	3	OSANA (FR) *EJO'Grady,Ireland* 8-11-4 (s) AndrewJMcNamara	5/2f	13 2
3985	4	ARCHIE BOY (IRE) *PaulFlynn,Ireland* 8-11-4 (s) DavyRussell .. 16	12/1	8 3
3946	5	Bergo (GER) *GLMoore* 7-11-4 APMcCoy	7/1	2 4
2647	5	Overclear *VRADartnall* 8-11-4 JackDoyle	33/1	1¾ 5
4295	1	Noble Alan (GER) *NGRichards* 7-11-4 BrianHarding	9/2 7/1	2½ 6
3811	2	See U Bob (GER) *PaulNolan,Ireland* 7-11-4 AlainCawley	10/1	2¼ 7
3895	1	Bedlam Boy (IRE) *FerdyMurphy* 9-11-4 GrahamLee	14 10/1	f
4054	1	Joe Jo Star *RAFahey* 8-11-4 BrianHughes	20/1	f
3811	4	Schelm (GER) *RonaldO'Leary,Ireland* 8-11-4 DJCasey	40/1	pu

2.15race The Stewart Family 10ran 3m53.14

The presence of Arkle-third Osana gives a direct line to the Cheltenham form and, though he wasn't at his peak, there's plenty of other solid yardsticks in this field to be able to mark Tataniano's performance as the best of the season in the division, particularly given the extra for which he was value; there was a sound pace, easing only briefly mid-race, though very few got involved. **Tataniano** exceeded even his early-season promise as he announced himself the best 2m novice around, slamming the Arkle third with even more in hand than the winning margin suggests; what's more, as a 6-y-o with few miles on the clock, he appeals as just the sort to develop into a Champion Chase candidate next season, particularly with the division having a more open look to it with Master Minded's domination apparently over; he travelled strongly from the front (took over after the fourth), jumping supremely well, and sprinted clear from 2 out, finishing with plenty left to give. **Osana** is undoubtedly at the top-end in the division, as his Arkle run showed, and it's possible that big effort had taken its toll, likely to have struggled with Tataniano regardless but certainly not seeming in quite the same form as at Cheltenham despite typically jumping well, unable to keep with the winner from 2 out; he's sure to win more races over fences, albeit whilst remaining vulnerable against the best. **Archie Boy** is most reliable, showing his form yet again returned to chasing, but this underlines his shortcomings to a large degree, losing his place after 4 out and rallying past weakening rivals late; there's always the option of reverting to timber again (still a maiden). **Bergo** had dominated inferior opposition previously and, whilst confirming his useful status here, there was also further indication his jumping is a cause for concern going forward, especially with valuable handicaps being the likely route for next season, always on the back foot here due to mistakes at the second and third and plugging on Without Seriously Threatening. **Overclear** isn't going to be easy to place, too high in the weights for handicaps and vulnerable in graded events, and he gave his running here after 4 months off without proving anything like good enough, an inadequate test compounding matters. **Noble Alan**'s merit was hard to gauge, and still is for that matter, achieving very little with 2 facile wins most recently and shaping better than the bare result upped in grade here, on the bridle and looking the only threat to Tataniano 3 out only to stop quickly, all possibly not well; he may yet get closer to his useful hurdling form in this sphere. **See U Bob** never looked like confirming the marked improvement he'd shown in a smaller field at Leopardstown, not helped by some sloppy jumping. **Bedlam Boy** wasn't up to this stiffer task, well held when falling at the last. **Joe Jo Star**'s jumping is evidently more of a problem than it initially looked, surviving a couple of earlier errors here but not one at the eighth as he fell for the second straight start; he may be best reverted to smaller tracks for handicaps this summer. **Schelm**'s consistency has been his strong point this season and this was too bad to be true, not jumping well and struggling from an early stage.

4564 John Smith's Dick Francis Aintree Hdle (Gr 1)   2½m (11)
(1) (4yo+) £91,216

4121²	KHYBER KIM *NATwiston-Davies* 8-11-7 PaddyBrennan	7/2		1
3569⁴	MUIRHEAD (IRE) *NMeade,Ireland* 7-11-7 PaulCarberry	10/1	5	2
4121³	ZAYNAR (FR) *NJHenderson* 5-11-7 (s) BarryGeraghty	11/8f	3	3
4121	Won In Tho Dark (IRE) *MissCJHarty,Ireland* 0-11-7 DavyRussell	20/1	sh	4
4161	Petit Robin (FR) *NJHenderson* 7-11-7 APMcCoy	12 10/1	hd	5
3644ᵃ	Quwetwo *JHowardJohnson* 7-11-7 DenisO'Regan	11 14/1	7	6
4121⁴	Celestial Halo (IRE) *PFNicholls* 6-11-7 (t) RWalsh	9/2 5/1		f

2.50race Mrs Caroline Mould 7ran 4m50.48

A smaller field than in 2009, though no dilution of quality with the second, third and fourth from the Champion Hurdle reopposing over this longer trip and Khyber Kim confirming superiority without needing to run to his best, though it would have been a close run thing had Celestial Halo not crashed out at the second last when travelling every bit as strongly in front; the pace was modest to halfway, things winding up only gradually, hence a relatively bunched finish. **Khyber Kim** reaffirmed his place amongst the elite hurdlers after his excellent second in the Champion, deservedly going one better straight away to gain a first Grade 1 win, and more should follow given how well he's held his form this season compared to previous ones; he travelled powerfully under a typically patient ride and was just beginning to throw down a challenge to Celestial Halo when that one came down 2 out, left with a relatively simple task as a result and making it count readily (eased late), clearly just as effective around this trip when the emphasis is on speed as he is 2m. **Muirhead** has tried and failed many times in top races, his very smart level good enough only for minor honours as here, travelling with typical menace to 2 out but unable to pick up like the winner; his failure to take advantage of easier opportunities this season has rightly led to his temperament being questioned. **Zaynar** is a high-class hurdler, his early-season Ascot rout of Karabak for one hard to knock, but there's a suspicion now his laziness is tipping towards temperament, admittedly turned out quickly but worryingly going in snatches throughout and dropping right back from 4 out before a late rally, his being slightly short of room 3 out (rider lost iron briefly) making little difference. **Won In The Dark** had one of his good days after shaping as if amiss in the Champion Hurdle, though never a threat after getting behind following a blunder at the fifth. **Petit Robin** will match the pick of his chasing form in this sphere when returned to 2m, going as well as any to 3 out and still in second jumping the last, patently failing to stay even with the emphasis on speed. **Quwetwo**'s defeat of Zaynar at Kelso shouldn't be judged as a fluke yet, but he wasn't up to this stiffer task, albeit on firmer ground than is perhaps ideal; his size points to a fruitful novice chase campaign next season. **Celestial Halo** has had his low points this season but looked back in form at Cheltenham last month and would have confirmed that had he stood up here, going strongly in front when diving at the second last, albeit with Khyber Kim beginning to loom up.

Hurdlers

Rating	Name		Rating	Name		Rating	Name	
174+	Big Buck's	/	149	Souffleur		168§	Twist Magic	
168	Binocular	3	148p	Peddlers Cross	4	166	Golden Silver	6
166	Time For Rupert		148	Aitmatov		165+	Master Minded	/
164	Khyber Kim	5	148	Dee Ee Williams		165	Albertas Run	
163	Celestial Halo		148	Jessies Dream		165	Nacarat	
163	Hurricane Fly	/	148	Kayf Aramis		164+	The Listener	
163	Zaynar	3	148	Menorah	2	163	Forpadydeplasterer	7
162	Punjabi		147p	Beshabar		163	Kalahari King	
162	Solwhit		147p	Get Me Out of Here		162	Don't Push It	
161+	Go Native		147	Andytown		161	Monet's Garden	
161	Karabak	2	147	Bouggler		161	Poquelin	
159	Bensalem		147	Cape Tribulation		160+	Joncol	
159	Diamond Harry		147	Head of The Posse		160	Tartak	
159	Donnas Palm		147	Micheal Flips		160	Tranquil Sea	
159	Lough Derg		147	Najaf		160	What A Friend	
158§	Tidal Bay		147	Ninetieth Minute		159	Black Apalachi	
158	Thousand Stars		146x	Reve de Sivola		159	Cooldine	
157	Medermit		146	James de Vassy		159	Herecomesthetruth	
157	Sublimity		145p	Rite of Passage		159	Planet of Sound	
156	Mourad		145§	Clopf		159	The Tother One	
156	Muirhead		145	Berties Dream		158p	Tataniano	6
156	Powerstation		145	Carole's Legacy		158§	Tidal Bay	
156	Quevega	/	145	Dancing Tornado		158	Carruthers	
156	Sentry Duty		145	Rigour Back Bob		158	Deep Purple	
155	Ebadiyan		145	Tell Massini		158	Garde Champetre	
155	Mr Thriller		145	Wymott		158	Madison du Berlais	
155	Oscar Dan Dan		144P	Captain Chris		158	Money Trix	
155	Starluck		144p	Alfie Sherrin		158	Mon Mome	
154§	De Valira		144p	Bobby Ewing		158	Our Vic	
154	Duc de Regniere		144+	Blackstairmountain		158	Vic Venturi	
154	Katchit		144	Ballyfitz		157	Barbers Shop	
154	Pettifour		144	Fionnegas		157	French Opera	
153	Won In The Dark		144	Golan Way		157	Joe Lively	
152	Bahrain Storm		144	Sir Harry Ormesher		157	Silver By Nature	
152	Dunguib		144	Summit Meeting		157	Voy Por Ustedes	
152	Fair Along		144	Wayward Prince		156p	Sizing Europe	4
152	Rock Noir		144	Western Leader		156	J'Y Vole	
152	War of Attrition		143p	Arvika Ligeonniere		156	Long Run	
151	Al Eile		143p	Oscar Whisky		156	Oh Crick	
151	Blue Bajan		143	Banjaxed Girl		156	Petit Robin	
151	Jumbo Rio		143	Farringdon		156	War of Attrition	
151	Luska Lad		143	General Miller		155p	Weapon's Amnesty	
151	Noble Prince		143	Mamlook		155	Newmill	
151	Quwetwo		143	Marodima		155	Schindlers Hunt	
151	Spirit River		143	Pause And Clause		155	Scotsirish	
150	Cousin Vinny		143	Torphichen		154p	Duc de Regniere	
150	Lie Forrit		143	Voler La Vedette		154	Captain Cee Bee	5
150	Tasheba		143	Wishfull Thinking		154	Casey Jones	
150	Trenchant			**Chasers**		154	Monkerhostin	
149§	Ashkazar		191	Kauto Star	2	154	Well Chief	
149	Petit Robin		182	Imperial Commander	/	153p	Somersby	
149	Ronaldo des Mottes		181	Denman	3	153	Dbest	
			169	Big Zeb	2	153	Free World	

153	Glencove Marina
153	Halcon Genelardais
153	Killyglen
153	My Will
153	Notre Pere
153	Taranis
152x	Dream Alliance
152	L'Ami
152	Master Medic
152	Miko de Beauchene
152	Oscar Time
152	Trafford Lad
151p	Punchestowns
151x	Mahogany Blaze
151	Big Fella Thanks
151	Calgary Bay
151	Chapoturgeon
151	Cornas
151	Fix The Rib
151	From Dawn To Dusk
151	I'msingingtheblues
151	I'm So Lucky
151	Made In Taipan
151	Mad Max
151	Niche Market
151	Osana
151	Siegemaster
150p	Tazbar
150+	Follow The Plan
150	Inchidaly Rock
150	Let Yourself Go
150	Mansony
150	Rare Bob
150	Sa Suffit
150	Shining Gale
150	The Sawyer
150	Tricky Trickster
149+	Pandorama
149§	Tamarinbleu
149	Ballabriggs
149	Church Island
149	Diamond Harry
149	Gone To Lunch
149	Hey Big Spender
149	In Compliance
149	Pasco
149	Takeroc
149	Watson Lake

Juvenile Hurdlers

147p	Soldatino
145p	Sanctuaire
144	Barizan
142	Alaivan
142	Sway
141	Carlito Brigante
140	Tarla
138	Notus de La Tour
138	Pistolet Noir

137p	Royal Mix
137+	Escort'men
137	Kotkidy
136	Orsippus
134	Gimli's Rock
133p	Orzare
133	Me Voici
133	Son Amix
133	Westlin' Winds
132p	Sang Bleu
132	Ciceron

Novice Hurdlers

152	Dunguib
151	Luska Lad
148p	Peddlers Cross
148	Menorah
147p	Get Me Out of Here
147	Najaf
146x	Reve de Sivola
145p	Rite of Passage
145	Berties Dream
145	Rigour Back Bob
145	Tell Massini
145	Wymott
144P	Captain Chris
144p	Bobby Ewing
144+	Blackstairmountain
144	Fionnegas
144	Summit Meeting
144	Wayward Prince
144	Western Leader
143p	Arvika Ligeonniere
143p	Oscar Whisky

Novice Chasers

158p	Tataniano
157	French Opera
156p	Sizing Europe
156	Long Run
155p	Weapon's Amnesty
154	Captain Cee Bee
153p	Somersby
151p	Punchestowns
151	Mad Max
151	Osana
150p	Tazbar
150	Inchidaly Rock
150	Let Yourself Go
149+	Pandorama
149	Diamond Harry
149	Hey Big Spender
148p	Weird Al
148	An Cathaoir Mor
148	Zaarito
147p	Sports Line

National Hunt Flat Horses

132	Cue Card
125	Al Ferof
123	Don't Turn Bach

121	Megastar
120	Dare Me
119	Bishopsfurze
119	Loosen My Load
118	Cottrelsbooley
118	Frawley
118	The Jigsaw Man
117p	Sprinter Sacre
117	Ghizao
116	Araucaria
116	Hidden Universe
116	Kerb Appeal
115	Tavern Times
114	Our Girl Salley
114	Quantitativeeasing
114	Summit Meeting
113p	Divine Rhapsody

Hunter Chasers

144*	Roulez Cool
136*	Paddy Pub
135p*	Nedzer's Return
135	Baby Run
134d*	Good Company
132*	Another Jewel
131*	Knighton Combe
130*	Cool Running
130	Southwestern
130	Turthen
129	Kilty Storm
129	Agus A Vic
128	Ice Tea
127	Templer
127*	Noakarad de Verzee
126x	Take The Stand
126	Trust Fund
126	Ofarel d'Airy
125	Robbers Glen
125	Silver Adonis

* Not achieved in a Hunter Chase

Racecourse Characteristics

The following A-Z guide covers all racecourses in England, Scotland and Wales that stage racing over the Jumps. A thumbnail sketch is provided of each racecourse's characteristics .

AINTREE

The Grand National course is triangular with its apex (at the Canal Turn) the furthest point from the stands. It covers two and a quarter miles and is perfectly flat throughout. Inside is the easier Mildmay course, providing a circuit of one and a half miles, which has birch fences. A major feature of the Mildmay course is its sharpness; the fences there are appreciably stiffer than used to be the case. The Grand National is run over two complete circuits taking in sixteen spruce fences first time round and fourteen the second, and, in spite of modifications to the fences in recent years, the race still provides one of the toughest tests ever devised for horse and rider. The run from the final fence to the winning post is 494 yards long and includes an elbow.

ASCOT

The triangular, right-handed circuit is approximately a mile and three quarters round; the turns are easy and the course is galloping in nature. The sides of the triangle away from the stands have four fences each, and the circuit is completed by two plain fences in the straight of two furlongs. After being closed for two seasons due to major redevelopment work, NH racing returned to Ascot in 2006/7. The fences are still stiff, though improved drainage means conditions don't get so testing as they once did.

AYR

The Ayr course is a left-handed circuit of one and a half miles comprising nine fences, with well-graduated turns. There is a steady downhill run to the home turn and a gentle rise to the finish. There is a run-in of 210 yards. When the going is firm the course is sharp, but conditions regularly get extremely gruelling, making for a thorough test.

BANGOR-ON-DEE

Bangor has a left-handed circuit of approximately one and a half miles. It's a fair test of jumping, with nine fences in a circuit, and the run-in is about a furlong. The track is fairly sharp because of its many bends, the paddock bend being especially tight.

CARLISLE

The course is right-handed, pear-shaped and undulating, a mile and five furlongs in extent. The track is a particularly stiff one and the uphill home stretch is very severe. There are nine fences to a circuit with a run-in of 300 yards. Perhaps due to the nature of the track, the fences are among the easiest in the country. A long-striding galloper suited by a real test of stamina is an ideal type for Carlisle.

CARTMEL

This tight, undulating, left-handed circuit is a little over a mile round. There are six fences to a circuit and the winning post is a little over a furlong from the turn into the finishing straight, which divides the course and which the horses enter after two circuits for races over seventeen furlongs or three circuits for three and a quarter miles. The fences are tricky, with four coming in quick succession in the back straight; the run of half a mile from the last fence is the longest in the country.

CATTERICK BRIDGE

The Catterick course is a left-handed, oval-shaped circuit of around a mile and a quarter, with eight fences and a run-in of about 280 yards. Races over two miles and three miles one and a half furlongs start on an extension to the straight and over two miles the first fence is jumped before joining the round course. Catterick's undulations and sharp turns make it unsuitable for the long-striding galloper and ideal for the nippy, front-running type.

CHELTENHAM

There are two left-handed courses at Cheltenham, the Old Course and the New Course. The Old Course is oval in shape and about one and a half miles in extent. There are nine fences to a circuit, with recent modifications for 2010/11 meaning there will now be two fences jumped in the home straight.

The New Course leaves the old track at the furthest point from the stands and runs parallel to it before rejoining at the entrance to the finishing straight. This circuit is a little longer than the Old Course and has ten fences, two of which are jumped in the final straight.

The most telling feature of the Old and the New Courses is their testing nature. The fences are stiff and the last half mile is uphill, with a run-in of just over a furlong.

The hurdle races over the two tracks are quite different in complexion, with only two flights jumped in the final 6f on the New Course. The four-mile and two-and-a-half-mile starts are on an extension, with five fences, which bisects both courses almost at right angles. The two-mile start is also on this extension, and two fences are jumped before reaching the main circuit.

There is also a cross-country course at Cheltenham, laid out in the centre of the conventional tracks.

CHEPSTOW

Chepstow is a left-handed, undulating, oval course, nearly two miles round with eleven fences to a circuit, a five-furlong home straight, and a run-in of 250 yards. Conditions can be very testing. With five fences in the straight, the first part of which is downhill, front runners do well here.

DONCASTER

The Doncaster course is a left-handed pear-shaped circuit of approximately two miles, and has eleven fences—including four in the home straight—with a run-in of 240 yards. Only one fence is jumped twice in races over two miles. The course is flat apart from one slight hill about one and a quarter miles from the finish. The track is well drained and often produces conditions which naturally favour horses with more speed than stamina.

EXETER

This is a hilly course, galloping in nature. Conditions can get extremely testing in midwinter and the exact opposite in drier periods, the course being without an artificial watering system. Its right-handed two-mile circuit is laid out in a long oval, with eleven fences and a run-in of around 170 yards. The chase course is on the outside of the hurdles one, but the inside track is often used on the home turn regardless of whether the races are over fences or not. The half-mile home straight is on the rise all the way to the finish.

FAKENHAM

Fakenham is an undulating, very sharp track, ideal for the handy, front-running type and unsuitable for the long-striding animal. The left-handed, square-shaped track has a circuit of a mile and a run-in of 250 yards. There are six fences to a circuit and, probably on account of most races being well run, the course takes more jumping than most which cater for horses of lesser ability.

FFOS LAS

The wide, galloping, left-handed circuit of 1½ miles, with a straight of just over 4f. It has no undulations but a very slight rise over the course of the back straight and the opposite in the home straight. There are short run-ins for both hurdles and chases. Early indications are that it is a very fair track, though there has been a tendency at the first few meetings for the races to be steadily run, meaning the fields haven't got stretched and large numbers of runners have still been in contention turning for home.

FOLKESTONE

The course is right-handed and approx-imately eleven furlongs round. The turns are easy, but the undulations can put a long-striding horse off balance. There are seven fences to a circuit, which are relatively easy, and the run-in is about a furlong.

FONTWELL PARK

There are two types of track at Fontwell, the hurdle course being left-handed, an oval

about a mile in circumference with four flights, and the chase course a figure of eight with six fences which are all in the two straight intersections linked with the hurdle course. Fontwell is not a course for the big, long-striding horse, and it can cause problems for inexperienced chasers.

HAYDOCK PARK

The 2007/8 season was the first since redevelopment work at Haydock resulted in a resiting of the chase course. All jump races are now run on the old hurdle course, using portable fences instead of the traditional ones, some of which had a slight drop on landing. There are four fences (instead of five) in the back straight, with the open ditch now the second there instead of the last, whilst there are still four fences and a water jump in the home straight. The 440-yard run-in is no more, however, its length significantly reduced as only the water jump is omitted on the final circuit. The new chase course has a tighter configuration than the old one and doesn't test jumping to the same extent.

HEREFORD

Hereford's right-handed circuit of about a mile and a half is almost square and has nine fences, of which the first after the winning post has to be taken on a turn. The home turn, which is on falling ground, is pretty sharp but the other bends are easy.

HEXHAM

Hexham has an undulating left-handed circuit of a mile and a half with ten fences. Although the fences are easy the course is very testing; the long back straight runs steeply downhill for most of the way but there is a steep climb from the end of the back straight to the home straight, which levels out in front of the stands. The finish is on a spur, which has one fence and a run-in of a furlong.

HUNTINGDON

The course is right-handed, oval with easy bends, and is a flat, fast track about one and a half miles in length. There are nine fences to a circuit, some of them rather tricky. Huntingdon favours horses with speed over stamina, sluggards seen to best advantage only under extremely testing conditions.

KELSO

The left-handed Kelso course has two tracks, the oval hurdle course of approximately a mile and a quarter and the chase course of approximately eleven furlongs. There are nine fences to be jumped in a complete circuit of the chase course; the last two aren't jumped on the final circuit and the first open ditch isn't taken at the start of the chases over four miles. The run-in, which is on an elbow, is a tiring one of 440 yards. The hurdle track is tight, with a particularly sharp bend after the stands.

KEMPTON PARK

Kempton is a very fair test for a jumper; it is a flat, triangular circuit of one mile five furlongs and is right handed. There are nine fences to a circuit, three of them in the home straight, and although they are quite stiff they present few problems to a sound jumper. After the laying of an all-weather course, which necessitated the removal of the water jump, NH racing returned in 2006/7.

LEICESTER

The right-handed course is rectangular in shape, a mile and three quarters in extent and has ten fences. Leicester is a stiff test and the last three furlongs are uphill. The run-in of 250 yards has a slight elbow on the chase course 150 yards from the winning post. Races over hurdles are run on the Flat course and the going tends to be a good deal more testing than over fences.

LINGFIELD PARK

Lingfield is about a mile and a half in length, triangular and taken left-handed, sharp, has several gradients and a tight downhill turn into the straight. Nine relatively easy fences are jumped on a complete circuit. Bumper races are now usually run on the all-weather track.

LUDLOW

Ludlow is a sharp, right-handed, oval track, with a nine-fence chase circuit about a mile and a half and a run-in of 250 yards. The fences are easy. The hurdle course, which runs on the outside of the chase course, has easier turns. Whereas the chase course is flat, the hurdle course has slight undulations but they rarely provide difficulties for a long-striding horse.

MARKET RASEN

There is a right-handed, oval circuit of a mile and a quarter, seven relatively easy fences and a run-in of 250 yards at Market Rasen. The track is sharp, covered with minor undulations, and favours the handy, nippy type of horse.

MUSSELBURGH

A right-handed oval track a little over a mile and a quarter in extent, almost flat with sharp bends, favouring the handy type of animal and also front runners. There are eight fences (four in each straight) or six flights of hurdles (three in each straight nowadays) to a circuit. The two-mile start is on a spur on the last bend.

NEWBURY

The oval Newbury course, with eleven fences to the circuit, is about a mile and three quarters in circumference and is set inside the Flat track, following a left-handed line. It is one of the fairest courses in the country, favouring no particular type of horse. The home straight is five furlongs with three plain fences, an open ditch (the water jump being omitted on the final circuit) and a run-in of 255 yards. There are seven hurdles to a circuit, four in the back straight and three in the home straight with a long run to the third last. The course is galloping in nature, with easy bends, plenty of room and few significant undulations.

NEWCASTLE

The jumps track is laid out inside the Flat course, its left-handed circuit of one and three quarter miles containing ten fences. There is a steady rise from the fifth last to the winning post and the course puts a premium on stamina, with the fences being on the stiff side. The ground is often testing here, too.

NEWTON ABBOT

Newton Abbot has a flat, oval, tight, left-handed circuit of about nine furlongs that favours the handy sort of horse. There are seven relatively easy fences to a circuit, and a very short run-in. The nineteen-furlong start over hurdles is on a spur after the winning post and the first hurdle is jumped only once.

PERTH

Perth is a right-handed circuit of one and a quarter miles, with eight fences to the circuit. The course has sweeping turns and quite a flat running surface. The water jump is in front of the stands and is left out on the run-in, leaving a long run from the last fence to the winning post.

PLUMPTON

The oblong-shaped course is only nine furlongs in circumference and has tight, left-handed bends, steep undulations, and an uphill home straight. The climb becomes pretty steep near the finish but the course is not a particularly stiff one; it favours the handy and quick-jumping types. There are six fences to a circuit and the run-in is 200 yards.

SANDOWN PARK

Sandown is a right-handed, oval-shaped course of thirteen furlongs, with a straight run-in of four furlongs. There is a separate straight course which runs across the main circuit over which all five-furlong races are decided. From the mile-and-a-quarter starting gate, the Eclipse Stakes course, the track is level to the turn into the straight, from there it is uphill until less than a furlong from the winning post, the last hundred yards being more or less level. The five-furlong track is perfectly straight and rises steadily throughout. Apart from the minor gradients between the main winning post and the mile-and-a-quarter starting gate, there are no undulations to throw a long-striding horse off balance, and all races over the round course are very much against the collar from the turn into the straight. The course is, in fact, a fairly testing one, and over all distances the ability to see the trip out well is important.

SEDGEFIELD

The circuit is approximately a mile and a quarter, oval, and taken left-handed. It is essentially sharp in character and the eight fences are fairly easy, though some uphill sections of the undulating ground, notably the final 150 yards, are punishing. The run-in is 200 yards.

SOUTHWELL

The Southwell track is laid out in a fairly tight, level oval of less than a mile and a quarter. In 2002/3 the circuit was divided into a summer and a winter track, with the slightly larger summer track on the outside of the winter one. The runners go left-handed. There are seven portable fences to a circuit which are stiff ones for a minor track. The brush-type hurdles can also catch out less fluent jumpers.

STRATFORD-ON-AVON

This sharp track is flat, triangular in shape and has a left-handed circuit of a mile and a quarter, taking in eight fences. One of the fences in the home straight was removed in the summer of 2007, but a water jump was introduced at the start of the following season just before the winning line and is obviously bypassed on the final circuit.

TAUNTON

The right-handed course is a long oval, about a mile and a quarter round, and has seven fences, four in the back straight and three in the home straight. The fences are easy enough but, due the the sharp nature of the track, catch out plenty more runners than might be expected. The bend after the winning post is tight and the chase run-in short.

TOWCESTER

Towcester is a right-handed course, a mile and three quarters round, and is the stiffest track in the country. The last mile or so is very punishing, with a steep climb to the home turn and a continuing rise past the winning post. Stamina is at a premium and conditions can get very testing. There

are ten fences on the circuit, two (small obstacles) in the finishing straight, but they seldom present problems, with the exception of the two downhill ones running away from the stands. The run-in is 200 yards.

UTTOXETER

The course is an oval of approximately a mile and a quarter with a long, sweeping, left-handed bend into the straight and a sharper one after the winning post. The hurdle course in particular suits the handier type of horse. There are minor undulations and the back straight has slight bends. The ground can get extremely testing, so that few horses act on it. There are eight fences, with a run-in of around 170 yards. Races of two miles, three and a quarter miles and four and a half miles are started on a spur on the last bend.

WARWICK

Warwick's left-handed course is a mile and three quarters round with ten fences to a circuit. Five of them come close together in the back straight and sound jumping is at a premium. The bends are rather tight and the track is a sharp one, favouring the handy horse. There is a run-in of 250 yards.

WETHERBY

The course is left-handed, with easy turns and follows a long oval circuit of a mile and a half, during which nine fences are jumped, the four in the home straight now on the inside of the hurdles track. It provides a very fair test for any horse, but is ideal for the free-running, long-striding individual with plenty of jumping ability.

WINCANTON

Wincanton is a level course with an oval, right-handed circuit of around a mile and a half containing nine fences. It is essentially sharp in nature and, as such, provides a stiffish test with regards to jumping. The run from the last fence is only about 200 yards.

WORCESTER

The course is laid out in the shape of a long oval of thirteen furlongs, flat throughout with easy, left-handed turns. There are nine well-sited fences, five in the back straight, four in the home straight, and a run-in of 220 yards. Brush-type hurdles are used at Worcester and can cause jumping problems. Severe flooding in summer 2007 caused considerable damage to both the racing surface and stands.

WE'VE GOT IT COVERED

On sale at these courses at most meetings
Available from timeform.com

TIMEFORM RACE CARDS ARE AVAILABLE
FOR EVERY MEETING EVERY DAY

£5 EACH AT TIMEFORM.COM
Or call 01422 330540 (24 hrs)

Index